CAMBRIDGE CLASS

General Ed:
J. A. CROOK, E. J. KENNEY

DEMOS: THE DISCOVERY O

DEMOS: THE DISCOVERY OF CLASSICAL ATTIKA

ROBIN OSBORNE

Junior Unofficial Fellow,
King's College, Cambridge

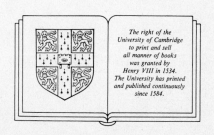

The right of the
University of Cambridge
to print and sell
all manner of books
was granted by
Henry VIII in 1534.
The University has printed
and published continuously
since 1584.

CAMBRIDGE UNIVERSITY PRESS

CAMBRIDGE

LONDON   NEW YORK   NEW ROCHELLE
MELBOURNE   SYDNEY

Published by the Press Syndicate of the University of Cambridge
The Pitt Building, Trumpington Street, Cambridge CB2 1RP
32 East 57th Street, New York, NY 10022, USA
296 Beaconsfield Parade, Middle Park, Melbourne 3206, Australia

First published 1985

Printed in Great Britain at the University Press, Cambridge

Library of Congress catalogue card number: 84–12170

British Library Cataloguing in Publication Data

Osborne, Robin
Demos.–(Cambridge classical series)
1. Attica (Greece)–Rural conditions
I. Title
938´.5   HN10.A8

ISBN 0 521 26776 5

AL

TO ARTHUR BROWN

CONTENTS

Part two: Supporting studies

Conclusion

MAPS

page

Map 2 is reproduced by courtesy of the American School of Classical Studies at Athens.

PLATES

PREFACE

Athens is the classical Greek city about which we know most from literary sources, and it has at the same time left us the richest collection of inscriptions; the territory of Attika has been long and relatively thoroughly explored. Athenian democracy explicitly acknowledged that most Athenians lived outside the 'city' of Athens, exploiting this fact in its own organisation. Despite all this, historians have never paid any great attention to the overall relation between the city of Athens and the countryside of Attika, to how the polis as a whole worked. This study attempts both to present the detailed evidence relevant to this question and to offer a preliminary analysis. The individual chapters are largely independent enquiries into various aspects of the relationship of town and country and the order in which they are presented here is to a large extent arbitrary, but, as the first and last chapters aim to emphasise, there is a coherent picture emerging from all the studies.

The book is a rewritten and enlarged version of my Cambridge Ph.D thesis of 1982, 'Rural structure and the classical polis: town—country relations in Athenian society'. All the chapters have been revised and chapters 1 and 7 are entirely new. In its present form the work was substantially completed in March 1983, although references to more recent publications have been made where that has been possible and appropriate. An earlier version of chapter 2 was awarded the Grote Prize in 1981.

This work would not have acquired its present form but for the kind assistance of Anthony Snodgrass, who supervised the thesis, David Lewis and Michel Austin who scrutinised it as examiners, numerous Cambridge colleagues who commented on chapters 1, 2, 4, 5 and 8 when they were given as seminar papers, and the editors of Cambridge

Classical Studies. The fieldwork which supports chapters 2 and 5 would not have been possible without the facilities and hospitality of the British School of Archaeology at Athens, and the work would not have progressed beyond the thesis stage but for the continuing support of King's College and in particular the stimulating encouragement of Geoffrey Lloyd and Simon Goldhill. That the work exists at all is in no small measure due to the critical support of Catherine my wife.

The transliteration of Greek is always a source of difficulty, and it will be apparent that mine has inconsistencies.

King's College, Cambridge   R.G.O.
St Mark, 1984

ABBREVIATIONS

The names of ancient authors are mainly abbreviated following the conventions of LSJ (where e.g. D. is used for the Demosthenic corpus), but in some cases a fuller abbreviation has been used (thus Xen. not X. is used for Xenophon and Arist. not Ar. for the Aristotelian corpus).

The following abbreviations of periodical and other titles may be less familiar to some readers.

AA	*Archäologischer Anzeiger: Beiblatt zum Jahrbuch des deutschen archäologischen Instituts*
AAA	*Athens Annals of Archaeology*
ABSA	*Annual of the British School of Athens*
ADelt	*Arkhaiologikon Deltion*
AEph	*Arkaiologike Ephemeris*
AM	*Mitteilungen des deutschen archäologischen Instituts; athenische Abteilung*
AR	*Archaeological Reports*
ARV^2	Beazley, J. D., *Attic red-figure vase-painters* (2nd ed. 1963)
FGH	Jacoby, F., *Die Fragmente der griechischer Historiker*
MIGRA	*Miscellanea Graeca*
PAA	*Praktika tes Akademias Athenon*
SEG	*Supplementum Epigraphicum Graecum*
SIG^3	Dittenberger, W., *Sylloge Inscriptionum Graecarum* (3rd ed.)

INTRODUCTION

CHAPTER 1

THE POLIS AND ITS *POLITAI*

A cautionary tale

On the second of Skirophorion, roughly midsummer, of 341, Euthykles, son of Euthymenides, of the deme of Myrrhinous, denounced for confiscation a tenement house belonging to Meixidemos of Myrrhinous, who was in debt to the public treasury of the Athenians. Meixidemos' tenement house (*sunoikia*) was in the Peiraieus, close by the Mounykhia promontory, immediately south of the house of Euthykles himself, just north of the house of Protarkhos of the Peiraieus, just east of the house of Euthymakhos of Myrrhinous, and west of the city road.[1]

Meixidemos' public debt had arisen from an evidently ill-advised willingness to go surety for various individuals who were undertaking public contracts: for Philistides, son of Philistides, of Aixone, who had contracted to collect the *metoikion* tax in 343/2 but had failed to produce his 6th, 7th, 8th and 9th payments of 100 dr., and had also undertaken to raise the 5-dr. tax in the mines but had not produced the 6th, 7th and 8th payments for this, of 125 dr. each; for Telemakhos, son of Hermolokhos, a metic living in the Peiraieus, who had taken a share in the raising of the 5-dr. tax for Theseus but had failed to pay up the 4th, 5th, 6th, 7th, 8th, 9th and 10th instalments of 100 dr., and had also undertaken the rental of a quarry in the Peiraieus but failed to pay the 4th and 5th instalments of the $115\frac{1}{2}$-dr. rent; for Kallikrates, son of Kallikrates, a metic living in the mining deme of Besa, who had taken a share in the raising of the drachma tax for Asklepios but not produced the 7th, 8th, 9th and 10th payments of 36 dr. 4 ob. As none of these debts had been met by the debtors or by Meixidemos the debt had been doubled. Euthykles' denunciation of the *sunoikia* was

1

the next step in the process of recovering the money. The *sunoikia* was bought by Telemakhos, son of Theangelos, of Akharnai, for 3,705 dr. 2 ob. Since this met the sum of the outstanding debts Meixidemos was presumably thus released from his obligations.[2]

We owe our knowledge of this case to an inscription found in the Agora at Athens and published in 1936,[3] but although cited in discussions of the process of denunciation of the property of public debtors (*apographe*) and in commentary on the Aristotelian statements in chapter 48 of the *Athenaion Politeia*,[4] Meixidemos' case has excited little interest. When it is examined in detail, however, it provides, not only in the manner in which the case is recorded[5] but also in the whole construction of the case, a very nice example of the nature of Athenian public life.

Euthykles son of Euthymenides, who denounces the property, is clearly not a disinterested party. He is both a fellow demesman of Meixidemos and his neighbour in the Peiraieus, where, together with Euthymakhos, they seem to form a little ghetto of men from that deme in the Mesogaia. Euthykles' family is known: his brother, Eupolemos, is found as *amphiktyon* in Delos just months later in 341/0, and ten years on is found as *tamias* of the *trieropoioi* (ταμίας τριηροποϊκῶν).[6] The fact that Eupolemos put himself forward for these posts, both of which have some connection with shipping and the sea, may not be unconnected with the base in the Peiraieus, but that Eupolemos undertakes public service at all must mean that he was not out of touch with the home village.[7] The preference for names commencing in Eu- which have connections with war (-polemos) and glory (-kles) makes it not at all unlikely that the Euthymakhos of Myrrhinous who is another of Meixidemos' neighbours is a relative.

Meixidemos' family is not certainly known,[8] and at first sight there seems little rationale to his apparently random financial commitments. However, although Philistides is from Aixone, a coastal deme some way south of the Peiraieus (modern Glyphada) and is not known to have interests in the

Peiraieus (we do not know where he was collecting the *metoikion*) he does have a rather roundabout connection with what is evidently an area of Meixidemos' interests. A Pausistratos son of Philistides appears in a mid-fourth-century list of the tribe of Kekropis, which is the tribe to which Aixone belonged, and although the name Philistides is not rare this Pausistratos is generally thought to be the brother of the Philistides here.[9] Pausistratos *is* a rather uncommon name, and so when it occurs in a mining lease it seems likely that the same man is involved.[10] That Philistides is found here to be raising a tax in the mines reinforces this connection. That Philistides' family had established mining interests may account for the link with Meixidemos, for that he also goes surety for a metic living in Besa suggests that he too was not without involvement in the area.

While Kallikrates' Besa connection is manifest he may also have links with the Peiraieus. For the tax which he is involved with is the tax for Asklepios, and although the occurrence of 'Asklepiakon' as a mine name may indicate that the cult had an active centre in the mining[11] region it is very likely that Kallikrates would have had some contact with the sanctuary of Asklepios in the Peiraieus, a sanctuary which was situated on Mounykhia.[12]

Telemakhos the metic's connections seem more straight-forward. He is based in the Peiraieus and his exploitation of a quarry is the exploitation of a local resource — indeed the quarry might have been one of those known on Mounykhia hill.[13] His collection of the tax for Theseus again may have strengthened the Peiraieus connections, for it is known that there was a cult of Theseus there.[14]

The men and activities with which Meixidemos is linked by his actions as a surety thus prove to be all connected with one of two local areas of activity — the Peiraieus and the mines. Since some prior contact is to be expected in order that Meixidemos should be willing to risk his property in their interests the links with these men are hardly surprising. More unexpected are the links with Telemakhos of Akharnai, the man who buys the *sunoikia*. That Telemakhos is more than simply a man who happened to buy the property at the auction is already suggested by the price paid: the sum paid by Telemakhos is exactly equal to the sum of the doubled debts of Meixidemos. Although the payment of the exact sum of the debt may be paralleled in one other known case of *apographe* (a case in which the purchaser is the brother of the man from whom the property is confiscated[15]) it is not at all a usual, let alone a necessary, feature of the *apographe* process. This clearly smacks of some sort of collusion, for not only is this sum the minimum one that will secure that no further item of Meixidemos' property is confiscated, but since men who denounced items of property for confiscation seem to have been rewarded with part of the proceeds after the sum of the debt had been subtracted[16] (a sum which they could choose to hand over to either the debtor or the public treasury[17]), the payment of the exact sum would seem to deprive the man who denounces of any reward for his action. It must further be presumed, since no one bid any higher, that Telemakhos had to pay over the odds for this property in order to meet the sum of the debts in this way.[18]

Fortunately Telemakhos son of Theangelos of Akharnai is a man who is not unknown from other sources, and it is possible to suggest why he chooses to bail out Meixidemos in this way. Telemakhos was a prominent man in the Athenian assembly in the 330s and 320s. Not only is he the chief instigator of honours for Herakleides of Salamis (on Cyprus) for the help he had given to Athens during a corn shortage,[19] but he seems to have been one of the many men who at one time or another proposed honours for Lykourgos.[20] He seems to have been the butt of at least one comic poet, Timokles, and Athenaios preserves a number of fragments from the comedies of Timokles which relate to Telemakhos and to the pot in which he boiled his beans. The essence of these jokes seems to be the mixed allusion to Telemakhos' windy rhetoric, his constant putting himself forward for allotted office, and his grandfather's famous foundation of an altar to Asklepios.[21] Telemakhos' grandfather was also called Telemakhos and his foundation of an altar is both epigraphically recorded and would seem to have given rise to the proverbial phrase Τηλεμάχου χύτρα.[22] That Telemakhos the grandson maintained the links with the cult of Asklepios is not directly attested, but it is far from unlikely, especially since Timokles' jokes rely on the identification of the two men. If Telemakhos (II) *was* a devotee of Asklepios then that would give him a link with Mounykhia and a context in which he might have got to know Meixidemos. Moreover it raises the possibility of a link with at least one of the debtors: the metic who contracts to raise the tax to Asklepios is named Telemakhos . . .[23]

Where does Euthykles of Myrrhinous fit into all this? Is he the annoyed neighbour (the use of *sunoikiai* as brothels is well attested) only too keen to interfere in the business of a fellow demesman, or is he too in collusion with Meixidemos and doing him a service by denouncing only *this* item of property and by doing so at a time when Telemakhos is able and willing to produce a large amount of ready cash with which to purchase it? The particular answer to this query is of little more than antiquarian interest; the importance of the case lies in the demonstration that it gives that action at law at Athens was not a disinterested matter: the men who appear on different sides in a court of law are men who are already involved with each other in one way or another.

This finding is amply borne out by the other cases of *apographe* of which we know in detail. In the case which followed before the same court in Skirophorion 341 property at Aphidna belonging to a man from neighbouring Oinoe is denounced by men from Aphidna and bought by Niko-krates of Rhamnous;[24] an earlier *poletai* inscription (*SEG* 12.100) gives a different sort of connection between the parties: Theomnestos son of Deisitheos of Ionidai denounces property at Alopeke belonging to Theosebes son of Theo-philos of Xypete. Theosebes has been condemned for *hierosulia* and given the nature of the names it is difficult to believe that either family is without priestly connections;[25] a naval list gives another case from the Mesogaia: Theodotos of Myrrhinoutta denounces property of Demonikos son of Apseudes, a fellow demesman.[26]

The speech of Apollodoros against Nikostratos ([D.] 53) provides a literary example: much of the speech is taken up with the charting of the history of the relationship between Apollodoros and Nikostratos and his brother Arethousios, a relationship begun in boyhood amity and co-operation but which has proceeded into a series of lawsuits. Apollodoros has secured a fine of 1 talent on Arethousios for *pseudokleteia* and this speech is an attempt to prove that the slaves Apollodoros has denounced in order to secure payment of the fine do belong to Arethousios and not to Nikostratos. Apollodoros feels that he has to justify his bringing of the *apographe* himself, and this he does in terms of his being the wronged party. However, he also feels that he has to point out that it is not that he has *had* to act himself: 'I was not a man so short of resources and friends that I would not have been able to find a man to make the denunciation for me' (53.1). It was open to anyone to denounce the property of a public debtor; however, the cases reviewed here very strongly suggest that in the event it was men connected with the victim, whether by friendship or hostility, by neighbourhood or common interests, who exercised the right.

Polis: city? state?

Meixidemos' case should caution us not, or not only, against offering to be sureties for the commitments of others, but against the all too easy assumption that classical Athens was much like a small-scale version of a modern city or even of a modern state. Athens did have a developed civic centre with specialised official buildings; it did have a sort of extramural 'green belt' made up of cemeteries (e.g. the Kerameikos) and wooded areas (e.g. the Akademy or Kynosarges); there was an active theatre and the arts do place a high value on natural representation. Even in the field of law the Athenians of the fourth century, at least, did make a distinction between laws and decrees: the everyday decisions of the assembly did not have the force of law and they could not simply undo the law. It is easy to latch onto these features and to treat classical Athens as the Edinburgh of the south, even as a more or less modern state.

Meixidemos, however, will allow none of that. For us, actions for public debt come into the sphere of criminal law, of state prosecution: classical Athenians did not have our distinction between civil and criminal cases,[27] and they did not have any office of public prosecutor. Neither the man who denounced Meixidemos' property nor the man who, by purchasing the denounced property for the requisite amount, effectively bails the debtor out, is disinterested. That in a *graphē* such as this the plaintiff is *ho boulomenos* does not mean that the prosecutor is just *any* Athenian, let along that he is somehow a 'representative of the Athenian state'.

Even those modern societies which might appear at first sight to be very like classical Athens prove crucially different in just this area. Thus Loizos,[28] whose study of a modern Cypriot village shows many areas of contact with traditional societies and thus with classical Greece, finds his villagers confronted with a concept of law whose implications they do not fully comprehend: 'The authority of the state, which seeks to monopolise the use of force, is an intrusive factor which has become more prominent in recent times and is directly related to modern efficient government. Yet as with other aspects of central government, villagers do not regard state intervention or the process of law as certain' (p. 118). Athens, the polis, was not simply a village, like Loizos' Kalo, and it did have some sort of central government, but there was no equivalent to the authority of the state, no attempt to monopolise the use of force. Such a monopoly of legitimate use of force has been seen as one defining feature of the state,[29] but the Athenians did not single out violence as creating a category of particular public concern. Harm to property or to the person was not necessarily open to prosecution by *ho boulomenos*, and in cases of homicide the rights to prosecution lay with the relatives of the deceased, who had the right to absolve.[30]

7

While it is frequently repeated that 'city-state' is a mis-nomer,[31] the complaints are voiced in terms of the lack of fit between 'city' and polis. The dangers inherent in the use of 'city' in a Greek context are indeed great, greater than is generally admitted,[32] and perhaps greatest of all in the case of Athens, where it may be totally unclear whether 'the city of Athens' refers to the *astu* or to the polis as a whole.[33] It is part of the burden of this work that the polis is a unity, that 'Athenians' live all over Attika, and that talk of the loyalty of the villages to Athens radically misconceives the nature of the polis.

It is, however, a further burden of this work that potentially the 'state' element of 'city-state' is no less misleading. Although much importance is often attached to the identi-fication of 'states' the term is not one that has any single widely recognised significance. 'State' may be used to refer to no more than the political aspects of a developed society. Without specification, however, such an 'innocent' use of the term is unlikely to be clear: other elements from the field of meaning of the word contaminate its significance. 'Polis' is, of course, itself another term with a whole field of meanings, but this similarity, far from warranting the interchangeable use of the two terms, only promotes misconnections.[34]

One indication of the degree of difference between polis and state lies in the fact that we cannot, and feel no pressure to, identify 'state' and citizens in the way that the polis was and was felt to be co-extensive with the citizen body. This identification is first found in the lyrics of Alkaios (fr. 112: ἄνδρες γὰρ πόλιος πύργος ἀρεύιος) and it became something of a topos,[35] but it was none the less an ideological commit-ment for all that, as is shown by its being, the basic assump-tion on which the Funeral Speech is built.[36]

Modern conceptions of the state may extend beyond the citizen body, as in those which stress the state as a hierarchical sociopolitical organisation, which will, of course, embrace disenfranchised as well as citizens;[37] or it may be divored from the citizen body, as in 'the distinctively modern idea of the State as a form of public power separate from both the ruler and the ruled'.[38] By contrast the polis not only is the citizen body, but it embraces all the interests of citizens. Aristotle's opening suggestion in book 1 of the *Politics* stresses the polis as a natural social unit existing for social functions: ἡ δ᾽ ἐκ πλειόνων κωμῶν κοινωνία τέλειος πόλις, ἤδη πάσης ἔχουσα πέρας τῆς αὐταρκείας ὡς ἔπος εἰπεῖν, γινομένη μὲν τοῦ ἕνεκεν, οὖσα δὲ τοῦ εὖ ζῆν. διὸ πᾶσα πόλις φύσει ἔστιν, εἴπερ καὶ αἱ πρῶται κοινωνίαι (1252a27ff.). When he later (book 3, 1276a22ff.) turns to the slightly different question of the conditions for identity of polis, he considers whether identity of *politai* is a sufficient condition for identity of polis, and stresses the importance of the way in which the citizen body is organised, of the *politeia*. *Politeia* is not simply a matter of the precise nature of the organs of government, it affects the whole question of the interrelation of members of the polis to each other, as Aristotle's analogy with different kinds of dramatic chorus makes clear. It is the impossibility of divorcing the *politeia* from the society that makes it evident to Aristotle that to change the *politeia* changes the polis; to his modern critics, however, who have no difficulty driving a wedge between state and society, Aristotle's remarks become opaque:[39] there is little attraction in claiming that the change from Fourth to Fifth Republic in France caused a new state to be created.

Athenian democracy represents the problem of the nature of the Greek polis in an extreme form. Extreme democracy, in its theory even if not in its practice,[40] does not tolerate inequality even to the extent of accepting that efficient government demands delegation of responsibility to offices and officials. Athens did have executive officials who were held responsible for their actions,[41] but these men were little more than the ciphers of a civil service. This leads to the elision of anything that could properly be termed an executive *power*, and reduces officers to individuals not distinct from the *demos*. Aiskhylos, in exploring the heightened moral difficulties produced by this reduction, in the *Suppliant Women*, expresses the nature of democratic rule clearly in the words both of king and of chorus. Thus the king, at 398–401:

9

εἶπον δὲ καὶ πρίν, οὐκ ἄνευ δήμου τάδε
πράξαιμ' ἄν, οὐδέ περ κρατῶν, μὴ καί ποτε
εἴπῃ λεώς, εἴ πού τι μὴ τοῖον τύχοι,
'ἐπήλυδας τιμῶν ἀπώλεσας πόλιν.'

and the chorus, at 698—700:

φυλάσσοι τ' ἀτρεμαῖα τιμὰς
τὸ δήμιον, τὸ πτόλιν κρατύνει,
προμαθὶς εὐκοινόμητις ἀρχά.[42]

At Athens popular sovereignty is more than just a constitutional dogma: Solon's law of stasis — the tone, at least, of which runs through fifth-century Athenian thought — obliged all citizens to take part in politics.[43]

In refusing to countenance intermediary distinctions between individual citizens and the citizen body the Athenians effectively refused to separate politics from other aspects of the life of the individual and of the community. The *politai* — all *politai* — are the locus of power, but they are also the locus of all other forms of independent social organisation and behaviour: although the *politai* constitute 'political society' there is no question of their existing solely for political purposes.[44] The polis embraces the *politai* in all their various manifestations and activities — τὸ ζῆν, whether εὖ or not!

Just as there is an inclination to use Meixidemos' case simply to determine the nature of the Athenian law on sureties or *apographe*, neglecting the extra-legal play of social and personal factors, so there has been a tendency to study the political, social, and religious aspects of Athenian life in isolation.[45] But as the concentration on the letter of the law has endangered our grasp of the crucially informal nature of legal action, so the myopic compartmentalising has seriously hampered understanding of Athenian religion (see below, chapter 8) and indeed of Athenian politics (chapter 4). Athenian actions can only be understood if they are seen in the context of the body of *politai*, the way they organised themselves, and the forces affecting their decisions.

Locating the *politai*

While it is not difficult to see that 'state' in any strong sense can have little meaning when applied to classical Athens, the location of the difference demands further investigation. Athens is not only not like a state, it is remarkable among Greek *poleis*. The difference is most notable in its exceptional size and its exceptional resources.[46] This study sets out to explore the peculiar nature of Athenian society starting from just these exceptional features: Athenian settlement and land use are described in chapters 2 and 3; the mineral resources in chapters 5 and 6. Chapters 4 and 7 attempt to assess the degree to which these features affected social organisation and political action, and in the light of the overall findings chapter 8 looks at the place of religion and attempts to put the study of religious practices at Athens on a new footing.

This study is only possible because of the unique historical and archaeological information available for Athens and Attika. In particular the Kleisthenic reforms not only opened the way to the radical democracy which undermines the equation of polis and state but also introduced a system of official nomenclature which appended a demotic to the personal name of the citizen.[47] This means that from a man's name alone we can, in theory at least, establish not only his family but also the locality with which he has inherited ties.[48] Since in addition the institution of the liturgy, and in particular the epigraphic record of those who performed liturgies, enables us to trace the moneyed class with some certainty[49] it is possible to analyse in some detail the operation of kinship, locality, and wealth as factors in Athenian social and political life and to gain some grasp of how these factors interacted.

Although much remains in dispute, the political aspects of the Kleisthenic organisation of Attika have been much studied, and, while the precise motivation of the distribution of demes into tribes and *trittyes* and the details of the *trittys* affiliation of a number of individual demes have yet to be certainly established, the skeleton is more or less clear.[50]

11

The work that has been done has concentrated on the constitutional theory and has worked at the level of the deme; the social implications and practical workings of the system established have not been fully investigated.

The fullest study of the deme which looks at the internal dynamics is now a century old, and although a very thorough piece of work which has stood the test of time remarkably well, it brings assumptions to bear which are far from unquestionable — as the very title *La Vie municipale en Attique* itself shows.[51] Most of the major conclusions reached by Haussoullier are considerably revised, and often contradicted, by those of this work.[52]

Despite the wealth of literary and epigraphic evidence, the historian who is interested in any aspect of Athenian life owes an ever-increasing debt to the archaeologist. Athens and Attika have long been a focus of more or less casual archaeological investigations, and the game of locating demes, which is generally one of relating scanty literary evidence to hardly less scanty material remains, has been one that has been played with considerable scholarly acumen and rigour of argument from Leake's early nineteenth-century investigations onwards. In the late nineteenth century the Prussian cartographers and then Milchhoeffer combed the Attic countryside closely and acutely, and their work has been continued by generations of American archaeologists under the guidance of Eugene Vanderpool.[53]

Field walkers of the twentieth century have the advantage of a secure data-base with which to compare their material findings. The German investigations in the Kerameikos and the American exploration of the Agora have produced detailed evidence for the changing material culture of the classical period, enabling more or less safe dating of relatively plain ceramic wares and even rather fragmentary inscriptions. This ability to fix the dates of surface finds, while on occasions inviting premature conclusions from insufficient data, promises to allow the detection of important historical changes in the settlement and exploitation of Attika.[54]

Despite the variety, and comparative wealth, of material

available to them, those familiar with the field archaeology of Attika have tended to use their knowledge only to ask certain rather narrowly constitutional questions. This work aims to strike out a new course and to take up the challenge which has been thrown out by investigators of the Greek polis working at a higher level of generality to investigate the relations between the *astu* and the *khora*.[55] The implications of the results are considerable, not only creating a picture of Athenian social relations that offers a new perspective but also revising the received conceptions about the working of politics and the relations between the actions of citizens in assembly and outside. If this undermines the unthinking alignment of Athens with distinguished Western

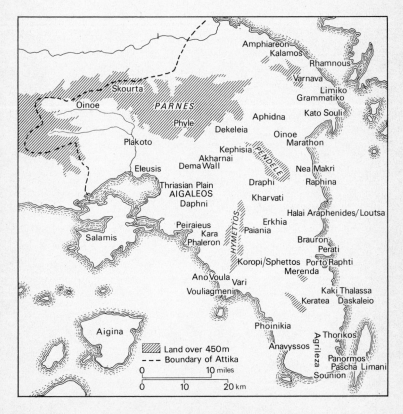

Map 1. A guide to modern and ancient Attika.

cities of the recent past it will have fulfilled its purpose. If it also creates a new and vivid picture of Athenians acting and reacting, and of the constraints within which these interactions took place, that will be a bonus.

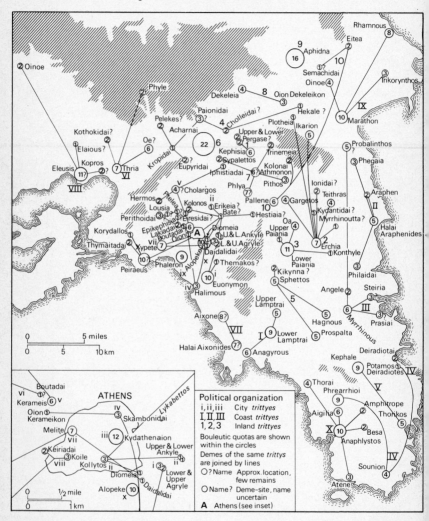

Map 2. The political organisation of Attika. From Traill (1975) map 2 (adapted).

CHAPTER 2

THE PATTERN OF SETTLEMENT OF CLASSICAL ATTIKA

The literary evidence

Isokrates was in no doubt about the settlement of early Attika: discussing the achievements of Theseus in the *Helen* he writes καὶ πρῶτον μὲν τήν πόλιν σποράδην καὶ κατὰ κώμας οἰκοῦσαν εἰς ταὐτὸν συναγαγὼν τηλικαύτην ἐποίησεν ὥστ᾽ ἔτι καὶ νῦν ἀπ᾽ ἐκείνου τοῦ χρόνου μεγίστην τῶν Ἑλληνίδων εἶναι (35). Thucydides and Philokhoros share a similar view of the state of Attika before the *sunoikismos*, and Aristotle regards settlement in villages as prior to the formation of *poleis*.[1] None of these writers, however, gives a clear explicit description of the nature of human settlement in Attika in the classical period.

Modern scholars not prepared to accept later imaginative reconstructions as historical fact have been in doubt about settlement patterns of all periods, and some have been prepared to lay aside what evidence there is in favour of imaginative reconstructions of their own. Thus it is that Detienne writes, with reference to Hesiod, that 'Un des traits les plus frappants de la vie paysanne au temps d'Hésiode, c'est l'isolement du petit propriétaire; il reste confiné sur son lopin de terre',[2] despite the fact that the *Works and Days* makes it clear explicitly in its two most famous lines

νάσσατο δ᾽ ἄγχ᾽ Ἑλικῶνος ὀϊζυρῇ ἐνι κώμῃ,
Ἄσκρῃ, χεῖμα κακῇ, θέρει ἀργαλέῃ, οὐδέ ποτ᾽ ἐσθλῇ

and implicitly in what it says about the community, that Hesiod lived in a village.[3]

For the classical period, where we lack the contemporary explicit evidence of a Hesiod, assumptions about settlement have tended to take the place of facts. Thus it is that Grote

15

talked of 'country residences', that Murray discusses how 'the peasantry' might become 'less able to live on their land', and that Snodgrass talks of 'smallholders'.[4] Those who have looked to the archaeological evidence to fill the gaps left by the literary sources have adopted no single model of settlement: some have regarded the material evidence as supporting a very scattered settlement pattern, others as revealing only or mainly villages, while the most recent investigators have tended to stress the variety of types of settlement, as if both village settlement and isolated farms were equally possible and viable ways of settling anywhere in Attika.[5]

Yet the question *is* important: patterns of residence do relate closely to questions of social structure, of agricultural exploitation, and, particularly in the case of Athens, to the very working of the political machine. Moreover there is evidence, both literary and archaeological, which enables an argued investigation. Pečirka claimed that 'Literary texts do not supply an unequivocal answer to the question about the existence of homestead farms in Attika',[6] but if we do not bias our answer by begging the question in this way the literary evidence is not unhelpful.

Two dramatic changes in the pattern of settlement in Attika in the classical period have at times been believed in: the *Athenaion Politeia* records Aristeides' advice to the Athenians to leave the country and dwell in the *astu*, and claims that it was accepted; more recent writers have often assumed that many remained in the city and did not return to their land after the Peloponnesian War (an idea often based on a misinterpretation of Xenophon, *Oikonomikos* 20.23). The claims of the *Athenaion Politeia* are refuted by Thucydides when he notes what a wrench it was for a large number of Athenians to have to uproot themselves and take temporary shelter in the *astu* at the beginning of the Peloponnesian War;[7] the allegations about the effects of the Peloponnesian War are surely refuted by the silence of the sources, for that the pattern of settlement can be so universally taken for granted strongly implies that no radical change in the pattern was perceived. It is therefore a safe assumption that whatever the nature of the settlement of Attika was it was more or less unchanged from the time of the Persian Wars down to the late fourth century, when our literary information begins to give out.

Of the minimal case that not everyone lived on the land they cultivated there can be little doubt. Euphiletos, the defendant in Lysias 1, has got himself into trouble precisely because of his reactions on finding his wife otherwise occupied when he returned ἀπροσδοκήτως ἐξ ἀγροῦ (11). His wife's new alliance had been advanced at the Thesmophoria ἐμοῦ ἐν ἀγρῷ ὄντος (20), where the implication must be that his absence lasted more than a day. Moreover Euphiletos' neighbours seem to be in a similar situation, for when he goes to seek help τοὺς μὲν οὐκ ἔνδον κατέλαβον, τοὺς δὲ οὐδ᾽ ἐπιδημοῦντας ηὗρον (23).[8] Whether or not these neighbours are out on some agricultural job it is clear that Euphiletos at least carries on an agricultural living from a town or village base.

The case can be put in still stronger terms: there is no clear evidence in the literature for anyone who lives and farms out on his own in the country. There are certainly some equivocal cases — for example the house and land of Apollodoros much discussed in [Demosthenes] 53 and which is certainly no ordinary farm but equipped with a rose garden and nursery[9] — but in many cases the evidence is clearer than it has been thought to be. Thus [Demosthenes] 55, which at first sight might be interpreted as a squabble between the owners of two adjoining farms, can be shown on closer examination to be simply a squabble between the owners of two adjoining pieces of land. For the speaker resorts to references to the family tombs and the vineyards on his land in order to dispute whether or not that land is a natural water-course (13), a rather weak argument which he could hardly have failed to strengthen by referring to a dwelling on the land if there had been one. Likewise the plaintiff has complained of damage to an old wall and to some grain: again reference to damage to a dwelling would make a better case and must surely have been made if there was a dwelling or if the grain had been in a dwelling. Moreover since it follows that the grain that was harmed was not in a house the presence of the grain, although puzzling, cannot imply the presence of a house.[10] Thus this speech would seem to be best read as a dispute between members of the same community who own adjacent pieces of land.

It is a product of this situation where the dwelling and the land are not necessarily contiguous that the term γείτων carries no implication of residence. The speaker of Lysias 17 calls as witnesses τοῦ Κικυννοῖ [χωρίου] τοὺς γείτονας, and it is the universal practice of *poletai* inscriptions, whether describing confiscated property or some property to do with mining, to define property by listing the neighbouring properties.[11]

That a division between *oikia* and *khōrion* is the norm emerges from various statements. [Demosthenes] feels it necessary to state explicitly when there is an identity of residence and place of agricultural activity: γεωργῶ δὲ πρὸς τῷ ἱπποδρόμῳ, καὶ οἰκῶ ἐνταῦθ' ἐκ μειρακίου (47.53). Similarly when the speaker of [Demosthenes] 55 says πάντες τε ὑμεῖς τὸ ἐκ τῶν οἰκιῶν καὶ τὸ ἐκ τῶν χωρίων ὕδωρ εἰς τὴν ὁδὸν ἐξάγειν εἰώθατε (26) he is assuming two separate instances, and this is an assumption shared with the rather similar passage in Plato's *Laws* which relates to the same problem of drainage of water. The Platonic passage comes in a section which deals with easements and relations between neighbours in general and opens (844c) ἐὰν δὲ ἐκ Διὸς ὕδατα γιγνόμενα, τὸν ἐπάνω γεωργοῦντα ἢ καὶ ὁμότοιχον οἰκοῦντα τῶν ὑποκάτω βλάπτῃ τις μὴ διδῶς ἐκροήν... Here again there are two possible cases envisaged: dwelling close together in a village and farming a piece of land that neighbours another, and these two instances are distinct.[12]

The Platonic law goes on to specify that disputes about drainage should be referred to the *astynomoi* if in the city and to the *agronomoi* if in the country. In this split between city and *agros* Plato adopts the division which is almost universal in the classical writers, the split between the city and an undifferentiated countryside. That a split is made in this rather crude way is indicative of prejudices and assumptions, an aspect of relations between the urban and the rural which has been quite thoroughly examined.[13] It follows from this that the *astu* was perceived to have features, advantages, not shared by settlements in the countryside, but this does not mean that there were no settlements: indeed that those settlements could be considered strongly comparable with the *astu* is implied by Thucydides when he notes that the people coming in from Attika to the city in 431 were οὐδὲν ἄλλο ἢ πόλιν τὴν αὑτοῦ ἀπολείπων ἔκαστος 2.16.2).

The negative evidence from the sources can be reinforced by a lexical analysis of the terms that might be thought to be appropriate for the description of an isolated farm, and which are themselves sometimes translated as 'farm'.

There is one passage in Greek literature where ἀγρός is almost certainly accurately translated as 'farm' and where it certainly encompasses reference to a building. At *Odyssey* 24.205f. Odysseus visits Laertes and τάχα δ' ἀγρὸν ἵκοντο καλὸν Λαέρταο τετυγμένον.[14] This usage does not reappear in classical texts, however. Rather it is a word which may cover the countryside in general (in opposition to the town), as in Aristophanes, *Akharnians* 32f.,

> ἀποβλέπων ἐς τὸν ἀγρὸν, εἰρήνης ἐρῶν,
> στυγῶν μὲν ἄστυ, τὸν δ' ἐμὸν δῆμον ποθῶν.

or may be used of farm land, but with the buildings carefully excluded, as when Thucydides has Perikles promise that if Arkhidamos leaves his property untouched whilst ravaging the rest of Attika he will make over to the polis τοὺς δὲ ἀγροὺς τοὺς ἑαυτοῦ καὶ οἰκίας. There are, of course, dubious passages where there may be buildings that are not referred to on land that is called *agros*, but in no case is this clearly so. Iskhomakhos' daily visits εἰς ἀγρόν will not yield evidence that he 'spent most of his time on his farm'.[15]

Although it may be used interchangeably with *agros*, as by Xenophon (*Hell.* 2.4.1), ἦγον δὲ ἐκ τῶν χωρίων, ἵν' αὐτοὶ καὶ οἱ φίλοι τοὺς τούτων ἀγροὺς ἔχοιεν, the word *khōrion* is generally used of any plot of land, whether or not put to agricultural use,[16] and tends to refer to smaller pieces of land

19

than *agros*. Thus Isaios uses *agros* of estates worth from one talent (8.35) to two-and-a-half talents (11.42), and *khōrion* for items of up to 7,000 dr. in value (2.34). The various epigraphical texts describing land tend to avoid the use of the term *agros* at all, except in the sense of 'in the country',[17] while *khōrion* is their regular term for a piece of land. Buildings do not seem ever to be subsumed by the term *khōrion* since their presence is regularly separately specified, as on *horoi* where χωρίον and χωρίον καὶ οἰκία form two separate categories of mortgaged property.

LSJ give 'estate, farm' as one of the meanings of γῆ, but the passages which they quote do not in fact support this meaning. Agricultural land can be security, and be bought to provide future income quite as well as a 'farm' can. *Gē* is the land itself, the basic resource which the farmer works (Xen. *Oik.* 1.8), and varieties of agricultural land are distinguished by qualifying *gē*: γῆ πεφυτευμένη and γῆ ψιλή are land planted with trees and arable land respectively.[18] Its use of a piece of rural property seems rather rare, and the instance at Lysias 19.42 refers to a very substantial piece of land, and has the dwelling associated with it separately specified.

Aristotle (*Pol.* 1263a5−8) uses γήπεδον as interchangeable with gē, Plato (*Laws* 741c5) as complementary to οἰκόπεδον, while it is defined thus at Bekker, *Anecdota Graeca* 1.32.1: γήπεδον·διαφέρει γήπεδον οἰκοπέδου. οἰκόπεδον γὰρ οἰκίας κατερριμμένης ἔδαφος, γήπεδα δὲ τὰ ἐν ταῖς πόλεσι προκείμενα, οἷον κηπία. The occurrence of a γεπ]έδο ἔμισυ at Mounykhia in the Attic Stelai (i³ 424.8) indicates that the term could bear a precise meaning. The link with gē and the contrast with *oikopedon* mean that *gēpedon* can hardly encompass buildings.

There are two terms which refer to land which may be considered briefly here, although there is little temptation to consider that they refer to farms. *SEG* 24.152.2 seems to record the leasing of some land of the type known as φελλεύς. Pollux includes φελλεύς in his list of bad soils (1.227), while Plato suggests that it is the product of γῆ πιείρα after erosion. Evidently stony (Harpokration s.v.), it was not good land for hunting, but could be grazed.[19] ἐσχατιαί seem to be marginal pieces of land but still land that was cultivable. Lewis[20] has discussed the evidence for this type of land, which is surprisingly common in the fourth-century epigraphic evidence. The scholiast on Aiskhines (p. 271 Schultz) associates it with land at the edges of demes (τὰ ἐπὶ τοῖς τέρμασι δὲ τῶν δήμων ἔσχατα κείμενα χωρία ἐσχατιαὶ ἐκαλοῦντο) and the marginal status is well illustrated by an epigraphical example not mentioned by Lewis: Προμηθίων: Αἰσχ[ρα]ι-[ου] ἐκ Κη: ἀπέγραφε: ἐ[σ]|χατιὰν Θρίαι: ἦι γε; βορ: [ἡ ὁδὸς ἡ] ἐπὶ τὸν κλευσ|ον ἄγο: καὶ τὰ ὄρη . . .[21]

There is in addition one term which does not refer to land but to a building, where the building has been thought to be a specifically agricultural one. Kent (1948, 297f.) discussing the Delos temple leases suggested that κλισίον should be translated 'farm'. In Attic literature the word is rare, and it is consistently implied that it is simply a shed or outhouse, not suitable for permanent habitation.[22] The *klision* which appears in a confiscation document (*Hesperia* 15 (1946) 185f.) in association with a house and a *khōrion* is in the deme Melite within the walls of Athens, and so hardly agricultural. It remains possible, however, that in parts of Greece, at least, this term was used for a temporary shelter in the fields.[23]

The classical Attic vocabulary is clearly rich in terms with which to describe land, varying the terms, albeit in a non-technical way, according to size, situation, and quality of the land described. That, by contrast, it has no term at all for the unit of a land with a house from which the land is worked must surely be indicative of the absence of such a unit from the countryside of Attika. Land does occur with a house associated, but this always seems to be seen as land and a house and not as a single unit, let alone as a 'farm'.

There is little sign of development over time in the literature. Menander's *Duskolos* might be though to provide a classic example of an isolated farmer, but in fact Knemon does have neighbours (23ff.) and the farm is adjacent to the shrine of Pan (a factor not to be underestimated, compare the Vari House). Moreover the position of Knemon's dwelling is clearly the dramatic counterpart of his δύσκολος nature, and

21

although he picks up traits of real life Knemon is hardly a typical Athenian; rather, he is a first-rate exemplification of the social disabilities which result from living in isolation. Menander's plays rely on an intense and intimate social life, so that the fact that at least three were set in Attic demes must be an indication that the demes remained close communities down to the last years of the fourth century.[24]

The archaeological evidence

If isolated farms are unknown in the literary evidence for Attika they are far from unknown to the archaeologist. Not only is the number of farms claimed from surface remains rapidly increasing, but two buildings thought to be farms have been fully excavated and published and others more summarily investigated. However, not all the evidence claimed to represent isolated farms is quite what it claims itself to be, and the important questions can only be answered by examining the 'farm' remains in the context of the full archaeological picture of the locality in which they are found.[25]

Two areas of Attika have proved exceptionally rich in claimed 'farm' sites: the Vari—Vouliagmeni area, and the area just north of Sounion at the very southern tip of Attika. Both these areas are also generally well investigated and have abundant remains of other types, and for that reason they will be treated as test-cases here.

The area around the modern settlements of Vouliagmeni and Vari

The remains in this area (map 3), along with those of the whole west coast of Attika, were examined in detail some 20 years ago by Eliot, and have recently been briefly re-examined by Lauter.[26] Archaeological activity in the area has been galvanised by the steady spread of Athens down this coast, and the increasing popularity of Vouliagmeni and Varkiza as tourist resorts.

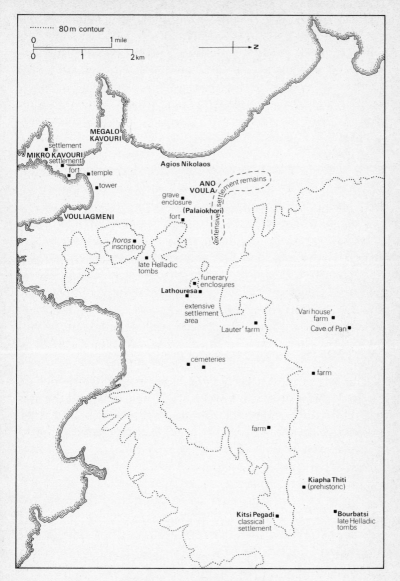

········ 80 m contour

MEGALO KAVOURI
settlement
MIKRO KAVOURI
settlements
fort
■ temple
■ tower

Agios Nikolaos

ANO VOULA
grave enclosure
(Palaiokhori)
fort ■

settlement remains

extensive settlement remains

VOULIAGMENI

horos inscription

late Helladic tombs

funerary enclosures
Lathouresa

extensive settlement area

'Lauter' farm

'Vari house' farm ■
Cave of Pan ■

cemeteries

■ farm

farm ■

Kiapha Thiti ■ (prehistoric)

Kitsi Pegadi ■
classical settlement

■ Bourbatsi
late Helladic tombs

Map 3. The Vari–Vouliagmeni area.

At Vouliagmeni itself the Mikro Kavouri peninsula[27] has, apart from prehistoric finds, a temple of Apollo Zoster (still visible) with an associated building interpreted as a priest's house.[28] Some 150 m away was a house with a tower where some thirty-six clay loom-weights were found. North-west and north-east of the temple were two further towers.[29] South of the temple, on the highest point of the peninsula, were traces of a fort, investigated by Mastrokostas but never published. Finds of Ptolemaic coins in the vicinity make it possible that the fort served as some sort of Ptolemaic base in the Chremonidean war.[30] Virtually nothing has been recorded from the area of the main modern settlement of Vouliagmeni, but classical sherds have been found near the War Memorial and late geometric pottery and a grave stele have been reported as 'from Vouliagmeni'.[31]

North of Megalo Kavouri, remains of an uncertain nature have been reported in the immediate area of the church of Agios Nikolaos,[32] but the greatest concentration of well known and excavated finds comes from the area immediately north and east of the junction of the Voula—Vouliagmeni and Voula—Vari roads — the area known to Eliot and earlier investigators as Palaiokhori. A great complex of human activity has been revealed in this area, with houses, some of them very large, tombs, a rupestral inscription, and a potter's workshop with two kilns. The remains stretch round the western and southern slopes of a low hill, and it is doubtful whether either the northern or eastern limits have been reached. Excavation continues in the eastern extension of the remains, in a triangle of land bounded by Odos Kalymnou, Odos Herakleidon, and Odos Dragatsaniou of the modern *demos* of Voula. Here a very compact residential area, with narrow streets and at least one tiny shrine, has been uncovered (pl. 2). This seems to have been occupied in the fifth century, at least, but further west along Odos Herakleidon a residence (?agricultural) of hellenistic date has been excavated, and since Eliot reported sherd material from the seventh century it appears that the general area was densely occupied from the archaic period onwards.[33]

The area of ancient structures also stretches south of the road to Vari (Leophoros Varis). A complex of buildings and tombs has been excavated in Odos Athenon, and a large number of walls are visible on the ground surface, especially in the area just east of the modern football pitch. This area has one very upstanding square structure which is probably funerary. The round structure interpreted by Papagianno-poulos as the theatre of Aixone, and reinterpreted by Eliot as a threshing floor belongs in this area.[34] As Eliot and others have argued, there seems little doubt that we have here the remains of the deme Halai Aixonides.

One of the most striking remains in the area has only recently come to light in published literature although it was noted in the sherd catalogue of the British School at Athens as long ago as 1958. On the summit of the height marked 102.5 on the *Karten von Attika,* Blatt VII are exten-sive remains of walls, including a rubble circuit wall creating a fortified akropolis site approximately 45 m wide and 115 m long. On the south side some 80 m of wall survives to over a metre high and from 1.9 to 2.2 m thick. The walls can be traced on the east and north sides also and the west end is precipitous enough to make walling unnecessary. Inside there are extensive traces of buildings and remains of roof tiles. The sherds in the British School Collection which come from the site suggest a late fourth-century or early third-century date, and this, together with the style of walling, supports an interpretation of this structure as connected with the Chremonidean War.[35]

The presence of this site does not affect the overall pattern of settlement of the area: there are the two basic clusters of settlement, one around the shrine on Mikro Kavouri (Cape Zoster), a shrine known from literary references to have been of more than local significance, and the other covering an area of at least 50 hectares north and east of Agios Nikolaos. The latter seems to have been a very mixed settlement, of varying density, with a cemetery on its southern fringe, and with some signs of ribbon-development on the roads leading north to Aixone and Athens and east to Anagyrous. Halai Aixonides was neither a particularly large nor a particularly wealthy deme;[36] the one unusual feature was the important sanctuary. The sanctuary clearly does not determine the choice of a nucleated main settlement here, and so this deme looks a good candidate for what a deme unconstrained by special factors looks like in terms of settlement pattern.

At Vari, however, which lies immediately to the east, just over the low foothills of Hymettos, the pattern of archaeological discovery has been rather different. This is in part a result of the modern settlement history, for Vari was a *metokhi* and has long been settled, while Voula and Vouliagmeni were still almost totally deserted in the nineteenth century. At Vari it is the cemetery finds that are most notable. Just before the pass leading from Ano Voula opens out into the coastal plain a number of classical funerary enclosures have been discovered.[37] East of the modern village two further extensive cemeteries have been partly excavated:[38] to the south of the road to Koropi a large number of tombs were dug in the early 1960s, revealing that the area had been used for burials from the eighth century to the fourth century; to the north of the road excavations in the 1930s had yielded material of similar periods, notable for the fine quality of the pottery. It seems possible that the two cemetery areas in fact join, and that burials took place over about a kilometre of land stretching south-east from the foot of Hymettos; a detailed study of the arrangement of tombs in the various periods would be invaluable but is impossible on the basis of published evidence.

Between the monumental grave terraces and the cemeteries lie a number of other remains. On the top of the hill Lathouresa, immediately south of the grave terraces, are quite extensive remains of walls and buildings. On the northeast tip there is a small shrine, while the summit has an altar and traces of adjacent buildings, surrounded by a further wall which may have rooms attached internally, while on the south-east spur is a complex of walls investigated in 1939 and interpreted as a shrine and twenty-five houses. The finds from the 1939 excavations included material from the archaic period, while the summit has yielded fifth-century sherds.[39] The remains on this hill clearly need to be considered together. They are united by all having religious

associations, and, given the lack of any natural water supply
on the hill, residence in any part needs positive proof.[40]

The lower eastern slopes of this hill form the site for the
modern village, and the ancient village may have been situated
here also. Traces of walls were noted in the nineteenth
century and more have been uncovered in recent years.
Whether the settlement extended as far as Agioi Pantes,
where some notable material was reported in the nineteenth
century but where there is little to be seen today, remains
doubtful.[41]

Vari is most remarkable, however, for the number of
isolated farms that have been claimed in the area. Three
were reported by Eliot, and of these the house below the
Cave of Pan has since been excavated, and Lauter has reported
another.[42] Only two of these, the excavated site and the
Lauter house, claim to be classical. The Vari house lies very
close to the Cave of Pan, in a sheltered position well into the
foothills of Hymettos and at the end of a ridge. The valleys
on either side of the house presumably gave a supply of
well-watered land, but this is by no means the best land in
the area, and it has now been given over to pines. The house
represents a considerable effort of construction: a terrace
was artificially cut and an outer enclosure constructed. Yet
occupation at the site appears to have been short: although
the excavators acknowledge (p. 373) that 'our collection of
sherds may not be totally representative of the occupation'
they argue that the quantity of sherds indicates 'a decade, or
at most two, of actual occupation' (p. 397). The presence of
a number of late fifth-century sherds is explained as indicating an earlier building which 'seems likely to have been
of slight construction'. The excavators further admitted that
'it contained no hard evidence . . . to prove that the house-
holder was an active farmer and carried on some of his work
under his own roof' (p. 418). It did, however, yield the
evidence that enabled a proof of the classical practice of
bee-keeping with ceramic hives for the first time.[43]

The Lauter house is a slighter affair altogether, covering
only 140 square metres compared with the 246 square metres

of the Vari house. It too lies on the rising ground of the low foothills of Hymettos, but in a much more exposed position, closer to the village and just above a shallow valley with a depth of good soil. The evidence as to date and purpose is exiguous. Of the few sherds on the site most are from storage vessels, but Lauter does report one black-glazed sherd and one base which he dates to the later fifth century.[44] Given the tiny size of the rooms it is far from certain that this was a permanent residence: it may have been a seasonal shelter, a store, and a fold for a few animals.

The other two 'farms' are known in less detail. On the north side of the modern road to Koropi, just before that road bends to sweep round Kiapha Thiti, Eliot found remains of 'a substantial and well-built farmstead with a large walled area behind it', with a cistern and sherds that were mainly Roman but included some hellenistic material. North-west of this, and virtually on the line between it and the Vari House, were some scanty remains indicating a house complex of the late Roman period.[45]

While it is unlikely that *none* of these sites was ever a farm, the evidence for classical isolated farming settlements in the area is clearly deficient, and the general pattern of settlement in the Vari area conforms closely to that around Vouliagmeni. Again the most notable geographical position receives a shrine with attendant buildings. Although there is not here a clearly excavated site, enough remains are known to be confident that there is a nucleated, village, settlement, especially in view of the concentrated cemetery finds. The scatter of isolated farms does not materialise: only two sites are classical, and of these the house below the Cave of Pan may have some rather strong connection with that cave sanctuary, while the Lauter house seems unlikely to have been permanently occupied by a family.

It is not impossible, however, that the hellenistic period saw some change in the pattern. The large hellenistic/Roman site reported by Eliot near Kiapha Thiti is not particularly isolated (it was probably near an ancient as well as the modern road, and is not out of sight of the village) but it does break away from the area of classical settlement. The presence of one new site hardly changes the overall pattern, of course, but the presence of a late fourth-century or hellenistic *horos* inscription on Kamini, the ridge between Vari and Vouliagmeni may indicate a new concern about territorial definition such as is likely to mark a dispersion of settlement.[46]

Sounion and Thorikos: the south-east tip of Attika

The mineral resources of the Laureotike and their re-exploitation in recent times have ensured that the whole area has been fairly closely examined (map 4). The upstanding remains of the temple of Poseidon have led to excavation in its immediate vicinity on Cape Sounion, and work on the fort at Thorikos has led to full-scale excavation of the Thorikos site by the Belgians. The result is a picture of the area in antiquity which, if not complete, at least has some pretensions to be without systematic bias towards one type of site.

The excavations at Thorikos continue, and much more certainly remains to be discovered, but the nature of the settlement has become tolerably clear. Originally known for its theatre and temple (possibly of Demeter, see below chapter 8), it is now apparent that domestic occupation and industrial activity took place together within a small area close by these. It is less clear how far the settlement spread down from the foot of Velatouri and across the plain. The plain has suffered from the accumulation of a younger fill, and complete archaeological investigation is never likely to take place. Some remains are known from the plain, of which the item of most interest here is a round tower. One tower complex has been dug in the settlement itself, and finds there suggested that for part of its varied life it was used as a farm. Two more round foundations, probably of a similar nature, were dug through by Stais, who thought them tholos tombs. The tower in the plain may be similar, but until it is actually investigated it is not

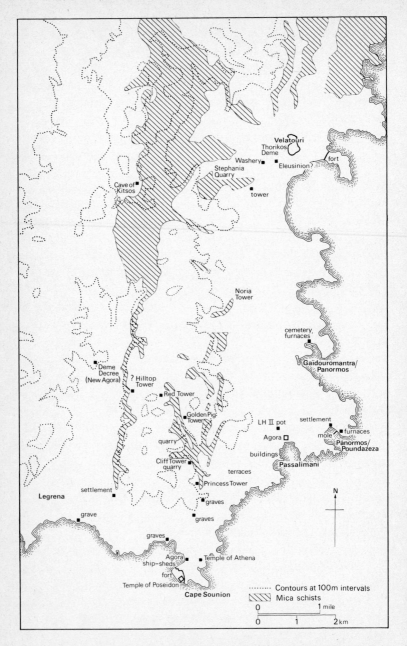

Map 4. The Sounion–Thorikos area (mining remains omitted).

possible to say either that it is a farm or that it is isolated.[47]

The coast immediately south of Thorikos has revealed remarkably little in the way of ancient remains, and unless all trace was destroyed in the nineteenth-century development it would appear that there was no ancient settlement at all on the site of modern Laurion. Between Laurion and Sounion, however, extensive and varied remains are known, which suggest industrial activity and a cemetery at Panormos,[48] industrial activity (some traces of which are now submerged) and a number of finds indicative of agriculture, including a farm and terrace complex occupied in the hellenistic period, at Poundazesa,[49] and some sort of settlement at Pascha Limani where an agora has been added to the archaic head, harbour and building remains, and hoard of late Roman coins already known.[50]

The Cape itself had in classical times temples of Poseidon and Athena, a *heroon* of Phrontis, and, from 412, a fort. This was later supplemented by some hellenistic ship-sheds.[51] There are some possible ancient terraces on the neck of the promontory and foundations so impressive that Thompson (1938, 75f.) wrote: 'The original construction gives the impression of good Hellenistic work. Its plan would be suitable as that of a small market place or Agora into which shops or storerooms were later incorporated ... As designed the building adjoined a dock.'

The mining leases locate works both 'in Sounion' and in certain named locations within Sounion. The placing of these regions is uncertain, but most of the Sounion mines seem certain to have lain in the Agrileza valley. The remains of mines naturally distribute themselves according to the availability of rich ores, while the washeries have their position partly dictated by the presence of water, and the Agrileza valley is riddled with cisterns. Two washery complexes here have been excavated recently, and the total spread of mining remains has been newly mapped by Conophagos.[52] The valley also has remains of two quite extensive quarries.

The remains which are of most interest here are the seven

towers reported by Young.[53] One of these towers was destroyed before he had a chance to examine it fully, and another he considers to have had a purely industrial use, but of the remaining five he remarks that 'we may safely conclude that these towers do, indeed, mark the sites of flourishing agricultural estates' (p. 142). If Young is right then these are the most certain examples of relatively isolated farms known from Attika.

In three of the five cases there is no doubt that the tower has some agricultural connection, because of surface finds on the site (including beehive sherds from the Princess Tower).[54] In addition the Cliff Top Tower has recently been revealed to have a series of rupestral inscriptions which seem to indicate residence, religious activity, and even burial (possibly), and to be surrounded by a field wall enclosing some 180 plethra (50 acres).[55] This vast area is by no means all farmland, for while the wall does run down to the valley on the north and east sides it also encloses the whole of one quarry and two entrances to mines. A connection seems likely between these mines and those that appear in the mining leases as on the land of one Timesios, for the rupestral inscriptions here show the farm being acquired by one Timesios from a defaulting debtor. The tower itself stands on a surface formed by quarrying, and the same applies to the nearby 'house', while several of the inscriptions are cut in quarry faces. All of this seems to show that the quarrying must have ceased before any of this activity began, thus dating the latter into the fourth century. This does not mean that all the post-quarrying activities on the site are contemporary: Waelkens has argued that the rupestral inscriptions are of varying dates, and it remains to be shown that the house and tower are part of a single development, or that either belongs with the threshing floor. There is no doubt that the site history is complex and we have no more right to assume that agriculture was ever the primary activity here than to assume that the worship of Hermes was.

This site can hardly be regarded as typical of an Attic agricultural establishment, and for that reason it is notable that it has yielded the first epigraphic evidence for the employment of an *epitropos*, although the use of such farm overseers is discussed at length in Xenophon's *Oikonomikos*. One possible reconstruction of the history of the site is that when the completion of the building work at Sounion ended the regular use of the quarry the land was bought by Aristomenes, either for agriculture or for its mineral resources, but that through this or some other venture he ran into debt. Timesios then came into the land, allowed the mining possibilities to be exploited by others and put in a bailiff to tap the agricultural resources — and no doubt to keep an eye on the miners.[56]

The site history of the other towers cannot be reconstructed in such detail, and it is unlikely that it is in all cases so complex. The proximity of the Golden Pig Tower to an area of very dense mining remains makes it doubtful whether the dubious evidence of a dwelling close by constitutes sufficient proof that it was a farm at all, let alone always or primarily. Young regarded these towers as manifestations of a more general phenomenon, but still felt it necessary to give special reasons for their presence in this area. He stresses that 'All five of these towers, then stood in good, if restricted, farming land' (p. 141).

A closer examination of the environment in which the towers are found reveals that this is more idiosyncratic than Young suggests. All three towers which Young is most confident to be the centres of estates stand on the upper marble. However, the field wall of the Cliff Tower encloses only a relatively small area of the upper marble, the area with the mine entrances, and the majority of its land lies on the mica schists of the valleys below. Similarly the Princess Tower is so sited as to be right by the ancient road, possibly then, as now, at a crossroads, but the good land below is on mica schists. Likewise the valley below the Golden Pig Tower. The other four towers Young mentions I have not been able to locate accurately on the ground, but the Yellow Tower certainly lies on schists while both Red and Hilltop Towers commanded soil on mica schists — even if the Red

Tower did not exploit it. The tower in the Noria valley may have been on mica schist, but it is more probable that it was on quaternary material.

All of this shows a preference for one particular rock type that is all the more remarkable since the areas of mica schist are very restricted. The preference for schist over marble is not surprising but the particular preference for *mica* schists is less expected. Mica is in fact very resistant to chemical weathering, but it does break up into small pieces relatively readily. The pattern of modern vegetation and the almost total limitation of modern cultivation to quaternary and mica schist areas shows that the ancient preference was soundly based.[57]

The towers are almost certainly contemporary with the exploitation of the mines, and it must be considered doubtful whether this land would have been used for arable purposes at all but for the demand created by mining. Given the density of mining works, any decision to exploit the land had to be a decision to exploit the land from farms outside the village settlement, for without presence on the land there would be little possibility of control. It is notable that a field wall was found necessary at the Cliff Tower, for there is little sign that such walls were a normal phenomenon in Attika.[58] Young talks grandly of 'towered country estates' but the Cliff Tower was evidently unattractive enough to deter the owner from residence. Thus while these may be good examples of relatively isolated farms they serve less to show that such farms 'must have been a common feature of the countryside' and more to suggest that only an exceptional conjunction of extraordinary demand and extraordinary geology would induce the Athenian to live and farm in isolation.[59]

The peculiarities of Sounion as a deme have not been exhausted by the explanation of the occurrence of these isolated farms. While Thorikos clearly conforms to the pattern of settlement seen above in the Voula and Vari areas, with a single nucleated settlement accounting for almost all the residences, Sounion has been seen to be extraordinarily spread about. It is symptomatic of this that as many as five agoras may be attested for the deme: the two possible examples, mentioned above, of which remains have been found, the two attested by the 'new agora' inscription (*IG* ii^2 1180), and the 'agora in Koile' attested in the Salaminioi inscription (*SEG* 21.527). It is possible that the latter was in the urban deme of Koile, and not in Sounion at all, but both the agoras of the other inscription must be in the deme, and unless the find-spot of the inscription is highly misleading at least the 'new agora' seems unlikely to be one of those known on the ground.[60] All these factors suggest that there may well have been more than one village in which men of Sounion lived. Kakovogiannis has recently suggested that the classical deme proper was sited at Pascha Limani, but that there was a subsidiary settlement, dependent on mining activity, at the top of the Agrileza valley.[61]

Mining and geology clearly play an important part in determining the very different pattern of settlement of men of Sounion from the pattern of settlement of men of Halai Aixonides, Anagyrous, or Thorikos. There is, however, also another factor. The major sanctuary at Cape Zoster attracted a small settlement away from the major nucleus, while the major centre had its own much smaller shrines, and there is a possible division between the religious and the political office holders in that deme (below chapter 4). At Vari, and still more at Thorikos, the shrines are of little more than local importance and their location is influenced as much by the pattern of settlement as that pattern is by their location. The sacrificial calendar from Thorikos, with its mixture of elements which we would separate out as 'religious' and 'political' well bears out the testimony to the entanglement of work, residence, and religion given by the remains on the ground.[62]

The sanctuaries at Cape Sounion clearly fall into the same category as the Zoster ones. That they were part of national religious life already in the archaic period is shown by the presence of a large number of *kouroi*, all dating to a short period at the beginning of the sixth century.[63] Although fragmentary, *IG* i³ 8 shows the body of Athenians as a whole taking an interest in the cult sufficient to care for its financial well-being by levying a small tax on shipping that put in at the Cape. This is the earliest of three cases in which funds were raised for cults in this way in the fifth century.[64] That particular groups of Athenians might also use the shrines at the Cape is shown by the way in which the Thorikos calendar provides for sacrifices there in Boedromion. The festival and associated ship races held off Sounion seem to have been open to all. All of this was more or less independent of the local community (although men of Sounion seem to be afforded a special treatment in i³ 8), and is largely the result of the prominence of the headland site.

For Sounion the situation is still more complex, for along with the adoption of the Cape as a focus for all Athenians there was another group within the deme which had apparently virtually taken over an area. This is the *genos* of the Salaminioi, about whose nature and activities in the fourth century we are well informed by *SEG* 21.527. This *genos* seems to have had a considerable stake in the area called Porthmos and the nearby Hale.[65] The *genos* included many who were demesmen of Sounion, but it was not identical with the deme. Whether there was *any* room left for a structure of shrines and observances which were the particular focus of the demesmen is at present unclear, but it seems likely that, ironically, the presence of major shrines will have weakened the sense of the men of Sounion that they were a religious community.

That Thorikos conforms to the settlement pattern found elsewhere is an indication that the unusual mineral resources of the Laureotike were not on their own enough to produce a dispersed pattern of settlement. The multi-centred pattern found at Sounion, with its scatter of isolated farms, is the product of the direct and the indirect action of partly interconnected geographical and geological circumstances,[66] and in particular of the ways in which they constrained and determined the extent to which demesmen formed a clearly-focused social group.

The making of a settlement pattern

The close examination of the literary evidence suggested that isolated country residences were at least not a phenomenon that Athenians of the fifth and fourth centuries chose to write or talk about. The review of the pattern of archaeological discovery in two very different areas of Attika, both moderately well investigated, has suggested that such isolated residences were indeed rare, and that the settlements designated by deme names were perhaps most frequently single villages, rather than a number of smaller groups of dwellings.[67] There were exceptions, however, areas which were politically single units but which were not single nucleated settlements. Sounion is one example, and the multiple foci of the deme are reflected in the occurrence of separately named regions all said to be 'at Sounion'. On that basis another exception would be the large deme of Aphidna, where similar local names occur, as for example in the description of a denounced *khōrion* as Ἀφίδνῃσι ἐν Πεταλιδῶν.[68] That such cases were few in number seems to be indicated by the fact that breakaway settlements (which often seems to be what the smaller of two demes which form a pair 'Upper X' and 'Lower X' is) do have political representation, and that the constitutional reforms of 307/6 did not give deme status to any new settlements.

On the one hand this finding is consistent with the general observation that completely dispersed settlement patterns seem to be a product of modern agricultural conditions, and with the absence of dispersed settlement patterns from more recent Greek settlement history;[69] on the other hand there is a contrast with the situation known from other parts of the Greek world, especially in the late classical period. Isolated farms are beginning to be well attested in the colonial Greek world, both in the Black Sea and in Magna Graecia,[70] and, despite literary evidence for the preference for 'town' life, surface survey is beginning to produce good evidence for isolated agricultural establishments in the southern Argolid, the Karystos area of Euboia, and to a certain extent in north-west Boiotia.[71] In the Ionian islands there is reason to believe that there was a change to a more dispersed pattern of settlement after the Peloponnesian War.[72] There may be a move to a more dispersed pattern in Attika too (above p. 28f.), but the evidence is not especially strong, and any move that there is would seem to be rather late. In the face of this it becomes important to try to account for the fact that Attika is so different.

The geography of Attika is peculiar in various ways, and since the shortage of acceptable land and the irregularity of its disposition were factors which produced isolated farms in Sounion there is a prima-facie case for seeing geographical factors as of major importance. Those who have discussed the problem in the past have laid considerable stress on the interconnections of settlement pattern and water supply, arguing that a dispersed settlement pattern is only possible when there is a large number of springs available. This factor seems to have been considerably overemphasised. The connection between exploitation of the countryside and the need for water is appreciated in both the Solonic and the Platonic easements, but although both realise that there *might* be difficulty in finding water on one's land neither envisages it to be unlikely that there will be water on a neighbour's land, indeed they assume that there will be.[73] There are areas of Atikka where water resources are not abundant, but the system of cisterns to enable industrial uses of water in the Sounion area shows that it was possible to provide water in large quantities even in an unpromising area if the demand was there. Furthermore there are equally areas of Attika which *are* well-watered, but there is no indication that these areas are full of isolated residences in the classical period. Nor is Attika exceptionally well or badly supplied with water compared with other parts of the southern Greek mainland, and thus water supplies will not explain why Attika is *different.*

The particular geographical factor which is picked out by the study of Sounion is the nature of the soil, and this will serve as justification for a longer examination of Attic settlement from a pedological perspective.[74] Of the four

demes examined in detail above Halai Aixonides is on rendsinas of a sandy/loamy nature, with some hard limestone
fragments; Anagyrous dominates a large expanse of loamy
fans of ejection from destroyed rendsinas and red soils;
Thorikos commands extensive alluvial fans, partly affected
by post-classical marine transgression at the coast, and the
background scatter of sherds seems to indicate that in the
Stephani valley, at least, cultivation was carried on up
beyond the quaternary area and onto the mica schists. By
contrast for Sounion the eastern coastal strip provides a
limited extent of eroded rendsina soils with an even smaller
area of alluvium behind, while inland the soils are very
patchy -- some rendsinas on the marble and some brown
forest soils on the schists.

The general or precise position of some eighty-five further
demes (excluding demes within the city wall) is more or
less certainly known.[75] The distribution of these according
to soil type is as follows (demes on two soil types are treated
as half of each):

Soil type	Demes on	Demes partly on	Bouleutai from
Alluvium	16	10	76 + 38/2
Rendsina in situ	2	2	10 + 9/2
Eroded rendsina	15	9	50 + 69/2
Rendsina with hardpan	11	11	61 + 36/2
Fans of ejection from rendsinas/red soils	11	6	53 + 31/2
Degraded solonetz red soil	2	0	8
Patchy rendsinas/red soils	4	1	9 + 8/2
Patchy rendsinas/forest soils	5	2	10 + 3/2
Eroded and transported rendsinas with hardpan/ alluvium	2	1	13 + 6/2
	68	43/2	290 + 200/2

The figures must be used with care: the areas of the various
soil types in Attika are not at all equal, for by surface area
the patchy soils cover the largest part of Attika, followed in

order by eroded rendsinas, rendsinas *in situ*, and fans of ejection from eroded rendsinas. Further the preference for settling on slightly elevated ground leads to a further under-emphasis on the rendsinas *in situ* in favour of the eroded rendsinas.

Some conclusions may nevertheless cautiously be drawn: alluvial soils are inhabited, and there may even be a slight preference for them; in general there is no great fussiness over soil type, for all the soils that are both cultivable and occur in broad enough stretches are settled. Furthermore, using bouleutic quotas as an indication of relative population, no soil type consistently supports larger settlements than another with the exception of the patchy soils. Thus it appears that only at the extreme, when soil type comes seriously to undercut the possibility of production at all does settlement size seem to be affected.[76]

It is the demes that are found on poor soils that are of greatest interest here. There are twelve demes on patchy soils according to the soil map.[77] Examination on the ground eliminates four of these that are in fact adjacent to considerable, if isolated, areas of good soil. Two of the remaining eight are only partly on patchy soil. The six that remain are Deiradiotai (if correctly sited at Daskaleio), Amphitrope, Besa, Sounion, the Kolonai and Korydallos. The occurrence of Deiradiotai in this list raises the possibility that the resources of the sea were important for marginal communities, although this site would also enjoy a limited alluvial coastal plain.[78] Besa, Amphitrope and Sounion all belong to the mining region and the Kolonai may be, in at least one case, connected with the exploitation of the Pendele marble quarries.[79] Only in the case of Korydallos, a tiny deme returning one member to the *boule*, is no special explanation for its existence forthcoming;[80] all the others were clearly not primarily dependent on agriculture.

Thus while the Athenians were not constrained to settle in villages by limited water resources, nor were they compelled to settle in any particular pattern by the distribution of agricultural land. Both water and soils allow equally of scattered or village settlement: geographical factors seem far from being determinant. Evidence from Xenophon and Theophrastos concerning how to deal with sandy and with waterlogged soils seems to indicate that there was some pressure on land in the classical period,[81] but the disinclination for farming in isolation seems to have meant that unless the returns were very high patchy soils would not be exploited. Even if this land was still used for pasture, this is a very remarkable state of affairs.[82]

Since geography did not enforce this pattern of settlement it must have been a product of human choice. That choice was not one that was economically 'rational': there is no doubt that a nucleated settlement pattern leads to cultivators having to travel further than they would have to in a dispersed pattern, and this is economically inefficient.[83] Such nucleated settlement patterns remain common in the Mediterranean today, and analysis of examples from South Italy has suggested that they persist because of the advantages villages give in terms of enabling political activity, diversity of employment, and greater concentration of and control over the family.[84]

The possibilities that the settlement pattern might be socially and politically determined is clearly attractive in the case of classical Athens: Athens was exceptional in being a very large polis, a democratic polis from an early date, and in having a system which recognised politically the existence of rural settlement.[85] The demes already existed before the Kleisthenic reforms,[86] and those reforms presuppose a nucleated settlement pattern. Demes were primarily communities, and in classical usage the name of the demesmen seems prior to the name of the deme, but the fact of a nucleated settlement pattern meant that deme names also 'meant' areas of land, so that, for example, metics could be identified by where they resided.[87] The whole working of Athenian democracy demanded that the demes continued to be communities, and without modern means of communication that was effectively a demand that people continued to dwell together in villages. The degree of identification with other members of the same deme demanded by the mechanisms of local and central politics will become apparent from the discussion of the demes as political units in chapter 4 below. The evidence that demesmen felt that there was a special tie between them in circumstances of all sorts is apparent on a general level from Aristotle's observation that demesmen form an example of a natural *koinonia* (*EN* 1160a), and there are particular examples of the deme being the arena to which one first looked for military recruits, the source of someone to mediate a loan for one, and of witnesses in a court-case.[88] Further aspects of this social interaction will be examined in chapter 7.

Once it is recognised that the settlement pattern is not simply the natural by-product of the geography, but that we are dealing with communities of people, it can be seen more clearly that the relationship between the various areas of human activity will never be a one-way one: the way men organise themselves to work the land, the way they organise themselves to celebrate natural and divine events, the way they organise themselves to relate to others in all spheres from marriage to foreign policy will all be inter-related, each will influence and be influenced by the others. To establish the nature of the settlement pattern is not simply to give the answer to an antiquarian enquiry, it is to offer a new perspective on a society at work, to destroy the old assumed framework of understanding, the framework of the state, of the separateness of the political, and to begin to build anew with an awareness of the complexity of the interdependence of human activity.

The size and the wealth of the demes

Given that the demes were in any case necessarily close and active communities, and that in most cases they were in addition single villages, calculating the order of magnitude of the population of the demes reveals a significant factor in the way in which demes perform, both socially and politically.

Kleisthenes' reforms provided for a council of 500 to be

manned by the demes. From the middle of the fourth century onwards the survival of epigraphic evidence has enabled the more or less secure calculation of the number of councillors provided by each deme, and the scanty evidence that there is from the fifth century seems to indicate that the quota was the same in the fifth century.[89] Deme affiliations in 507 probably depended upon self-identification with a locality, which must normally have meant that they depended on residence, and subsequently a man retained the demotic he inherited regardless of whether or not he continued to live in his ancestral community.[90] Demes must have grown at different rates, so that by the late fourth century the relationship between population and bouleutic quota will not have been constant, but nevertheless a deme must have remained above a certain minimum size if it was to fulfil this political obligation. The use of the bouleutic quota as a basis for the calculation of the citizen population and of the size of the demes thus provides a minimum figure which must have been already reached by the late sixth century and must have been maintained thereafter (it is not unlikely that it was considerably exceeded).

As a check on these minimum figures it is possible to gain some knowledge of the actual population of the demes in the late sixth century from the lists of men who served as public arbitrators, who were men in their sixtieth year.

The use of bouleutic quotas and *diaitetai* lists for the calculation of population is not new, but previous calculations have been less than rigorous.[91] Following the admirable demonstration of Hopkins, the calculations here are based on the UN model life tables for persons from under-developed pre-industrial countries with a life expectancy at birth of *c.* 25 years.[92] Since the 500 *bouleutai* were drawn from citizens over 30 who had not already served more than once, there effectively had to be 250 thirty-year-old citizens available each year.[93] On the model life being used here, men of thirty form about 1.5% of the total male population, so that some 16,000 males are required to produce the 250 thirty-year-olds (cf. table 1).[94] This requirement may also be expressed as the demand for a male population of 65 to produce one new *bouleutes*, so that a deme needs to have a male population of 32.5 × bouleutic quota. Thus the largest of the demes, Akharnai, returning 22 *bouleutai*, needed a population of 715 males, while the 'average' deme of 3.7 *bouleutai* required about 120 males.

It must be stressed that these are minimum figures which take no account of the fact that there may have been, in theory at least, a property qualification for office,[95] nor of unwillingness to serve. Although it is true that 'a deme is not a big enough unit to have a constant annual birth and death rate' this is less important for this calculation of the theoretical demands for *bouleutai* than it is for calculations from the actual figures of *diaitetai*.[96]

Males in their sixtieth year form *c.* 0.5% of the model male population. The one surviving complete list of *diaitetai* (ii² 1926) has 103 names and this would imply a male population of 21,000. Demes which figure in more than one list support the evidence of this overall figure that the minimum population demanded for bouleutic purposes was comfortably exceeded in the late fourth century: thus Paiania seems to average about three *diaitetai*, yielding a male population of about 600, compared with the 390 needed for the *boule*, while Kollytos averaging *c.* 2.5 would have a male population of *c.* 500, compared with the 100 needed for the *boule*. At the same time, however, there are many smaller demes which are absent from the appropriate part of the lists.

The figures derived from the *diaitetai* lists must again be minima. The Aristotelian *Athenaion Politeia* makes it clear that selection was made according to the eponym and since only ephebes acquired age-group eponyms it seems that only ephebes became *diaitetai*. It is generally thought that only men of the hoplite class served as ephebes, and this seems to be justified.[97] Thus, as Gomme, Sundwall, and Lewis had already argued, not all men of 59 served as *diaitetai*. The corollary of this is that at least at the end of the fourth century it would have been possible to fill the *boule* from the hoplite class.

Above these minimum figures we are reduced to speculation, but the evidence that men did in fact serve twice in
the *boule* is limited,[98] and it may be a reasonable working
assumption that the Athenian male citizen population was,
at least in the fourth century, sufficient to man the *boule*
with men serving just once. This would give a total male
population of 33,000 of whom between 20,000 to 21,000
would be over 18. The minimum population of a deme would
therefore be 65 males.

If we simply double the figure for the total Athenian
population the smallest deme becomes a community of at
least 130 people, the largest a large village of about 1,500.
Even the smallest deme will have constituted much more
than simply a family unit, and many will have been comparable with the leading market towns of medieval England,
places like Sudbury, Loughborough, Stamford, and Wisbech,
of which 'few can have contained more than 1,500 souls'.[99]
In view of this it is hardly surprising that we find the demes
constituting important and quite independent social groups.
The difference between a community living in groups of
this size and one scattered in isolated farms is a fundamental
one.

The bouleutic quotas can be further employed to give
some indication of the distribution of wealth through Attika.
Subjective judgments have not infrequently been made
on this matter but the establishment of a catalogue of
propertied men which is based on secure, if demanding,
criteria of wealth and which, if not complete, is not regionally
biased, through the work of Davies (1971), enables a more
scientific assessment to be made.[100]

Taking the number of wealthy men attested per deme
from Davies' work[101] and dividing this by the number of
bouleutai provided by that deme gives a crude index of the
wealth of the deme. The results are shown in table 2. The
figures for individual demes are clearly too subject to the
effect of individual chance attestations to be taken too
seriously, but the results for groups of demes are of more
interest. The pre-eminence of the Mesogaia reinforces belief
in the landed basis of much Athenian wealth, while the

comparative poverty of the Thriasian plain may indicate the degree to which men from other demes, resident in Athens, had a stake in its exploitation (cf. chapter 3).

Two notably poor groups of demes should be noted here, as a preliminary to two following chapters (6 and 8). The mining demes have a low index figure of 1.19, while the group of all the demes from which owners of land in the mining region come has an index of 1.89. On the basis of this it would appear that mining did not create wealth for the local community but did attract attention from the propertied class. The second poor group of demes is that possessing important religious sanctuaries (Rhamnous, Marathon, Halai (both), Phlya, Philaidai, Sounion, and Eleusis). These together have an index figure of 0.96, which is lower than that of any region. From this it might be suggested that major sanctuaries were more a drain on local wealth than a source of enrichment. But it is equally possible that the presence of a shrine may have led to the ascription of too large a bouleutic quota by causing the deme to be thought of as larger than in fact it was.

The positive evidence afforded by these calculations for the links between wealth and agriculture provides an appropriate point from which to launch an enquiry into the local aspects of Athenian land-holding.

CHAPTER 3

THE PATTERN OF LAND-HOLDING IN CLASSICAL ATTIKA

In a society grounded in agriculture social relations and settlement patterns are bound to be related to patterns of land-holding and land use. The relationship is not a simple one, however: land use may be a determining factor in the settlement pattern, but it may be itself determined. Thus some recent anthropological work has produced examples of settlement patterns being altered by social changes, and of land use changing in the wake of these.[1]

Attika is virtually the only area in classical Greece where enough information has survived to allow work on the relationship between land use and settlement pattern. While other parts of Greece have produced some detailed information for small areas[2] there is a large body of data for Attika relating sporadically to the whole territory. These data are not easy to handle, however. That uniquely Attic body of writings — the corpus of the Attic orators — contains a considerable body of information, but this information is not only patchy, it is systematically biased towards the richer levels of society. This corpus is supplemented by a number of epigraphic documents, lists of confiscated property drawn up by the *poletai*, lists of land transactions of public bodies carrying a small tax (ἑκατοστή), individual markers of property mortgaged (*horoi*), and records of land leased out.[3] At present archaeology can offer, to supplement this, only the dubious 'farm area' marked out by the field wall at the Sounion Cliff Tower, but further field work may yield a little more information from this quarter.[4]

The literary sources

The evidence from literary sources is heavily context-dependent, and this is both an advantage and a problem. It adds useful social information about the owners and their milieux, but also means that information about property is only given when it is relevant to the point at issue. Court conditions should ensure that items of property mentioned did exist, but they also make it impossible to trust the details given of property size or value. Since references to isolated items of property are of little use unless the location is given, and the only references of great value are those where a large amount of the individual's property is described (for it is never possible to be sure that the list is complete[5]), the existing bias towards the wealthy in the orators is in fact being magnified, and the picture resulting must be of limited value.

In five cases the single item of property mentioned in the literary source plausibly represents the whole property of the owner in question.[6] In nine of the sixteen cases of multiple property-holdings we are told the location of at least part of the property. In seven of these nine cases the demotic of the owner is known. One of the seven, Timarkhos, certainly has property in his native deme (Aiskhin. 1.97f.), while Euktemon of Kephisia at least had a 'farm' in the neighbouring deme of Athmonon (Is. 6.33). Apollodoros has property spread through three demes, one of which may be his own deme of Akharnai ([D.] 50.8). The other four do not appear to have any property in their own deme, although Dikaiogenes' property 'in the *astu*' might be in his deme of Kydathenaion, and the property ascribed to Aristeides' son Lysimakhos may not have existed at all.[7] Although from Isaios 11 it appears that none of the Bouselids had property in the native deme, one item of property is of particular interest: at 11.44 a *khōrion* at Prospalta, which appears to be identical with the estate of Theopompos' brother-in-law Khaireleos, is in the hands of Theopompos himself. Davies (1971, 89) notes that 'the process by which Theopompos came to possess this in his own name (rather than his wife's) is obscure'; given that Theopompos 'can only be described as a thorough-paced scoundrel' (ibid., 84) it cannot be certain that the process was legally above-board, but this movement of property is perhaps indicative of the sort of way in which property found its way into the hands of men of other demes.

The two owners of multiple holdings of property whose demotic is not preserved are also of interest: the unknown speaker of Lysias 17 mentions property at Sphettos and Kikynna, demes in the same *trittys* which were probably neighbouring,[8] and this looks like a holding built up by more or less local accumulation; Kiron in Isaios 8 has two houses in the city and an *'agros'* at Phlya 'easily worth a talent', of which Davies remarks, 'It may be a coincidence that his farm lay in the deme of his brother-in-law Diokles, and of course we cannot infer that Kiron's demotic was also Phlyeus' (1971, 314). This is strictly true, but the findings of this chapter should give some reason to assert that it is indeed very probable that this was his deme.

Two of these multiple holdings are of land alone, but since one of these is the dubious property of Lysimakhos and the other that of Lysias 17 where only disputed property is mentioned both must be discounted as representative of typical complete estates. More convincing is the one case where the property consists entirely of *oikiai*: Komon has a house in the Peiraieus (D. 48. 12, 27), 'industrial' slaves, and an unknown sum of ἀργύριον φανερόν at the bank of Herakleides, and we may have here a member of the small class of Athenians whose wealth had no grounding in agriculture.

In all the other cases both land and residential property are involved. The two longest and most interesting lists are of the properties of Stratokles and Timarkhos: Stratokles has *agroi* at Eleusis and Thria, and houses at Eleusis and Melite (as well as a long catalogue of cash invested and movables, Isaios 11.40–3); Timarkhos has an *agros* at Amphitrope, *khōria* at Alopeke and Kephisia, an *eskhatia* at Sphettos, two *ergasteria* in Laureion, and a house 'behind the polis'.[9] These are clearly two contrasting estates: Stratokles' property has a focus in the Thriasian plain, a focus which, if Thompson is right, may have been built up by purchase, and which is certainly consistent with the way in which Stratokles seems to order his financial affairs very efficiently;[10] Timarkhos' property has no such consolidation of locality and none of type of property, for it does not focus on the native deme of Sphettos, and Timarkhos is prepared to sell the property at Alopeke which seems to have been his mother's family home (cf. her desire to be buried there, Aiskhin. 1.99). In so far as this collection has any rationale, that comes from the mining interests. Despite the differences between the two estates they are linked by the part that inheritance has played in forming them: this is explicit in the case of Stratokles and probable in the case of Timarkhos, and the differences lie in the choice of whether or not to exploit the inherited situation.

There is some pattern to the location of types of property in these literary estates. In all the multiple holdings where locations are known at least one *oikia* is found in or adjacent to the *astu* or in the Peiraieus.[11] The distribution of land shows a remarkable preference for the plain of Athens and the Mesogaia, but the sample is impossibly small for any statistical analysis.[12]

The literary sources thus give a picture of multiple property-holding scattered about Attika, with residence in the city always included. This is, however, a picture of the very topmost sector of Athenian society: nine of the sixteen men we have been considering earn a place among the liturgical families. Of the rest the speaker of Isaios 2 bore deme liturgies, and Aristophanes bore polis liturgies from insufficient property.[13] The speaker of Lysias 17 is not poor, just unknown — his father made a two-talent loan. Only three cases remain, Lysimakhos, Komon and Timarkhos, and there the evidence is insufficient to show liturgical status but does not show poverty.

The epigraphic sources

The Attic Stelai

The 'Attic Stelai' record the properties confiscated from those condemned over the mutilation of the Hermai and profanation of the Mysteries in 415 BC, and the men involved were again members of a rarefied sector of society. The property confiscated from a single individual was not all sold off together,[14] so that here again we can never be confident that we have a complete register of the property of one man in the extant fragments. The condemned were, on the whole, relatively young men, who presumably had not taken charge of the family lands, and this gives the information a particular importance. It also renders less surprising the fact that only Polystratos of Ankyle owns land in his own deme.[15]

The multiple property units of a single owner do not conform to a single pattern: Euphiletos of Kydathenaion has property spread about very thinly, with foci in the north Mesogaia and in north-east Attika,[16] while Pherekles of Themakos had accumulated a number of items relatively close together near the *astu.*[17] One anonymous figure has a whole collection of houses on cultivated land at unknown locations,[18] and another has a collection of land all at Athmonon.[19] While the strong impression is that multiple land-holding is the norm among this group,[20] the nature of the items owned varies enormously, with some agricultural estates, some possible commercial speculation, and quite a lot of apparently random accumulation of plots of seemingly useless ground.

The poletai lists

The *poletai* were the officials responsible, among other things, for selling off property denounced for confiscation because a man had incurred a public debt or had been condemned in a court to a penalty which involved or consisted in loss of property.[21] They were probably responsible for the 'Attic Stelai', although there are considerable formal differences between these and the later records for which the *poletai* are more clearly responsible. It is clear from the reference in Pollux that the 'Attic Stelai' were already in antiquity seen as a special group of records.

The earliest of the records which can be certainly attributed to the *poletai* (they were found in the area of the *poleterion*) are another special group: the records of the confiscation of property from the Thirty and their associates in 402/1.[22] These records may share with the 'Attic Stelai' the prominent part played by demarchs (although their restoration in line 11 of stele 3 is not certain), but in general they are far closer to the fourth-century *poletai* lists: single units of property are separately denounced and sold, and the buyers are recorded: the units of property are located by their neighbours. A sales tax is, however, exacted. Because of the similarity in format, which means that the same types of information are recorded, the information from these fragments is here included with the information from the later *poletai* lists.

One complete stele is preserved which records the sale of one confiscated property and details of the leasing of a number of mines (*SEG* 12.100) and there are extensive fragments of another much longer inscription. The other extant fourth-century *poletai* documents deal only with the leasing of mines and not with sales of property. There is one third-century *poletai* document from the year 283/2, but as extant this seems to be concerned mainly with extracting from his surety the price for the purchase of a confiscated property which the purchaser had failed to pay for.[23] Thus outside the documents dealing with property confiscated from the 30 and their associates the corpus is very small.

In bare statistics all these inscriptions together provide six (possibly eight) examples of ownership in the hereditary deme, six (possibly seven) of owning property in a neighbouring deme, and thirteen (possibly fourteen) where there appears to be no local connection.[24] Two of those owning property in their own deme only get mentioned as neighbours of a confiscated property, while in a third case a neighbour's son buys a confiscated property in his own deme.[25] The most interesting of the men who own land in their own deme is the pro-Macedonian politician Philokrates, whose property was confiscated and sold in 342/1 after he had been impeached by Hypereides for offences against the polis, had been condemned to death and had fled into exile. The stone which records the sale of his property is unfortunately badly damaged, and this, coupled with the property being sold off in more than one go, makes it impossible to be certain that we can reconstruct a complete register of his holdings. He certainly seems to have a whole group of properties in his own deme of Hagnous, one with a house, the others land alone without any indication of its use. He also has a house in the city deme of Melite, and two *ergasteria* next door to it. Here seems to be a clear picture of an agricultural base in the country supplemented by 'industrial' interests in the *astu*. It is of interest that some of the property at Hagnous was bought by a man from neighbouring Myrrhinous, while the commercial interests in the town passed into the wealthy family of the now elderly Hipponikos. That the *ergasteria* were a worthwhile purchase for such a man may indicate their size.[26]

The evidence given by Philokrates' case for the importance of ties of locality is complemented by that of the other cases where we have detailed information, and which were discussed in chapter 1.[27] The lists also give some support to the picture suggested by the literary evidence. For example, land in the hands of men with no apparent local connection with it is very largely to be found in the area of the *astu*. There is a little evidence here also for the rich accumulating land with scant regard for its location: Are[saikhmos Tlepol]emou of Euonymon, a man known to be propertied, buys 4 plethra of land which is possibly at Aphidna, while property in Salamis and at an unknown location may be bought by the same man, Meletos son of Megakles of Alopeke.[28] Despite these cases there is much in this corpus to support the suggestion that property-holding outside the native deme was almost always in addition to holdings within it (as can be seen where the records are most complete). Multiple holdings are certainly the rule among those from whom property is confiscated, and seem to be being built up by those purchasing. Local men are, however, far from being beaten out of the market and they seem to take their opportunity to consolidate existing interests, albeit unsystematically.

The leases

Unlike the other classes of inscriptional evidence employed in this chapter the land leases are not a clear group of documents already seen as such in ancient times: it is only modern analysis which has grouped these. Leases made by various bodies will be considered together here, although distinctions between them will be noted. All the leases used here date from the fourth century, but they range widely within that century.[29]

Leasing is clearly a very different matter from buying. Not all land that is leased is agricultural, but whatever its nature it seems safe to assume that the person who leases land will exploit, or at least enjoy, it directly. The leases give no information by themselves about the total property of an individual, but they do give a picture of the pattern of land acquisition for use.

The data about who leases what from whom have been expressed in table 3. Two features emerge very clearly from this: land to be worked productively figures much more largely among the cases where the lessee is from the deme where the property is located than among those where he is not; with religious property the reverse is the case. Rural locations attract local lessees, city locations men from outside. Demes tend to lease to their own members, but we cannot tell to what extent this is the result of social pressure. Demosthenes can assume that those who take up leases on deme land will be members of that deme (D. 57.63), and the arrangements for leasing the quarry at Eleusis are such that it effectively had to go to a demesman, for the demarch made the lease 'at a meeting of the demesmen to the man giving most'.[30] There are three cases of a person from another deme having at least a share in the leasing of property from a deme, but none of these is quite a normal transaction: for the Peiraieus theatre and the property at Teithras the man from outside is only a joint lessee with a demesman, while the Rarian field has strong religious connections and is not handled in the normal way.[31]

When outsiders take up leases the motivation is sometimes difficult to assess. We may assume that the *ergasterion* in the Peiraieus was a commercial venture, and the theatre there may also have been,[32] but the leases of religious property are a real problem. The duties of the lessee of the *hieron* in ii[2] 2501 are made very clear, but the benefits less so. The lease of the garden of the hero Iatros does give permission to build, and that might have been part of the attraction for the neighbour who took on the garden.[33]

When productive land is leased the question of motivation does not arise in the same way. Two leases give a fairly detailed description of the nature of the ground, its cropping potentials, and the buildings on it.[34] In both cases the land must have been farmed for some length of time previously since both vineyards and other tree crops (olives at Aixone, unspecified in the Dyaleis lease) are present, and in one case there is a house on the land. The Prasiai lease also has a house on land, and here (*SEG* 21.644) much of the extant lease is taken up with the catalogue of movable property in the house; how the deme came to be in possession of this fully furnished house is not at all clear.

There may be a social distinction between men who lease property locally and those who take it elsewhere. Only one of the men who take property in their own deme is otherwise known: Moirokles Euthydemou, lessee of the quarry at Eleusis. He is the son of the priest of Asklepios (ii[2] 4962) who had himself been involved with a quarry at the Peiraieus (ii[2] 47), and the family is clearly of some local standing, for Moirokles proposes a deme decree (ii[2] 1191) and his son becomes demarch, but there is no evidence that this family bore any liturgies.[35] By contrast three of the men who lease property outside their own deme are not only known but are of liturgical class: Hypereides of Kollytos, lessee of the Rarian field, Diopeithes of Sphettos, lessee of the shrine of Athena (ii[2] 2501), and Arrheneides of Paiania, lessee of

'Athena's marsh'.[36] Thus although their value is less clear to us, it is properties with religious connections which attract the wealthy. Their motives may well not have been purely financial: holding these lands conceivably brought a certain social advantage. However, the proximity of the two Athena sanctuaries to the *astu* suggests that it is not the case that propertied families used such leased property to extend the geographical area of their interests and influence.

We do not have a criterion for poverty as we do for wealth, and thus we cannot be sure what is happening at the other extreme. That the property at Prasiai had a fully equipped residence attached might be taken to suggest that this was intended for a propertyless family, but such an inference is not secure. Similarly a house in Kydathenaion is taken by a metic who could not have had landed property in Attika, but this does not mean that the man was poor. The leases of religious bodies seem indeed to be traditional in character, but the leases of demes are as yet impossible to assess with certainty.[37]

The hekatostai *inscriptions*

The *hekatostai* inscriptions are a group of documents of a single date in the late fourth century which were set up on the Akropolis to show the payment of a tax of 1% on some land transactions by demes and religious bodies. That much now seems more or less certain through the work devoted to these stelai by Andreyev and Lewis. It remains unclear, however, exactly what is happening to the land that is in question, why these public bodies are making the transactions, and just what the *hekatoste* is.

Some of the bodies disposing of property are demes, some religious bodies, but urban locations are seriously under-represented, and it is certain that not all demes, nor all religious bodies, were involved. The demes are arranged in tribal order and the prices too have an order: they are largely divisible by $12\frac{1}{2}$. The peculiarity of the latter feature has led to suggestions that a fixed price per unit area is being charged for the land, that sale by auction at fixed intervals is involved, or that the capital value of the land has been calculated as $12\frac{1}{2}$ times the annual rent.[38]

None of these suggestions is free from problems: all involved either a fixed price or a manipulated auction (for which there is no Athenian parallel). Auctions are the standard method for sales in Athens, whether conducted by central bodies or by demes.[39] The value of auctions lies in the way in which they reduce the possibility of accusations of bribery, and such accusations would surely have followed if auctions were not involved in these cases, for here there are instances of very valuable properties being acquired by the very officials responsible for disposing of them.[40]

Although there is insufficient evidence to claim that 8% was the 'standard' classical Athenian rent, it is clear that rents were often of that order.[41] This raises the possibility that the *hekatoste* might be 1% of the value of the property rather than 1% of some purchase price, and that what was paid was 8% of the value of the property (the value of the property being itself calculated by multiplying the sum paid by $12\frac{1}{2}$). This would account for the periodicity of the figures given in the texts. If this is the right explanation, then it is hard to see what transaction could involve paying 8% of the value of a property except renting that property for a year.[42] It is possible, therefore, that we have here another set of property leases, albeit leases made under slightly special circumstances.[43]

The evidence of these stones is biased by their preservation. The arrangement in tribal order means that what is preserved is not a random sample. On the basis of Lewis' reconstruction of the original stelai it seems that there were about 120 entries on each of three stones; of these thirty-three are preserved from stele 1, sixty-four from stele 2, and thirty-three from stele 3.[44] This weights the sample towards the demes of tribes V-X, and particularly towards the inland *trittys* of Aiantis. The bias is compounded by the fact that the location of all demes of Aiantis is known.

Lewis noted that there was a distinction between demes

and other territorial bodies, which disposed of property on the first and second stelai, and religious bodies which figured in the third; the information from the stelai can be divided up accordingly. The statistics are given in table 4. These reveal a bias towards men of the same deme as the property, which is hardly less strong among leases from religious organisations than it is among the leases of demes, and is only weak in the leases of non-deme territorial bodies. This strong bias towards the hereditary deme aligns the *hekatostai* inscriptions with the leases and against the various sale documents, giving considerable support to the idea that they do record leases and not sales. In contrast to the leases, however, there is no real difference here between the types of property acquired by men of the same deme and the types acquired by outsiders.[45]

In eighteen of the sixty cases where the demotic of the lessee of the land is known the individual lessee is otherwise known, and in seven of these the family is of liturgical status.[46] With two exceptions these propertied men acquire land in their own deme.[47] The known individuals who do not merit inclusion in the liturgical class are all, nevertheless, fairly wealthy men.[48]

The evidence provided by this corpus of inscriptions is invaluable for the demonstration which it gives that the tie with the hereditary deme was still strong in the 320s, even for the wealthiest men in Athenian society. This contrasts with the picture given by the literary sources, which seemed to be of such wealthy men acquiring a firm base in the *astu* and some landed property within reach of that. This difference might be explained in terms of a change of habit in the fourth century, with the hostile political environment of the last years causing retrenchment, but it is most likely that the *hekatostai* inscriptions are not that late, and it seems very probable that what we have is rather the contrast between two different source of information, which do not pretend to record even the same *type* of data.

This raises the problem of *why* lease documents should produce a different pattern from sales documents. The possibility of social pressure has already been canvassed, but the case is less strong for the *hekatostai* inscriptions where the cases of men who are not local leasing from demes do not seem peculiar.[49] Since local officials are in charge of the leasing in the *hekatostai* inscriptions it might have been done locally, and the cases where the officials in charge themselves acquire the property suggest that there may have been a good deal of scope for informal pressure and patronage.[50]

A practical factor may have distorted the picture: while the leases show a marked shortage of non-local people among the lessees of purely agricultural properties the *hekatostai* inscriptions have very little property that is not either *khōrion* or *eskhatia*, and in addition many of the lots are very small. These small lots prove of interest even to the most wealthy of lessees, but they are unlikely to have been of use to those who did not already have a local base.[51]

The horoi

Finley (1952) has shown that the evidence from the *horoi* relates to the wealthiest section of society. He further maintained that the bias in the pattern of discovery of *horoi* meant that no analysis based upon their data could reveal 'the ratio of rural to urban holdings and the relative frequency in the various demes and districts' (1952, 59) and as a result did not make any use of the local information from these stones. Although the bias does exist something can be done, and the discovery of new stones since 1952 gives a further justification for a re-examination of the evidence that the corpus provides.[52]

Three types of property (land, house, land and house) occur far more frequently on *horoi* than any others, and analysis here has been limited to those categories.[53] The stones from the Agora have not been excluded, despite the undoubted bias which they give to the sample, because it is unlikely that they came from outside the area of the *astu*, and because the properties they attest must at least have existed. The statistics are given in table 5.

As could be expected, *horoi* of land alone have a strong bias towards the countryside, while *horoi* of houses alone are found exclusively in Athens and two rather exceptional demes — Eleusis and the Peiraieus.[54] Houses with land have an even stronger bias towards the countryside than land alone. The distribution of these two types differs sensibly in one other way also: *horoi* of land and houses are notably infrequent in the area of the plain of Eleusis, although *horoi* of land alone are strongly represented there. This may reflect a different pattern of land exploitation as a result of the proximity to the city.[55]

There is a striking pattern to the relations between the origin of creditors and the location of the property mortgaged to them: local creditors are well represented for land with house(s) and for house(s) alone, but weakly represented for land alone. It seems that those mortgaging land alone would always have had further land associated with their residence, and would be likely to find a creditor where they resided. It seems probable also that holdings furthest from the residence would be the most readily mortgaged.[56] This is consistent with the complete absence of *horoi* for houses alone outside urban areas, which surely implies that all houses elsewhere belonging to this wealthy class either had land associated with them or were not susceptible to mortgaging.

A view of the whole patchwork

The complete body of information on land-holding in Attika has one consistent bias: it all relates to the wealthier sector of society. Many of the landowners are known to have borne liturgies, and where the owners are unknown there is nothing to justify the conclusion that they are poor. Only in a small body of the leases is it at all probable that the lessee in question is anything but rich. The conclusions that can be reached are therefore only conclusions about the habits of the rich.

The various sources give different types of information

— literary sources are generally evidence for the existence of an estate, not for its acquisition, and the same is true of confiscation documents; the *horoi* are evidence for the most dispensable items of a man's property (perhaps for the whole of it in some cases); the leases and *hekatostai* inscriptions, along with the incidental information from some confiscation documents, give some view of patterns of acquisition. The composite picture which emerges from all this is not inconsistent: the picture of holdings scattered round Attika given by the literary sources receives some confirmation from lists of confiscated property; the leases stress the other side, also visible in the confiscation documents although only glimpsed in the literature, that men did retain a primary interest in having actively cultivated land in the hereditary deme.

The confiscation lists possess at least one very clear picture of an estate made up largely of fragmented holdings within a small area: the estate of Philokrates of Hagnous at Hagnous.[57] The willingness to have and to work such fragmentary holdings must be the explanation behind the practice of wealthy men renting tiny plots of farm land which is revealed by the *hekatostai* inscriptions. This latter phenomenon also suggests that agriculture was still a profitable enterprise in Attika in the 320s.[58]

The lease documents reveal a strong bias against acquiring agricultural land at any great distance from the hereditary deme. This may be a product of the rather insular nature of deme society which these same leases certainly attest and for which there is a quantity of further evidence,[59] but estates such as that of Philokrates make it likely that there was a definite tendency to limit one's farming to a restricted area.

However, not only do literature, and probably the *horoi,* attest wealthy men with land in the plains of Athens or Thria, which might be supervised from a residence in the *astu,* but some men certainly did have land distant from their deme which needed cultivation. Where we have evidence property exchanges and inheritance within the family seem to be often responsible for these plots. Inheritance must have been a major factor in the formation of most classical estates, and thus patterns of land-holding bear indirect witness to patterns of marriage and of adoption (on which see below chapter 7).

When men did possess distant plots we simply do not know how they dealt with them; there was some private leasing but we are ill informed as to its nature or extent.[60] Distant plots may have been the most readily mortgaged. Although estates in the Mesogaia and the plains of Athens and Eleusis are very well represented by these sources the evidence does not show Athenians who were already rich building up large estates here, away from their own deme. These areas do have the best land in Attika, land that has been intensively exploited in recent times and which is the best known archaeologically (witness the large number of *horoi* found near Spata). It should be noted again that the estate of Philokrates at Hagnous was the estate of a man of Hagnous, and when sold off it passed into the possession of a number of men, some local, some not.

Work on present-day societies has revealed a correlation between a fragmented pattern of land-holding and a clustered pattern of settlement. One explanation for this is that fragmentation of land-holding makes it no more worthwhile living in one location than another, and hence the more sociable option is adopted.[61] There are, however, other advantages: fragmentation may lead to inefficient exploitation, but it does spread risks, and it is notable that fragmented farm-holdings are most persistent today in Mediterranean regions where the degree of interannual climatic variability makes agriculture still a precarious business.[62] Chapter 2 has argued that a nucleated pattern of settlement may have been adopted, or at least maintained, for its social advantages. A fragmented pattern of land-holding can be associated with agricultural advantages. However, these two independently justifiable strategies of rural land use are also interdependent: each facilitates the other. The evidence surveyed above reveals no sign that the fragmented pattern of land-holding was seen as a disadvantage: there is no attempt to consolidate holdings, no consistent pattern of acquisition of land by a neighbour. There is a tendency to acquire land in a single area, but this land is not continuous, and it forms, rather than consolidates, a fragmented holding.

Information on land use supports the contention that fragmentation represents a more or less conscious agricultural strategy: the leases which specify land use show no clear move towards monoculture — these farms have a little of everything. This situation on leased property can be compared with the mixed products of the estate of Phainippos ([D.] 42) and the mixed produce from the various confiscated estates which appear in the Attic Stelai.[63] If such an agricultural strategy is being adopted this itself constitutes a good argument for subsistence agriculture still being the farming model at the end of the fourth century.[64]

Not only do the quite independently argued conclusions about the patterns of settlement and land-holding support each other in this way, but the way in which men can be shown to continue to have firm local interests itself argues for a strong deme identity such as is most easily created in a nucleated settlement. The correspondence between pattern of land-holding and pattern of settlement must not, by its neatness, lead to over-simplification: agriculture was a basic economic activity, but it was not the only source of living. It has already been suggested in chapter 2 that two other economic activities — mining for silver and quarrying for stone — may also have had an effect on the settlement pattern, and it is to a detailed examination of these that chapters 5 and 6 are devoted.

CHAPTER 4

DEMES AND DEMOCRACY: LOCAL POLITICS AND THE POLITICS OF LOCALITY

First and foremost the deme was a political unit, both itself, within limits, autonomous, and a part of the political organisation of the polis. Not only can the political aspect not be ignored in any consideration of the part played by locality and local connections in Athenian society, but an adequate conception of the deme as a local as well as a political unit is indispensable for any study of the working of democracy on the ground. Previous work, both on democracy as a whole and on the demes themselves has concentrated on the demes as institutions;[1] this chapter builds on the findings of the rest of this work to suggest that the implications of the current orthodoxy about the nature of Athenian democracy are unacceptable, and to argue that the demes, if viewed as social groups and not merely as a framework for institutions, can provide the basis for an understanding of democracy which is more in accord with the empirical evidence.

Who ran the polis? Modern fallacies and ancient practice

Current notions of the nature of Athenian democracy owe much to the work and ideas of M.I. Finley, and it is he who is cited as authority for such statements as 'The citizens of the emerging Greek city-states were accustomed both to participate fully in the actual government of their country and to engage in active deliberation of constitutional issues.'[2] Finley's own expression of his views notes the relatively small size of classical Attika, that only about a third of the citizen population of perhaps 40,000 adult males lived in the city, and that the rest lived in villages. 'Ancient Athens', he concludes, 'was the model of a face to face society.'[3] The notion of a face-to-face society is one that has been eagerly taken up by ancient historians, but what does it mean? The phrase was coined by Peter Laslett in an article written in 1956 to which Finley refers.[4] That article begins: 'On a dull Sunday afternoon the situation of most Englishmen is likely to be that of sitting at home in his family . . . Now the family is a face to face society.' Laslett suggests that the important mark of such societies is that crises will be decided by everyone meeting together discovering 'what his appropriate behaviour is', 'to a large degree it will be a matter of personal response, expressed not in propositions, but in exclamations, apostrophes, laughter and silences . . . it is a question of total intercourse between personalities, conscious and unconscious' (p. 158), and he goes on to talk of 'intuitive psychology'. Laslett suggests that this model fits the polis 'with never more than 10,000' citizens (p. 163). Whether or not the model is appropriate for such a polis, can it really be accepted for classical Athens?

This absurd model has been so widely adopted at least partly because it filled out the older view that at Athens power was actively exercised by the whole people. The fallacy beind this view was already exposed by Aristotle (*Pol.* 1292b 11ff.): οὐ δεῖ λανθάνειν ὅτι πολλαχοῦ συμβέβηκεν ὥστε . . . τὴν μὲν κατὰ νόμους εἶναι πολιτείαν δημοτικωτέραν, τῇ δ'ἀγωγῇ καὶ τοῖς ἔθεσιν ὀλιγαρχεῖσθαι μᾶλλον. Both ancient and modern scholarship has laboured to produce a very detailed constitutional description of classical Athens, and this description has too often been read as a description of political practice; however, that all adult males could attend the assembly does not mean that all did.[5]

The overrating of the importance of constitutional provisions goes hand in hand with a rather uncritical concept of political power. Certainly the assembly had sovereign power and consented to or dissented from the motions put before it, but this final responsibility is not the same as effective power to initiate the policy. The assembly's decisions were quite firmly tied, even constitutionally, to the matters and motions which were brought before it, so that on a second dimension power rested in the hands of those who brought

65

the motions. On a third dimension even these political activists can be seen to have their hands tied by the structure and norms of the society, by the established practice shaped by the totality of previous measures which had succeeded, or failed, in gaining the assent of the people.[6]

The factors which shape the third dimension are notoriously difficult to assess, although this study should shed some light on some aspects of it, but it is possible to go some way towards revealing the second dimension. From the year 352/1 onwards Athenian decrees record the demotic as well as the name and patronymic of the proposer. Only when the demotic is given is secure identification possible, but the demotic also enables some measure of geographical distribution to be made. Thus for the last thirty years of full active and independent Athenian democracy it is possible to say something about the social circles from which those active in politics came.

The epigraphic evidence used in this analysis consists of the eighty decrees from these years which preserve at least the demotic of the proposer. Fifty-seven proposers are involved, from thirty-nine demes. Forty-four of the fifty-seven have at least one identifiable name, and of these thirty-three (75%) are otherwise known. Four men are only known from more than one source because they proposed more than one decree: Hierokleides of Alopeke proposed two decrees when *bouleutes* in 349/8, Kallikrates of Lamptrai made one proposal as *bouleutes* and one from the floor of the assembly, and Brakhyllos of Erkhia and Demosthenes of Lamptrai both made two proposals in the assembly.[7]

Eight proposers are only otherwise known for holding some office: Euboulides of Halimous was demarch apparently in the same year as he was *bouleutes*; Polykrates of Phegaia and Theodoros of Alopeke both made their proposals from the floor of the assembly, although both were *bouleutai* — Theodoros in the year of his decree, Polykrates thirteen years after his; Nothippos of Diomeia made his proposal when *bouleutes*, and his son Lysias was later *grammateus* in 307/6; Phyleus of Oinoe and Phileas of Paionidai are both known as *hieropoioi* and the former certainly proposed his decree as *bouleutes*; Epiteles of Pergase has rather more extensive religious connections: he is found in charge of a festival at the Amphiaraon, and twice as *naopoios* at Delphi: his decree is itself to do with an *arkhetheoros*.[8] The eighth man is Kephisodotos of Akharnai. This man is only otherwise known as an *exetastēs* at Sounion in 298/7, but in his case alone the circumstances in which he came to propose his decree are tolerably clear. The decree honours Herakleides of Salamis and is rather complex: Telemakhos Theangelou got the assembly to commission a *probouleuma* about Herakleides; Kephisodotos is responsible for this in the *boule*; and when the matter returns to the assembly Telemakhos proposes the amendment. Telemakhos is from the deme of Akharnai, and it looks very much as if he suborned a fellow demesman who was in the *boule* that year to do the spade-work for him there.[9]

Four proposers come into a class which might be called 'moderately well-known'. Philotades of Pallene, responsible for a proxeny decree, comes from a political family: his grandfather was *hellenotamias*, his father *bouleutes* at the dissolution of the 400, his brother *grammateus* in 363/2, and his son *hieropoios* in about 330. Phanodemos of Thymaitadai is the Atthidographer; not inactive in politics he has particularly close associations with the Amphiaraon; the decree of which he proposes part also honours him. The son of Kteson of Kerameis has a father known from the Diadikasia documents and as a witness for Apollodoros, and a sister who married a man with property in Ikarion.[10] All these three men propose their decrees as members of the *boule*. The fourth man in this class seems to have spoken from the floor of the assembly, and he is the most interesting figure in the group. Prokleides of Kerameis was a *diaitetes* in 330/29 and his grandson is responsible for the Mesogeioi decree of c. 260. His decree of 328/7 praises one Androkles for his performance as priest of Asklepios. Not only does Androkles come from Kerameis, but Prokleides' son is known to have made a dedication to Asklepios in the city at just about this time. There can be little doubt that there is a local and personal basis to Prokleides' political activity. This family is certainly not poor, and of the other three in this category the families of Philotades and Kteson are almost certainly rather wealthy, and that of the Atthidographer hardly likely to be less so.[11]

The eighteen remaining proposers (55% of those otherwise known, 41% of the identifiable names) are all very well known. In two cases, those of Kephisophon Kephalionos of Aphidna and Philemon of Oe, the prominent connections are military, but in the remaining cases the men are well-known to us precisely because of their political activities.[12] One of these men is particularly relevant to our present concerns: Hegesippos Hegesiou of Sounion. He himself was responsible for a decree concerning Euboia of 357/6 and appears in the sample for a decree honouring two Akarnanians; one brother, Hegesandros, proposed a decree about Andros in 357/6 having been *tamias* of Athena in 361/0; a second brother, Hegias, both has a son, Hegesias (II) who was *tamias* of Athena in 349/8, and himself is one of the seven oath-takers from the Sounion branch of the Salaminioi in the agreement of 363/2. More descendants are found in the *boule* in the third and second centuries. The family does not feature among owners of land in the mining leases, and its links with the deme seem to have been traditional and political.[13]

Twelve (66%) of these very well known men are certainly wealthy and there is little doubt of the wealth of the other six not in Davies' catalogue.[14] The sample as a whole strongly suggests that still in the fourth-century political power lay effectively with a rather restricted and wealthy social group. Although the necessity for a *probouleuma*[15] may have been intended not only to prevent precipitate action but also to prevent any single man gaining a monopoly of political action, it is not clear from this analysis that men were encouraged by service as *bouleutes* to take the shaping of policies into their own hands, and it appears, on the contrary, that activity in the *boule* came to rest with well-known, and generally wealthy, men. Four of the eleven proposers not otherwise known, four of the eight known for office-holding, and three of the four moderately well-known men made their proposals as *bouleutai*, exiguous evidence which, for what it is worth, suggests that more active men were *more* inclined to limit their proposals to the *boule*. There are some men who seem to have been emboldened by action when *bouleutai* to take further action later — one might point to Kallikrates of Lamptrai (above p. 66) — but there are equally men who are prepared to speak up on the floor of the assembly years before we know them to have entered the *boule* — e.g. Polykrates of Phegaia (above p. 66). That the *boule* did not serve to open up the political machine to the people emerges still more clearly from the geographical origins of these men.

Wealth was not evenly distributed in Attika (chapter 2), so that a bias to the wealthy must also be a local bias. There is, however, a geographical bias of a more important kind. Map 5 gives the results of returning proposers to the deme or origin. Some sort of bias towards city demes might have been expected, but here 28% of those localisable come from demes in or very near the *astu* and some 85% from demes no further away than Lamptrai — that is, from demes within fifteen miles of the Pnyx.[16] Demes near this limit are, however, particularly heavily represented, giving a sort of 'fringe effect'. Using bouleutic quotas as a measure of population distribution we find that 39% of *bouleutai* come from the area outside the circle, which is represented by 15% of the proposers. Chapter 3, showed that while most Athenians retained a strong interest in their home deme, many wealthy men did have a second residence in the *astu*; yet despite the fact that most of the proposers come from just that wealthy group the local bias remains, and it seems likely that the bias amongst men who simply attended the assembly, and never spoke, was still stronger.

The strength of the local bias among political figures is very clearly brought out by comparison with the distribution of those who held the office of general. That military officials

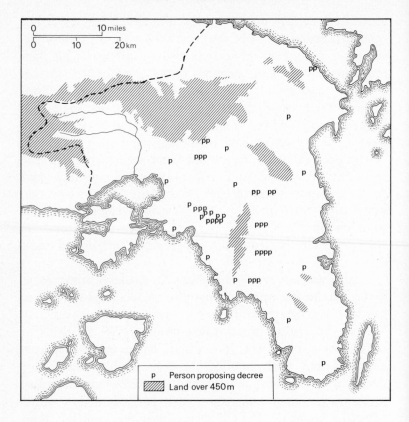

Map 5. The origins of those proposing decrees in the assembly 352/1–319/18.

were to a very large extent drawn from the propertied class is clear both from theoretical statements and from analysis of those actually selected;[17] the geographical distribution of generals is given in map 6. The distribution is clearly much less biased towards the *astu*, a result consistent with the selection of generals for their skill and with the failure of military demands to respect locality. The weighting here is produced by the existence of οἴκοι ἐστρατηγηκότες.

That political power lay with a socially and geographically limited group should cause no surprise. The literary background is given by Aristophanes: *Georgoi* fr. 1 has a farmer offering a political activist 1,000 dr. if he will refrain from

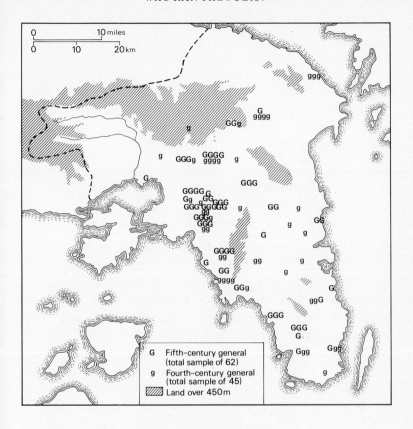

Map 6. The origins of generals.

pressing him into service in some *arkhē*. Aristotle explicates some of the factors behind the failure of farmers to be active politically, and he regards this as a positively good thing, claiming that the best democracy is that where farmers make up the sovereign body, since they only attend the absolutely necessary assemblies, and do not meddle with the laws (*Pol.* 1292b 25ff., 1318b 9ff.). Athens is generally assumed to be Aristotle's model of the worst form of demo-cracy, where the ἄποροι have more leisure than the well-off and become sovereign rather than the law (*Pol.* 1293a10). The findings of this section indicate that Athens in fact had elements, at least, of the 'best democracy'.

Modern political theorists have taken Aristotle's line of reasoning one stage further and have argued that apathy is necessary to the well-run state, so that politics in effect are left to 'experts'. Prima facie the findings here might suggest that the example of fourth-century Athens offers some support to such theorists; a closer look at the other end of the political process, at the demesman in his deme, casts some doubt on this.

Demos and *demoi*: the polis as demes

Membership

In the classical period the demes were responsible for the constitution of the *demos* in a very literal way: the demes accepted a man as a citizen, although there was a central appeals procedure. The demes scrutinised boys of 18 and according to [Aristotle] were concerned first with their age, and only then with their birth (*Ath. Pol.* 42.1, cf. 26. 4). This order, neither natural nor efficient, suggests that the demes were already responsible for recognising citizens before Perikles' Citizenship Law of 451/0: until then scrutiny of birth might well be superfluous, for only one citizen parent was necessary, and the *oikos* from which a boy came would be clear enough to fellow demesmen. The system which grew up for a simpler society will then have continued when the rules changed: the demes continued to operate with an open ethic while officially the citizen body had become a significantly closed group.[18]

The demes did keep lists of their members, but lists that appear to have been of a peculiar sort. Our sources appear to refer to this document in various ways, as *lexiarkhikon grammateion* (e.g. D. 57.26), *koina grammateia* (*SEG* 2.7.20f.), or simply as the *grammateion* (D. 44.37). To judge by the *grammateion* of *SEG* 2.7 this was not just a list (as it has generally been assumed to have been): there the honorific decree for Kharisandros is to be written up in it. The *lexiarkhikon grammateion* was certainly kept by the demarch and from this reference it would seem to be just his minute book.[19] Such a book would certainly record all accessions to the deme, in an inactive deme it might record little else, but it was not a public document. This means that there was no public list of demesmen and no public list of citizens. Awkward to handle as such a list might have been it would have been feasible if desired. That it was not desired is another indication of the open ethic of the deme: lists mark out those listed as different, normally as worthy of a peculiar honour or dishonour, so that a list of citizens would imply that their position was peculiar; non-inscription, in contrast, suggests that the demesmen felt no problem about their self-definition. Such has indeed been one conclusion arising from the earlier chapters.

This situation in the demes contrasts markedly with that in the phratries and *genē*. Both these groups were of undoubted importance in Athenian social life, and both based their membership on descent. The *genē* were essentially religious groups, and by the classical period the members of a single *genos* might be scattered all over Attika. While there do seem to have been registers of members there could also be uncertainty over membership. That *genē* were closed groups was essential to their religious rôle.[20]

The phratries share with the demes both the strong connections with a single locality and the membership by descent. Many phratries have names of a patronymic type — ending in -idai — and some names of demes in this form may have been phratry names. However the concern of the phratry was rather with the perpetuation of the *oikoi* of the *phrateres* than with limitation to strict descendants, but this concern did not lead to their being open groups. Rather they show an obsession with membership problems: a law related by Philokhoros and the longest and best preserved phratry decree relate to this. The elaborate procedure in the Demotionid decree reveals clearly how the *phrateres* regarded themselves as a privileged body.[21] Despite the local links, which are strongly present in this decree, and despite the fact that phratries might own land all over Attika, the phratry is an exclusive group, to such an extent that increasing the number of phratries is a democratic reform.[22]

The institutional form in which the conflict between kin and neighbours over who is to be interested in birth and death takes place is through the phratry and the deme. The deme looks after the *bureaucracy* of becoming a citizen, while the Apatouria is the ritual of the phratry. Homicide obligated the *phrateres* to extend the family in seeking vengeance on the killer; the deme, through the demarch, had to clear up the corpse. Thus the deme assumes the general civic responsibility, the phratry looks after its own.[23]

To be a member of a *genos* or a phratry was to set oneself apart from some or most of one's geographical associates, while to be a demesman was normal, expected, and meant joining them. The deme as an essential basis of democracy was founded upon the principle of equality, and it was active in all those areas of life where men could plausibly be claimed to be equal; the *genos* and phratry upheld privilege and inequality, and where the importance of blood ties or the physical variations involved in growing up were paramount, there these exclusive groups were supreme.

Deme offices and officers

Since the act by which a man was recognised as a member of a deme was also the act by which he became a citizen, uniformity of procedure was essential. Even here the case of Euxitheos suggests that different demes might interpret the criteria for citizenship in different ways. Where the deme was still more fully autonomous variation was still greater. Physically the demes were far from uniform: theatres, palaestrae, gymnasia, might or might not be present:[24] likewise a few demes had to endure the more or less permanent presence of soldiers manning a fort, and the sort of effect that this might have will be discussed in chapter 7. Such factors must influence the number and nature of deme officers, but they affect the superstructure rather than the structure, and it seems clear that in all demes one official was of especial importance, and that official was the demarch.

The institutionalised powers of the demarch were very considerable: he was the president of the assembly, and was responsible for calling it, regulating the opening oaths, the order of business, and the voting. He might then assume some executive responsibility: he summoned those honoured with *proedria* to that privilege, and generally announced honours and saw to the inscription and setting up of stelai recording the grant.[25] For all this the demarch might himself be honoured, and the amount of power makes it unsurprising that one honorific inscription reveals that the demarch was chosen by lot.[26]

The demarch also represented the deme in its relations with other groups. The rôle is seen in his involvement in various religious activities: thus he helps to see to the policing of the Thesmophoria at the Peiraieus, prosecutes breaches of custom in sacrifice or ritual, and may be closely involved in the sacrifices themselves – providing victims, assisting priests and *hieropoioi*, and distributing meat to demesmen.[27]

These religious responsibilities bring the demarch into contact with another group – the *demos* as a whole and its representatives in the form of central bodies and officials. According to a tradition handed down by the scholiast on Aristophanes' *Clouds* 37 and the Souda (s.v. *demarkhos*), both depending on the same source, the demarchs controlled the procession at the Panathenaia. Demosthenes 44.37 certainly shows that they distributed the *theorikon* to members of their deme who attended this 'carnival' and ii² 334.24ff. shows that meat from the sacrifices had to be distributed to each deme according to the numbers sent by that deme.

It may be through his religious responsibilities that the demarch became involved with the *aparkhē* for Eleusis: in the late fifth century he handed over his deme's contribution to the ἱεροποιοί Ἐλευσινόθεν Ἐλευσῖνάδε, and while in the fourth century the *boule* and tribes became involved it is still the δήμαρχος who handed over the grain ἐκ τῆς ἐπ' Ἀμφιαράου.[28]

The *aparkhē* responsibilities are also consistent with the financial tasks performed by the demarch. Not only does the demarch make sure that deme *tamiai* distribute money as commanded by the deme assembly, he also collected the *enktetikon* tax from non-demesmen owning land in the deme (presumably, since there was no land register, checking doubtful cases with reference to the *lexiarkhikon grammateion*); he played a large part in the renting out of deme property, and in some cases at least the rent was paid to him; at Aixone he is made part of the committee which regulated the removal of olives from a piece of rented ground.[29]

All these duties are more or less local, but they are closely connected with others which are not. The demarch's duties in chasing up debts appear to be notorious, and Euxitheos claims that it was his over-zealous performance of this task which made him unpopular with fellow demesmen. Debts could only be chased up effectively when backed up with the threat of court action. It is thus not surprising that the demarch is responsible for listing the property of public debtors and other offenders, and registering it for confiscation.[30] ii[2] 1196 is an example from Aixone of demarch and *sundikoi* taking action in the central courts over debts and pledges.

In two clear cases in the literature the demarch is brought to account through the central legal procedure for the decisions of the deme: both cases concern deme membership, and as holder of deme records the demarch is the natural target. Both cases may hide the full reality: [Aristotle] says that demes chose five men to defend decisions over membership in the courts, and the demarch may have been but the most prominent of the five.[31]

The demarch thus had a very widely ranging set of duties, some of them straightforward and routine pieces of bureaucracy, others carrying a large amount of influence and responsibility. The demarch was not only the indispensable centre of business within the deme, he was also a key figure in various aspects of the working of central government. This makes it less surprising that in procedures for appointment and dismissal the demarch seems to be assimilated to a central official.

In the matter of elections there is no doubt that the preliminary selection of candidates and the *dokimasia* were both carried out by the demesmen. [Aristotle] notes that the demarch of the Peiraieus was appointed by lot by the *boule*, and this was clearly exceptional in some sense. The recently published decrees from Eleusis suggest that it was only exceptional in being in the hands of the *boule*, not in happening in the city. For the Eleusis decrees concern a matter strictly of deme concern – the quarry which is rented out is at Eleusis, the funds are for sacrifices at Eleusis, and the procedure employed ensures that a demesman takes the lease – but the payment for the quarry is to take place on the occasion of the elections when the demesmen hold an 'agora' in the Theseion, in the month of Metageitnion. [Aristotle] notes that 'formerly' some offices had been divided among the demes and had been allotted in the Theseion, but not only does his use of 'formerly' imply that this situation no longer obtained at the time of the Eleusis decree, the phraseology of that decree ought to mean that it is an agora of men of Eleusis, not of all the demes (or even of all the demes of one tribe). Further it is difficult to see what the allotment of non-deme offices can have to do with the payment of rent to the demarch. The allotment in question here ought to be the allotment of the demarchy, and this occasion may be chosen for the payment because failure to pay up would be a great embarrassment on so public an occasion. Given the central responsibilities of the demarch it makes sense for the final selection procedure to be removed from the deme in order to limit the scope for corruption. It may be significant in this context that the meeting of the deme of Halimous which was solely concerned with the scrutiny of the status of the members was also held in the city.[32]

Deme officers were not exempt from scrutiny at the end of their period of office. *Euthunoi* are attested in a large number of demes, and these are generally assumed to be deme officers, separate from the central *euthunoi*. This may be right, but there is some evidence that points the other way. The number of regular deme offices seems to have been very limited, and separate boards of *euthunoi* in each of 139 demes seems a bureaucratic top-heaviness out of character with the rest of deme government. The *koinon* of the Tetrapolis in the third century certainly distinguishes its *euthunoi* from its magistrates, and the way the central *euthunoi* refer certain matters to the κατὰ δήμους δικασταί may imply dealings with demes. In addition the Thorikos calendar connects *euthunoi* and Horkomosion and if this Horkomosion was a building rather than a sacrifice it is likely to have been the building of that name near the Theseion in the *astu*. This feature, like the others, would be most easily accounted for if the *euthunoi* were central officials. Given that the demarch is seen as important enough to central administration for his final selection to be removed to the *astu* it would be surprising if the final scrutiny was left to the demes. On the other hand many of the matters which might be examined at the *euthuna* would be matters of only local concern, and outsiders might be suspected of being inadequately motivated to see justice done. The demes seem to have sought to counter this by imposing stringent conditions on the *euthunoi*: Halai Aixonides has its demarch extract an oath from the *euthunos* and his *paredroi* that they will carry out the examination according to an earlier deme decree; Myrrhinous not only makes the *euthunos* swear that he will not be corrupted into letting officials off, but he has to obtain the consent of a special commission of ten, voting in secret, before he can end the *euthuna*.[33]

The extra-deme activities of the demarch, and the fact that all judicial proceedings would be central lessen the extent to which the central *euthunoi* would be seen as interfering. All deme officers would be examined, but how many there were varied from deme to deme. *Tamiai* are widely attested, although their number seems to have varied, and they were simply treasurers without powers of initiative. *Kerukes*, basic to civilised political life, are also common, but their job is a menial one. Other magistrates occur in just one or a limited number of demes, and there is no reason to suppose that they were general: thus individual demes give us *grammateis*, an *antigrapheus*, a *logistēs*, and an *horistēs*. There are also special committees, varying in number of members, which are clearly set up for special tasks — two are concerned with leasing land, one with building.[34]

It is tolerably clear that the number of officers in a deme was small, and that with the exception of the demarch the officers were purely administrative; they executed decisions, they did not help to frame them. The very extent of the responsibilities of the demarch is indicative of the limited range of other officers available. The failure to delegate is in contrast to the practices of central administration, but there is little doubt that combining responsibilities in a single individual both was a realistic measure in view of the number of men available to hold the office, especially in a small deme, and considerably facilitated relations with central administration.

The assembled deme

The limited competence of most deme officers is only a counterpart of the limited activity of the deme acting as a whole. While some demes seem to have structured their meeting on the model of the central assembly, as with the *kuriai agorai* at Aixone,[35] the issues which got discussed seem rarely to have risen above the routine. The deme decrees, which alone provide evidence on this question, cover a rather limited range of subjects (table 6): demes honoured their own members and men from outside for outstanding services, concerned themselves with finance, providing themselves with income through the renting of land and spending that income on the honours they gave and on the religious observances of the demesmen which they subsidised, and intervened to see to the proper execution of religious activities. All are internal matters: only the lease of land by Eleusis to Thria involves another community, although a decree may assume the powers of the central body to enforce its threats. Far from resisting central administrative powers the demes might even honour men for their execution of central duties.[36]

Apart from the general requirement that they should not contravene the law, demes do not seem to be formally limited in what they do: certainly they both impose taxes and relieve individuals of those taxes, and, if the argument about the *euthunoi* being central officials is right, demes could impose close control on central officials. Demes make loans to their members, and make by-laws, penalising their breach. It is doubtful, however, that the demes themselves ever had any judicial authority.[37]

The relations between deme and central government may have been related less by formal means and more by traditional means. Deme decrees are marked by a very traditional language: in their unchanging expressions they reflect both one another and the central decrees, and there is little doubt that the uniformity of language both annexes for the demes some of the prestige of central government and limits the initiative of the deme; the partly formalised expression of political persuasion conditions and limits the possible response as well as the possible expressions, and in allowing such formalisation the demes accept a social hierarchy and even a social control.[38] Demes did go to court in Athens, but they did so to argue about individuals, and in disputes over land or religious matters: there is no evidence for a deme attempting to change its position in relation to central forces. The argument here, reinforced by findings below, is that the lack of friction is not despite the closeness of the relationship, but precisely because it is so close.

Delegation from the centre

The most important contribution of the demes to the machinery of central government undoubtedly lay in their selection of men to serve in the *boule*. Each deme produced a given quota of *bouleutai*, but the means by which the deme arrived at its selection is not known. Prominent political figures manage to be *bouleutai* in times of crisis with a suspicious frequency, and this suggests both that competition with the deme was not particularly strong, and that there tended to be enough men willing to serve in any year for a man not to be forced to serve his two years at times outside his control. Bouleutic service was a very heavy chore necessitating virtually permanent residence in the *astu*, and it is not surprising that there is some evidence that the members of the *boule* were not a random sample, socially, of the whole δῆμος.[39]

There seems to have been a period when the demes played a similar part in the selection of other magistrates: in [Aristotle's] time they only retained this rôle for the φρουροί (νεωρίων?) but previously they seem to have been in on the preselection of candidates from which the tribes allotted the archonships and on the allotment of other offices (the exact nature of which is not clear). Involving the demes was a way of overcoming the problem of locality and of geographical barriers, ensuring that the δῆμοι were indeed the δῆμος from which these officers were chosen. But involving the demes also meant involving small groups where relations were not anonymous and where more or less corrupt practices were difficult to prevent, and it was such practices that led to the demes losing their role in these elections.[40]

The demes retained a rôle in the selection of *diaitetai* (public arbitrators). These were men of hoplite status, probably, who were in their sixtieth year, and they were drawn from all the demes; the demes must have been involved at some stage in the identification of the men of the requisite age, and inscribed lists of these men survive. The arbitrators were divided into groups for each tribe, and they might arbitrate for a tribe other than their own, although it is not clear whether there were any fixed criteria governing which individual arbitrators of the tribal group received which cases, and it is possible that men with relevant local knowledge could be chosen if they were available.[41]

Cases involving less than ten drachmai went to the *kata*

dēmous dikastai, inaugurated, according to [Aristotle] by Peisistratos and certainly travelling round the demes in the late fifth century. The institution may have been less an interference with local judicial action (for which there is no good evidence) and more an attempt to regularise a difficult situation, where the parties involved might choose to use either the central courts, an inefficient procedure in such cases, or attempt to settle the case within the deme. These forty men seem again to have been divided by tribes, but there is no way of telling whether or not they judged the cases of men of their own tribe.[42]

Demesmen chosen as magistrates, by whatever means and for whatever duties, acquired a greater or lesser task to fulfil, but that task was also, to some extent, its own reward. The same is true of liturgies, which are burdensome obligations but also a source of honour and prestige, and from time to time men undoubtedly did choose to bear a liturgy when not strictly obliged to do so. Apollodoros' report of the mechanisms by which the *proeisphora* was raised, on one occasion at least, suggests that *bouleutai* were made responsible for listing those liable in their own deme ([D.] 50.8).

The deme seems to have been exploited also to raise and organise those who served in military forces. The one reference to service in deme units may be corrupt, but demarchs and bouleutic representatives could certainly be used to draw up lists of men liable for naval service ([D.] 50.6f.) and demesmen certainly formed informal military units: Philon is denigrated in Lysias 31.15 because he failed to contribute money to the war effort or to arm any of his fellow demesmen; Polystratos calls fellow demesmen to witness that he took part in all the campaigns as a sign that he is *demotikos*; Mantitheos uses as an argument in his favour the fact that 'when the demesmen had gathered to leave on campaign' he provided money and urged other to do so also in order to enable poor men to serve. All these examples suggest that the deme had at least an informal rôle in army recruitment, a rôle which it will have acquired not through any control that demes had over foreign policy, for they had none, but because army service was both a social and political act and the deme was the one division of the polis which was at once a social and a political unit.[43]

Formally and informally the government of the polis relied on the confusion of δῆμος and δῆμος: men appointed by a central mechanism are responsible for local action (so *diaitetai*, *kata dēmous dikastai*, and *euthunoi* (perhaps)); men appointed by the demesmen have obligations to the polis as a whole (so demarch, so also *bouleutai*); directly as demesmen or indirectly as members of tribes the members of the demes are responsible for at least the preliminary selection of many central officials; service towards war efforts, with money or person, was, at least on occasions and informally, organised both through the institutions and the social pressures of the deme. In all this there is little in the way of a clear system, rather there is an entanglement, but it is this entanglement which ensures the 'watchful supervision' which the effective, but barely acknowledged, devolution of obligation demanded. Small units are manageable: this constitutes both their advantage and their drawback, for they can be managed for good or corruptly; large units cannot be managed, as large units, either by legitimate or illegitimate means, but the fact of belonging to a large unit creates a control on smaller units. The Athenian polis broke naturally into local units: by political recognition and artificial organisation into *trittyes* and tribes the local deme units were tied in to the polis as a whole; the various institutions of government exploited the small units to manage the whole polis; but no institutional description will explain the government of the polis, for the nature of the institutions in practice is determined by relations at a still lower level − the relations of the individuals within the small deme units.

Who ran the demes? The personnel of local politics

The question of who ran the deme is in part a question about what sort of man became demarch. Haussoullier believed that the rich dominated deme politics, and that being demarch was a schooling for taking part in central political life, while Sundwall (1906, 57) thought that he could demonstrate that 'die Begüterten ein entschiedenes Übergewicht in den Demen haben'. The data now available put a very different complexion on things.

Table 7 gives the statistics: forty-two demarchs are known, all but two from before 300. Of these 39% are otherwise known, compared with some 60% of those proposing decrees in or being honoured by the deme being otherwise known. Of the sixteen otherwise known demarchs only two certainly come from wealthy families: Demophanes, demarch at Rhamnous in the middle of the fifth century seems an ancestor of the man of the same name who was syntrierarch about a century later; Euthydemos of Eleusis is the father of the Moirokles who rents the quarry, and the family is clearly wealthy, although it is not known to have borne liturgies.[44] Euthydemos' family has very strong deme interests and this is a pattern found with other demarchs also: at Eleusis the demarch Gnathis (ii² 1186) is father of Timokedes who proposes that the peripolarch Smikythion of Kephale be honoured (ii² 1193); Onetor, demarch in ii² 1191, may propose ii² 1192; at Aixone the son of Philotheros is among several people honoured in the year his father was demarch (ii² 1197), and at Teithras Euthippos is honoured for his performance of religious duties – presumably carried out in his capacity as demarch (SEG 24.151, 153).

A number of other demarchs can be connected with men representing the deme as bouleutai: Kleokhares Kleodoridou, demarch of Rhamnous in 262/1 was son of a bouleutes of 281/0 and brother of a man on a deme committee in 236/5, while a related branch produces a bouleutes, Antiphilos, in 336/5 and the proposer of the 262/1 measure, Kleokhares; Thoukydides of Ikarion was demarch and, in 330, diaitetes while his nephew and son served together in the boule in 304/3; Arkhias, demarch of Halai Araphenides, may be related to Apollodoros Arkhiou, bouleutes for the deme in 341/0; Antipatros, demarch of Sphettos, is the father of

Phoxias, *bouleutes* in the third century; Prokles of Sounion may be the father of the *bouleutes* whose name is imperfectly preserved in Meritt and Traill (1974) 88.8. The most well-known man of this class is Euboulides, demarch and *bouleutes* of Halimous and the opponent in Demosthenes 57.[45]

Just a few men have connections with service outside the *boule*: a descendant of Kybernis, demarch of Halimous, proposed a decree in the assembly; Euainetos of Rhamnous has a descendant as *grammateus* in the early second century; Euthydomos Euthydomou of Melite, as well as being connected to a woodworker on the Erekhtheion, seems related to a man who was both *sungrapheus* and belonged to a college of ten magistrates during the fourth century.[46]

This limited sample of demarchs is surprisingly consistent: most of these men are of no more than moderate wealth, and their interests are very heavily deme-based. When they are found serving the polis it is largely as *bouleutai* or *diaitetai* – among their fellow demesmen. Few, by contrast, are found active in the assembly, and only one family is at all likely to yield a 'full-time' politician (n. 44 above). Thus while their position makes the demarch a bridge between deme and polis, the individuals who take the office do not independently take much part in the running of the polis; and while the office carries much local power, the holders of the office are not men of high social status.[47]

Although the group of demarchs overlaps with the groups who propose or are honoured in deme decrees both these groups include men who are much better known to us. Men whose other connections are predominantly local are again prominent: the sons of Khremes, archon in 362/5, are responsible for no fewer than three decrees surviving from Aixone (ii² 1198–1200); Glaukides Sosippou of the same deme moved two measures in the same year, and his father was buried in the deme;[48] Euktemon of Halai Aixonides was syntrierarch in 322 (ii² 1632.180f.), but his brother married a local girl (ii² 5525) and his father proposes ii² 1174 and appears with his son's father-in-law (and the two proposers mentioned in ii² 1175) on a list of men chosen by the deme to see to the creation of a statue of Aphrodite and praised for the result (ii^2 2820).

Men whose only connection with central administration is bouleutic appear again, but there are other men who are rather more heavily involved in the polis: uncertain, but attractive, in the identification of Astyphilos Philagrou of Halai Aixonides, proposer of ii^2 1175, *bouleutes* (ii^2 1743), and father of Menyllos, whose marble funerary lekythos survives and who with his father appears on the list ii^2 2820, with the Philagros syntrierarch in 322 (ii^2 1632.192), and the Astyphilos who proposed the decrees ii^2 42 and *Hesperia* 2.2f. no. 3; Theodorides of Athmonon, who proposes ii^2 1203 is clearly related to the sons of Theodoros who figure in a deme list, probably of financial contributions, and is the grandson of the Theodorides who appears in the *diadikasia* document (ii^2 1929.24), and the brother of Simos, who pays a naval debt in the 320s (ii^2 1631.662), with whom he appears in a list of Kekropis of the mid-century (ii^2 2385). Both these men clearly belong to rather wealthy families, and the same is true of Euthemon and Glaukides, already discussed.[49]

Still greater wealth is found in the families of the men honoured by the demes: Pheidippos, who seems to have to pay part of the expense of inscribing the decree which honours him (ii^2 1182), was the son of Apemon, victorious *choregos* for Pandionis in the boys' dithyramb at the Thargelia in the early fourth century (ii^2 1138.17f.), and himself contributed to the cost of a dedication by the *boule* at the Amphiaraon in 328/7 although not a *bouleutes* in that year; Neoptolemos of Melite, honoured for his services to the Artemis Aristoboule shrine (*SEG* 22.116) is called 'excessively rich' by Demosthenes (21.215) and served in a number of religious capacities, as well as lending money as head of a group of *eranistai* attested by a *horos* recently recovered from Laurium; Philoxenides of Aixone, honoured as a *choregos*, also appears as a creditor on a *horos*, and his daughter married the orator Lykourgos; Demokrates, another honoured *choregos* of that deme was from the very well-off family of Plato's Lysis, which had connections with the local cult of the Herakleidai, and to which Kallias the priest and his son, also honoured, may belong.[50]

More humble men also find themselves honoured by the demes, and there is some overlap with the demarchs and proposers,[51] but it is nevertheless tolerably clear that the men honoured by demes are of greater wealth and standing than the men who propose deme decrees, while the men who propose those decrees are themselves often of much higher standing than the demarchs. Not only do those honoured and those who propose command greater wealth, they also show a much more active interest in central government and administration, while those who take the office of demarch are in general inclined to restrict their official activities to those closely associated with the deme. While it may be the case that most actions which would earn honours required a financial outlay it is not the case that wealth prevented service in the deme: more than an economic factor is at work here, a social facet of political life is revealing itself.

Although the findings here go directly against the position maintained by earlier scholars in the field they should cause little surprise, for the earlier parts of this work have shown that different patterns of behaviour are found amongst the more and the less well-off, whether in terms of extra-deme financial commitments (in the mines or in the *astu*) or in terms of preferred marriage partners. The rich saw the whole polis as their field of activity, while those less well-off were also less mobile. The demarch was certainly a big fish, but the pool was rather small, and some of the things he had to do were of a rather menial nature. The demes might prove a convenient source of honours, whether for oneself or for another who could be subtly obliged in this way, but too close an involvement with the deme could implicate one in the more sordid aspects of everyday life, and seriously hamper one's freedom to take a full part in other groups. This necessarily rather ambivalent attitude of the rich man towards his deme was one of the essential bases upon which democracy stood.

Demos and *demokratia*: formal and informal mediation of power

Despite the ethos of openness and equality which both demes and polis embraced, social factors did affect political activity. The nature of the groups of those who took the political initiative was heavily influenced by their social and geographical origin, while the locally important, if largely administrative, office of demarch was of limited appeal. There is a seeming contradiction here that in fact underpins the working of democracy.

Constitutionally the deme was the basis of the democracy: through the small group of the deme, men were selected to run the larger group of the polis, and a man needed to acknowledge his deme and be acknowledged by it if he wanted to take any full part in political life through magistracies. The nature of the settlement pattern encouraged deme solidarity, and the institutional incentive to the maintenance of deme ties reflects, and is reflected by, the continued possession of the major holding of land in the ancestral deme.

Demosthenes 57 shows only too clearly that getting too much involved in offices in the deme was very far from being a step on the road to prominence in the polis as a whole. Those who are prominent in polis politics are the rich who keep ties with their deme which are traditional in form: these men are those who are honoured by the demes. Neoptolemos of Melite provides a type case: this man is honoured by his deme for the restoration of the shrine of Artemis Aristoboule founded by Themistokles, an act unlikely to have been without political overtones, but one which was independently justifiable in traditional terms; although not among those who proposed extant decrees, Neoptolemos is known as a friend of Meidias (D. 21.215) and close associate of Lykourgos (D. 18.114), and his various religious activities earned him central honours also ([Plut.] *Mor.* 843f., cf. *SIG*³ 296.4); in the light of the *horos* found recently (n. 50) he is almost certainly a man with land in the mining region (ii^2 1582.122). Here is a man who is known to be rich (cf. ii^2 1628.384f., 418; 1629.904f., 938f.), who is active in deme and in central politics, and who is attracted to the one economic activity which mixed men from a large part of Attika, the mining of silver.

While the notion of a 'face-to-face' society is absurd as a picture of Athens as a whole, it is of value in considering the nature of smaller groups. Every Athenian was part of the total network of Athenaioi, but also part of a number of partial networks, of which the most important politically was the deme. These partial networks are not discrete: relations were not specific, contact might be made at different times with the same people for different purposes or with different people for the same purposes.[52] Of this complexity the honorific decrees are born: religious or social actions oblige the political community. But honours also oblige, and this is just the type of situation where patronage is inevitable.[53] By honouring Neoptolemos the demesmen of Melite established a relationship, but this was a relationship not just with him but with the networks of which he was part. Through Neoptolemos demesmen of Melite had access to circles of the wealthy active in the mines, men from many parts of Attika, and to the circle of political figures around Lykourgos.

It happens that Melite is a city deme, but the pattern and its possibilities are no less clear for that. The deme is a vertical group in which men are united by locality and not by social status; individual demesmen are part of a number of horizontal groups which may be more or less well-defined. In the case of the rich it is tolerably clear that the horizontal group was quite well-defined: these men were united in the bearing of liturgies, in activity in the mining area, in having some property in the city — all links which did not respect locality to any high degree. Moreover the rich were also united in a more physical way through the practice of inter-marriage, which results in the complex web of kinship connections partly explicated in chapter 7.

That wealthy men made political use of their local

connections seems clear enough from the use of an Akharnian *bouleutes* by Telemakhos of Akharnai (above p. 67). The argument here is that as recipients of honours the wealthy were obliged to make accessible to men linked to them by locality the links they had which were established by their wealth: their horizontal group provided the bridge by which not only they themselves but also other members of their deme could make contact with men who were active in politics, and by these links both the social and the geographical barriers to political activity could be breached, even if they could not be broken down totally.

The mediation of power involved here is informal, but it may be strengthened and supplemented by the formal institution of the *trittys*. In the *trittys* demes of the same tribe in the same general area were united. The precise rôle played by the *trittys* in Athenian political life still requires elucidation, but the *trittys* seems to have been a real enough unit to own property and even to have cults. The most important political rôle of the *trittys* may have been in electoral procedure: the *trittyes* are known to have played a part in the election of tribal officials and it is probable that they were important intermediate links between demes and tribes in elections where the tribe is the responsible unit.[54] Although this cannot be demonstrated it does seem likely that Athenians felt a closer bond with other members of the same *trittys* than they did with fellow tribesmen as a whole, and closer links with tribesmen than with the mass of the citizen body.

In the light of this it is at least interesting that when the men who proposed measures in the assembly are examined from the point of view of the *trittys* of origin the sample used above has twenty-two out of thirty *trittyes* represented compared with thirty-nine out of 139 demes. Not all the unrepresented *trittyes* are distant from Athens — they include the *trittys* constituted by Phaleron, the city *trittys* of Erekhtheis, and the coastal *trittys* of Kekropis.[55] If the *trittyes* were perceived as real groups they clearly did help to bend the geographical limits, for in very few *trittyes* were there no men able and willing to take an active part in politics. This process is considerably aided by the anomalous *trittyes*: precisely because they are not natural geographical units these tie together distant parts of the countryside and help to ensure that at least some members of the *trittys* can gain easy access to the *astu*.

Athenian democracy was founded upon a belief in equality, and all citizens could in theory take a direct and equal part. To a certain extent this ethos could be enforced by the institutions: thus most citizens must have served at least once on the *boule*.[56] To a large extent, however, geographical constraints and social inequalities intervened, and although a large number of citizens probably did attend the assembly (Hansen (1976)), political decision-making rested in the hands of a restricted portion of the citizen body. Constitutional changes altered the appearance of the Athenian political system very markedly, but they could not of themselves alter peoples' preferences and perceptions of the polis, and thus did not as radically alter the seat of political power. Democracy did create two important new 'front men' for the Athenian remote from the *astu* and the possibility of personal political action. One was the *bouleutes*, a man at the very hub of political activity, able to see what was going to happen in the assembly, able indeed to determine, to an extent at least, what was going to happen, and able to report back to the deme and to represent the deme in the *boule*. A second was the demarch, a man with roots very firmly set in the deme and little more than an executive cog in the machinery of central government, but nevertheless the man who had to face the consequences of unilateral action whether on the part of the deme or on the part of the central executive officers. Both these, for a year at a time, were important live wires regulating the temperature of politics local and central. But besides these there continued a more stable front man, the propertied man whom the deme found itself having to honour in its decrees. Ironically it is precisely through the very traditional social relations, formally ignored by the demes but implicitly acknowledged in many of their actions, that the inequalities in the access to power were most effectively mitigated. All citizens did have access to the true centre of power, but indirectly, and the access was all the more effective for being indirect. The deme was the essential link, forging strong bonds of service and obligation between men of various social circles, and connecting the humble demesmen to the network of the well-to-do through which the main power flowed. Through the demes, what was in theory a direct democracy was in practice a subtle representational one. In the deme, in the local unit which men could not refuse to acknowledge without losing their political identity, local acts and local obligations, formal and informal, came to form the essential backdrop for central obligation and central action.

CHAPTER 5

ATHENIAN STONE RESOURCES AND THEIR EXPLOITATION

Although he will be mainly interested in the mines, Xenophon regards the stone quarries of Attika as a major resource: πέφυκε μὲν γὰρ λίθος ἐν αὐτῇ ἄφθονος, ἐξ οὗ κάλλιστοι μὲν ναοί, κάλλιστοι δὲ βωμοὶ γίγνονται, εὐπρεπέστατα δὲ θεοῖς ἀγάλματα (*Poroi* 1.4). There are three main sources of information about quarrying in Attika: written sources, literary but above all epigraphic, give some information about specific uses of particular quarries for particular building projects; buildings themselves preserve quarried stone which may be traced to the quarry of origin with more or less certainty; and the quarries themselves may continue to exist to the present day and preserve traces of the classical activity. In some cases the information from more than one source may relate to a single quarrying project.

The physical remains

Apart from the Pendele and Hymettos quarries which have been known and visited since the seventeenth century, the quarries of Attika have not traditionally been an object of great interest to travellers or classical archaeologists. The quarries which have been noticed were very much noted 'in passing' and even the great German observer of the Attic countryside, Arthur Milchhoeffer, was less than thorough in recording traces of quarrying. Descriptions of the remains only began to be at all adequate or detailed in the mid-nineteenth century with Fiedler's description of the remains on Pendele (1840, 30ff.), and the first man to take an interest in the sources of stone in any systematic way was the geologist Lepsius, with his *Griechische Marmorstudien* of 1890. Even since then close study of the ancient traces with

93

the aim of discovering the methods employed, type of block removed, and extent of working, has been limited in Attika to the American work on the Pnyx quarries, done in the 1930s, and some recent work in the Peiraieus.

Ancient sources distinguish stones by their place of origin, but since quarrying methods and the nature of the use can be expected to vary with the geological type of the stone marble quarries, limestone quarries, and quarries for other stone will be treated in separate groups here.[1]

The most important classical marble quarries were undoubtedly those on the west slopes of Pendele.[2] Lepsius in the 1880s claimed to find traces of twenty-five ancient quarries, and estimated that some 400,000 cubic metres of marble might have been cut from them. He believed that the only ancient exploitation of the mountain had been on this slope, but while this does seem to be true of the classical period there were quarries on the north-east slopes towards Rapendosa and Dionyso, in the archaic period, as the discovery of an unfinished *kouros* showed.[3] Today modern quarrying has removed almost all the traces of ancient working, except in one particular area: this is the area of the Spelia quarry, the largest of the ancient quarries noted by Lepsius, and distinguished by the Byzantine church in the mouth of the cave which gives it its name. A paved ancient quarry road, beside which still sits an abandoned column drum, leads down from this quarry.[4] All quarry faces necessarily show the state of the quarry at the time of its latest exploitation, but Lepsius noted both in the Pendele quarries and in the stone from them used on the Akropolis that the quarrying had been done in a mechanical rather than an experienced way: the stone had been removed in horizontal and vertical planes rather than according to the natural grain of the stone. Such a method of stone cutting is not only more difficult, it also leads to an inferior endurance to weathering.[5]

In contrast to those on Pendele the quarries on Hymettos are quite widely scattered, mainly along the north-west slopes. It is unclear how many ancient quarries there were, and almost impossible to distinguish between quarries worked in the classical period and those only worked under the Romans. The quarries also vary in shape and size: there are some major ancient quarry faces, but there are also some areas of extensive shallow working.[6] Today the most visible and most extensive ancient remains lie on the slopes behind the Saketta army camp and immediately north of the Megale Rheuma. The strange structure known as the 'Dragon House' is situated here, and there are traces of terraces which supported the ancient quarry road (pl. 5); some of the workings are certainly Roman, however, and some are even more recent.[7]

The quarries in the Agrileza valley can be more securely dated to the classical period. There are two separate areas of quarrying, one in the immediate vicinity of the Cliff Tower, and the other across a spur valley to the north. The Cliff Tower quarry has extensive traces of shallow workings running along the top of the cliff for at least 200 m. Among the traces is a ring cutting apparently marking the spot from which a drum for a column of the Poseidon temple was removed (pl. 6). The building of the Cliff Tower and attendant house upon the quarry face suggests that once that temple was complete it was apparent that there would be no further demand for this marble. Lepsius claimed that here again the blocks were removed 'mechanically' in horizontal and vertical planes, without regard to the nature of the marble, but in fact the marble naturally splits in just this way.[8]

In the vicinity of Thorikos two further quarries exploit the upper marble of the Laureotike. There is a quarry on Velatouri hill itself, and another just to the west near the summit of the hill Stephani (pl. 7). The latter was reported by the mining engineer Kordellas, but apparently has not been examined since: however, the traces of quarrying are very clear there, although the workings do seem to have been shallow and limited.[9]

The only other marble quarries lie in north-east Attika: Papageorgakis has reported quarries of uncertain date on Kotroni, south of Marathon, and Milchhoeffer noted quarries by the coast immediately north of Agia Marina.[10]

95

Among limestones the most prestigious and widely used was the 'black' limestone from Eleusis. There were quarries at Eleusis itself, those on the north side of the Akropolis being visible today, but it is not clear whether these produced the requisite type of stone, and it is possible that the stone came from quarries to the north of Eleusis.[11] There is a similar doubt as to whether or not the 'stone from Akte' can or should be associated with particular quarries, or whether it may simply refer to all stone from the area of the Peiraieus. Several quarries are known right on the coast north and west of the Peiraieus, including some workings of considerable size which are now submerged. Strabo (C. 395) appears to refer to those towards Salamis and in the region of Perama. Further quarries are known inland. Recent excavations have revealed that there were small-scale classical workings in the Peiraieus itself, on Mounykhia hill and elsewhere, in the late classical and hellenistic periods. The quarries here are very shallow, but remaining trace suggest that blocks of some size ($1-1.5 \times 0.75$ m) were removed. It seems possible that this contrast indicates that we have here one-off workings of the stone resources of their own plots of land by private individuals to supply some public project.[12]

Quarrying is known at several other points along Aigaleos, particularly in the area of the pass at Daphni and at Profitis Elias Khaidari, but the city had limestone resources even closer to hand: at any early date both the Akropolis and Lykabettos were exploited, and the workings on the Pnyx have been thoroughly investigated.[13] The Pnyx quarry was created by the reshaping of the assembly place, and the stone from it was used for that. Because of the limited exploitation the methods employed are particularly clear, the lower part of the main quarry trench remaining intact. From this wide trench others only $0.2-0.3$ m wide were sent out perpendicularly, to reach a further trench parallel to the first and some 3.0 m out. The blocks were then removed by inserting wedges into slits chiselled about 0.15 m long. These slits were on one side of the block only, thus obviating the need for wide trenches all round, and the narrow trenches appear to have been produced without it being necessary for a man to be able to get into them. Further quarries are known on the saddle between the hill of the Pnyx and the Hill of the Nymphs.

In rural Attika only one limestone quarry has been claimed — by Milchhoeffer on the west coast at Phoinikia. A road has now been driven through this area, and no certain traces of the quarry are visible.[14]

All three non-limestone quarries in Attika are coastal. The *Karten von Attika* mark two quarries lying just north of Anavyssos, and these prove on examination to be of a soft conglomerate stone. The only merit of this stone is that it is easy to work, and given the relative desertion of the southern part of Attika from the Roman period to the twentieth century it is extremely unlikely that these quarries should be anything other than classical. That this stone should be exploited at all when the limestone mass of Mt Olympos and the marble resources of the Laureotike are so close is remarkable.[15]

The two other quarries in question are of a similar sedimentary sandstone, and lie close together on the east coast of Attika. One is just above the Mycenaean cemetery at Perati. Briefly mentioned by Iakovides, the workings here run for some 60 m up the hillside. They seem to have been shallow, more so than the Anavyssos quarries, with a maximum face height of about 1.5 m (pl. 8). It is likely that the stone from Steiria which figures in an inscription about building, probably at Eleusis, in the fifth century, came from this quarry.[16] The destination of the stone from the other quarry is completely certain: this is the quarry just north of Brauron which provided stone for the Artemis sanctuaries at Brauron and to the north at Loutsa. Here again the workings are quite shallow but extensive (pl. 9). This quarry is well known and was reused for the stone for the restorations at Brauron, but it has never been fully published.[17]

The use of stone in buildings

It has recently become clear that distinguishing stones of similar geological nature and determining their origins is not as simple as has been thought in the past, but for the historian it is essential that the attempt be made, for it is not enough to know about the movement of a few distinctive types of stone: there must be enough information to determine what was generally the case. In future the combination of isotopic analysis and petrological examination may yield reasonably certain data,[18] but meanwhile the historian who works with data from Attika is in a privileged position: the richness of the epigraphic record and the very distinct nature of Pentelic marble help greatly in distinguishing building stones.[19]

Two stones, which appear in the inscriptions as *lithoi arouraioi* and *lithoi Agryleikoi*, cannot be traced to their quarry of origin at all. In the former case the only clue to the origin comes from the fact that they were used at Eleusis, and we do not even know what sort of stone it was.[20] The latter stone is almost certainly to be identified with Kara limestone, whose use in buildings has been noted, but modern quarrying in that area has removed all trace of any ancient workings.[21]

In general only the stone of buildings of or later than the great Periklean building programme can be assigned to a quarry with any certainty. Earlier buildings are of course known, but archaeologists have generally classed their stone, unhelpfully, as 'poros'.[22] It is known, however, that the foundations of the Peisistratid temple of Athena on the Akropolis, and of the pre-Periklean Parthenon were of Kara limestone, and imported marble is thought to have been used for the sculptures of the Athena temple. Hymettan marble appears to have been used for the roof-tiles and *sima* of the Hekatompedon and is the only Attic marble to make an impact in archaic sculpture (despite the unfinished *kouros* on Pendele).

The Periklean buildings on the Akropolis used Pentelic marble almost exclusively; Eleusinian black limestone was used decoratively in the Erekhtheion frieze (where Lepsius has argued that the pinned figures were of Pentelic, not Parian, marble), and a small amount of Aiginetan stone was used for backers in the Erekhtheion. The Propylaia again has decorative use of Eleusinian stone. Outside the Akropolis the account of Stuart and Revett suggests that the temple on the Ilissos used Pentelic marble exclusively,[23] but the Hephaisteion has a bottom step of poros, Aiginetan architrave backers, and Parian sculptures.

In the Agora the picture is rather different. Many buildings have foundations of local blue-grey limestone, some possibly from the Akropolis itself: among such are the Old Bouleuterion, Metroon, and the fourth-century temple of Apollo Patroos. Grey poros is found in the New Bouleuterion and the lower part of the Tholos, where it is surmounted by a string course of Hymettan marble and then by brick. The Stoa Basileios uses stone from Peiraieus and Aigina, and the newly excavated Stoa Poikile had steps and foundations of 'hard poros limestone', with a poros bench, poros triglyphs and marble metopes. The late fifth-century South Stoa used poros and unbaked brick. Only the probably Periklean Stoa of Zeus Eleutherios made extensive use of Pentelic marble (on a poros foundation and with a step of Hymettan marble).

Excavation has shown that houses in the *astu* often had footings of stone, which is generally blue-grey limestone or soft yellow poros. The city walls, about which we are well informed by Thucydides, for the fifth century, and by inscriptions, for two periods in the fourth century, made extensive use of brick, but Thucydides (1.93.5) makes it clear that the Peiraieus defences were wholly of stone from the first. The records from the 390s specify only *lithagogia*, but those for the work on the Peiraieus fortifications in 337/6 specify that 'those who have contracted for the cutting of stone for the walls are to cut stone from wheresoever each contracts', and the contractors are also responsible for the shaping and transport of the blocks (ii² 244.47ff.). There is no fussiness about the type of stone used.

Epigraphic evidence from Eleusis shows that Aiginetan and Steirian stone were used in the fifth century, Pentelic and Aiginetan planned for and Pentelic and 'Aktites' used in the Telesterion portico in the fourth century, and Eleusinian used in repairs to a tower.[24] Excavation has revealed the use of Eleusinian limestone in house foundations, the sixth-century town and sanctuary walls, and the fifth-century temple of Plouto. Poros was used for the upper part of the Periklean precinct wall and in the *telesterion* in both the sixth century (with Kara limestone and, possibly, Parian marble) and the fifth century (with Eleusinian stone and Pentelic marble).

Elsewhere the range of buildings known at any one site is more limited. In the Peiraieus Philo's arsenal, which may have been the first building of its type in stone at all, uses Akte stone for walls and columns, Pentelic for the *hypertonaia*, Pentelic or Hymettan, at the builder's discretion, for the *parastades*, and Hymettan for the roof. The fourth-century temple of Zeus similarly combines Hymettan and Aktites.[25]

At Sounion the foundations of both temples in both building periods are of poros (i.e. in this case, local conglomerate), and the fifth-century part of the fort wall is also of this stone. The superstructure of both temples, however, in the fifth century, as possibly in the earlier buildings, was of Agrileza marble. That marble also appears in the hellenistic additions to the fort and the hellenistic ship-sheds. Marble is used with poros in the temple propylon and in the adjacent *andron*, while a small temple beside the main temple of Athena, thought by Abramson to be the *heroon* of Phrontis, has a statue base, possibly reused, in Eleusinian limestone.[26]

The temple building and the theatre at Thorikos employ local marble, but despite the proximity of the quarries many of the domestic buildings, and in particular the tower building, appear to employ fieldstones.

Brauron has extensive use of local sandstone, but imports marble for the metopes, while the temples at Rhamnous use the marble from Agia Marina exclusively except for the cult statue of Nemesis, which appears to be of Parian marble. Local marble is also extensively used in the fort and the funerary monuments.[27] At the Amphiareion local limestone and poros are the materials most used, with some interior and decorative use of marble.

It is not possible to identify with certainty the stones of

buildings which have not received recent close attention, but there is certainly no clear case of a fort not using stone quarried practically on the site — as is occasionally quite obvious, as at Plakoto.[28]

Some of the individual cases deserve fuller study, however, as for example the fort at Oinoe (Myoupolis) and the nearby tower beside the road from Thebes to Eleusis: both of these structures employ both limestone and conglomerate, but while in the fort the fifth-century part (the tower in the west wall) is of limestone and all the later work conglomerate, in the tower the very lowest courses are of limestone but the upper are of conglomerate, without any great change in building style, and with drafted corners throughout.[29]

The 'Tomb of Sophokles' at Dekeleia furnishes a further instructive case of a local and easily worked stone being employed where another stone would have given a better result. Here a particularly nasty conglomerate spoils an otherwise imposing monument (pl. 10).[30]

The siting of quarries and the movement of building stone

The siting of quarries is obviously determined by the requirement that a suitable stone be present. All four of the areas of Attika where marble is accessible were exploited, but all to a limited extent. The Rhamnous (Agia Marina) and Sounion (Agrileza) quarries seem to be quite closely tied to specific building projects, and the way in which the Cliff Tower and adjacent house were built on the former quarry surface indicates clearly that further demand for the stone was not envisaged in that case. The same may well be true of the Thorikos quarries on Stephani; nothing links this quarry closely with the Thorikos temple, but the marble from it is of better quality than most of that from Velatouri itself, and the Stephani quarry, which certainly had a rather limited exploitation, would be a very suitable source for that building.[31]

The quarries of stones other than marble are almost all either coastal or closer to Athens than the sea is. Despite this their exploitation is doggedly local. Most are shallow workings and a relatively small amount of stone has been removed. Often they can be tied to a specific building programme, as at Brauron. The one-off nature of the working of many of these quarries comes out from a study of the techniques employed. Given the limited tools available there was clearly a limit to the possible ways in which stone could be quarried, but it is nevertheless notable that the remains of workings in the Agrileza, Thorikos (Stephani), and Hymettos (Dragon House) marble quarries differ not only from the limestone quarry of the Pnyx but also from each other. The differences may in part be due to the peculiar demands made of each quarry (witness the ring and curious hemispherical cuttings in the Agrileza quarries) but cannot be entirely accounted for in such a way. All these are quarries with shallow workings; in the Spelia quarry on Pendele, where the vertical surface was cut back, not the horizontal dug down, a different technique again was employed.[32]

The nature of the quarries was closely linked with the standard of the building: not only did the use of stone from upper layers of a quarry lead to inferior weathering, but it has been argued that at Rhamnous the attempt to use up all the stone from a newly opened quarry led the builders to use up small and irregularly shaped pieces of stone from the very topmost layers of the quarry, hiding them in parts of the building where they would not be seen.[33]

When the buildings, rather than the quarries, are made the first object of attention the local bias becomes still more obvious. Excepting Eleusis, even sanctuaries outside Athens employ as their main building stone material found within 4 km of the site. The local stone was used even in preference to importing marble, if there was no marble locally, as the example of Brauron shows, for although Bouras (1967) suggests that the local stone at Brauron has structural advantages the fact that it gets no further afield than Loutsa militates against this being a major factor.

At Eleusis local stone *is* widely used, but there is a willingness to import stone for important sanctuary buildings. The

stone imported is not, however, generally marble, but limestone from the Peiraieus, Steiria, and Aigina; the reason for
this would seem to be the convenient coastal position of
Eleusis for obtaining stone from these coastal sources. One
striking feature is that stone from Aigina behaves as if it were
local, and is employed at Athens, Eleusis, and the Peiraieus:
this too must be a product of the fact that it had to be
moved by sea, the distance of transport then becoming of
minor importance.

In Athens itself there is a very clear division between sanctuary and other buildings. Marble is rarely used outside
sanctuaries, and even inside them other stones are as a rule
found in foundations and invisible parts. The use of local
blue-grey limestone shows that the preference is for local
stone, not just for stone that is easily worked.

It is stone that is used decoratively, not structurally, that
travels to other parts of Greece: Pentelic marble and Eleusinian
black limestone.[34] Even these stones are very often found in
connection with Athenian workmen: Pheidias at Olympia,
Timotheos at Epidauros. Burford found a similar association
beween Argive black stone at Epidauros and the presence of
an Argive architect.[35]

The organisation of the building-stone industry

The preference for local stone resources and the tendency for
a particular quarry to be linked to a particular building
project complicate rather than simplify the organisation of
quarrying. Some information about arrangements at both the
quarry and the building site is provided by epigraphic
sources, and this information has recently received an
important supplement.

Three cases are known of the renting out of quarries in
Attika.[36] One of these enters the records because the entre-
preneur and his surety failed to pay the rent demanded
(above pp. 1–3). This quarry was at the Peiraieus and the
rent the large sum of 115½ dr. a month. There is reason to

believe that the contract for the quarry may have been for only half the year.[37]

The second case is the least helpful: all we know is that certain sacrifices at the Peiraieus Asklepieion were paid from the income from the quarry, and it may be that the quarry in question is one of those known archaeologically on Mounykhia hill, close to the site of the sanctuary. The sacrifices that are paid from the quarry rent are not regular, and there is no means of telling whether or not the income from this source was regular.

The third case provides the greatest amount of information. The renting out of a quarry to provide income for the cult of Herakles 'in Akris' is the subject of the two decrees from Eleusis discovered in 1970. The exact location of the sanctuary of Herakles in Akris and of the quarry is not certain, and the quarry is leased by the demesmen of Eleusis. The lease is for five years, the shortest period that any deme property we know of is leased for, and the rent is 150 dr. a year, considerably lower than that of the Peiraieus quarry.[38] The quarry is referred to as such, and so had presumably been worked on a previous occasion, but it certainly had not been rented out before, since the deme honoured the man who suggested the leasing for making the suggestion. The decrees are datable to 332/1, and so come at the beginning of the major building programme in the sanctuary at Eleusis.

It is difficult to tell how typical these three cases are of the usual method of working a quarry. The shortness of the leases is suspicious. Further, it is odd that leasing a quarry was a novel idea to the Eleusinians. Strangest of all, Moirokles, who takes on the Eleusis quarry lease, is the son of the Euthydemos who has to do with the quarry in ii[2] 47. This makes it highly unlikely that what we have here is a random sample of a common phenomenon, and probable that leasing out quarries was not a normal activity. How the Peiraieus quarry lease fitted into the fiscal structure of the polis, and why *that* quarry came to be the subject of a public lease remains unclear.

The powers that be at Eleusis assume the right to lease out

their quarry just as they might lease out land for farming. The important question is whether or not the land on which other quarries were sited was owned, and whether land not owned by a private individual would automatically be considered to be public property. It certainly is not clear that assumption of public rights to stone resources is behind the public lease of the Peiraieus quarry, and the probability must be against 'automatic' public ownership. In this situation quarrystone would cost nothing at all in the majority of cases, and there would be no limit on exploitation.[39]

This suggestion receives some support from the building accounts. These record the payment for stone in a variety of ways, but the general pattern is for it to be recorded as payment for *lithotomia*, to *lithotomoi* (as particularly in the Parthenon accounts), or in the form of a *timē* for the stone followed by a list of the names of the quarrymen. In all the cases the context makes it clear that we are dealing with payments for cutting the stone, not with a price paid for ready-cut blocks. There is no reference in the Attic accounts to direct payment for the stone as such.[40] Payments made to *lithotomoi* seem, at first glance, to exclude the possibility of a middleman and with it the idea of a contractor covering his rent by labour charges, but this argument is weakened by the fact that the only names of quarrymen that we have look very likely to be slave names, and if these men are slaves then clearly the formula of payment 'to the *lithotomoi*' is a fiction.[41]

The variety of payment formulae support the evidence of the leases which suggest that demand for stone fluctuated and there was no regularly organised industry. The earlier findings about the local use of stone are consonant with this, and it can be demonstrated in detail from the building accounts. If some assumptions are made about the likely daily wage of a quarryman and about the relationship between payment and the time taken to extract the stone, it is possible to deduce from the information given in ii² 1672 that the whole of the major Eleusis building programme of 329/8 provided the men who quarried *lithoi arouraioi* with only some sixty-nine days of work.[42] Even in the quarries of Pendele the situation is not very different. Pentelic was widely used in the new portico for the Telesterion at Eleusis, a building project which was long meditated (cf. ii² 204) and was finally carried out in the twenty years or so following 335 BC. Each column drum for the portico will have taken about one man-year of labour to quarry, and it is known from ii² 1673 that twenty-three drums were delivered in the year 333/2. If this was the normal annual number then it will have taken six years to complete the order. The capitals, also of Pentelic marble, seem to have been delivered somewhat later. Thus the whole of this major order would seem to have been within the capacities of just twenty-three quarrymen.[43] A similar sum can be done for the major order of the first half of the fourth century, the provision of Pentelic marble for the tholos at Epidauros, with the result that that order appears to have provided no more than four years' work for a team of thirty-five quarrymen.[44]

From all this it appears that even in the quarries of Pendele the demand for marble for building fluctuated considerably, and even at its peaks in the fourth century was not great enough to keep a force of more than, say, fifty men employed. Of course there was also, in the Pendele and Hymettos marble quarries, as not in others, some constant demand for stelai for epigraphic and sculptural purposes, but this cannot have kept more than a handful of men continuously employed. As a result the number of skilled men available when demand did pick up will have been small. All the evidence from the stone industry is against the assumption that a great premium was put on skilled work.[45] Opening up new stone resources for new building projects will have made it impossible for anyone to have a particular skill in handling the stone to be used. On the Akropolis there is no specialisation on the part of the masons: Simon, a metic living in Agryle, is responsible for the placing and dressing of Pentelic marble, Eleusinian limestone, and Aiginetan stone for the Erekhtheion.[46] In such a situation it is not surprising that the quality of work of both sculptors and masons visibly improved as the Periklean building programme went on.

The 'one-off' nature of much Attic quarrying is revealed also by the *ad hoc* transport arrangements. In 394/5 and again in 330/29 Boiotians are found involved in transporting stone.[47] The Parthenon project had to employ *hodopoioi*, and they are still being employed in the 430s.[48] More surprisingly the authorities at Eleusis not only had to do some road building, probably at Eleusis, when it wanted to transport the column drums, but also had to do quite extensive road clearing at the Pendele end, which would seem to imply that no major movement of Pentelic marble had been undertaken for some time. Even once the project is under way the contracts for transport have no single form. In 333/2 the transport of the column drums was apparently put into the hands of a limited number of contractors, and payment is on a day rate. The 329/8 accounts, by contrast, have examples both of single payments for the quarrying, placing, and transport of the stone, and of separate payments for transport on a job price. Both types of contract are found even with reference to a single type of stone.[49] In the Parthenon accounts all the payments are broken down, with quarrymen, *kuklopoioi*, those putting the stone on the *kukla*, those dealing with *lithagogia* from Pendele, and those responsible for the *litholkia* to the workshops on the Akropolis all being paid individually.[50]

The variation of form within the Eleusis records is matched by the variation in the personnel involved. Of the men who provide transport and/or stone in 329/8 only one is a native of Eleusis, and while one other man, Neokleides of Kephisia, is employed in more than one capacity, it is only the native who is employed in more than one prytany.[51] There is little sign here of the presence of an indispensable pool of skilled labour: outsiders come in for a contract and then disappear again, and the shape and size of contract are determined by the inclination of the available contractor.

Quarries as local social forces

It has become tolerably clear that quarrying was not a major regular industrial activity. Buildings of all sorts prefer to use local stone. The demand for any particular stone was sporadic, and many quarries were opened for a single project. In such a situation owning a quarry could not become commercially viable, and it is not surpising that the only commercial quarries that are known occur in special circumstances, and even then one of them may have led to a bankruptcy.[52] The organisation and personnel of stone transport and provision strongly suggest that these were occasional and subsidiary activities for those who took them.

The strength of the preference for local material was almost certainly connected with the cost of transport. On the basis of the reconstruction of the cost of drums for the Eleusis portico (n. 43) the cost of transport will have been on average just over $\frac{2}{3}$ of the quarrying cost.[53] This is roughly the proportion found also for the Akte stone used at Eleusis, which cost 100 dr. to quarry and 60 dr. to transport.[54] The *lithoi arouraioi* used at Eleusis, however, have a quarrying: transport: placing ratio of 7:9:6.[55]

The consequences of this local preference were far-reaching. As already noted it excluded the possibility of the development of any high degree of special skill in a particular material. All that the quarrymen could provide was manual labour. We do not know enough about the labour force for these short-lived local projects to prove the case, but the personnel may well have been local, especially if the work was seasonal, as the transporting of the Eleusis column drums, at least, seems to have been.[56] If this is the case then it may be that the variations in quarrying technique are a result of this. Certainly the use of local men and the short life of most quarries would give little scope or incentive for technological developments. It was no doubt the limited requirements for skill that enabled so many monumental buildings to go up all round Attika in the later part of the fifth century.

The small demand for skilled men means a small demand

for outsiders. The Eleusis accounts do show men from out-side floating into and out of the picture, but they also show that local men could and did get involved, and the deme decree of 332/1 assumes that a demesman will be interested in taking out the lease of the quarry, as indeed one was. Such quarrying activity was hardly a force for social interaction.

The Pendele quarries provide a different case. Here there was some constant demand, although only building projects on a large scale would employ many men. That demand may have been enough to affect the pattern of settlement, if the Kolonai demes are rightly placed in this area.[57] Certainly the quarries caused some disruption of established practices, for they produce the one metic who is listed as living in an area rather than in a deme; this is 'Manes living at Pendele' re-corded, appropriately enough, in the Eleusis accounts, where he is paid for sharpening stone-working tools.[58] Such is the extent and the limit of the social interaction brought about by the quarries: it is metic manual workers, not important Athenian propertied families who are attracted into the area, and the involvement of metics may well be linked with the insecurity of the business and the remoteness of the quarries of Pendele from good agricultural bases.[59]

Manes from Pendele and Simon from Agryle (who featured earlier in the account) show one way in which there was some movement of men engendered by building programmes: both these men seem to have followed the stone out of the quarry and onto the building site (although Simon is found turning his hand to other types of stone also). Only with Pendele, however, will such a path have led the workman far afield, and in general far from encouraging the movement of men from one area to another within Attika or any real change in patterns of settlement, the adherence of all locally important building programmes to local resources will have served to reinforce the strength of local feelings of identity and have contributed both marginally to the economic welfare of the local people and substantially to the social standing of the group as a whole, and in particular, no doubt, of those individuals who pushed the projects through. This is

reflected in the whole ethos of the inscriptions which pains-
takingly lay down the specifications for the buildings which
are constructed, and nowhere is this more clear than in the
relatively minor project at Kynosarges in the early fourth
century, where the detailed instructions about the nature and
material of the structure are themselves a monument to local
pride (ii^2 1665).

That quarrying proves to be no great force for change,
that the social requirements bulk large and the technological
resources are constrained by them, is a finding of no mean
importance.[60] Not least, it provides a contrasting backdrop
against which the exploitation of the silver mines can be
considered.

CHAPTER 6

PATTERNS OF EXPLOITATION IN THE ATHENIAN SILVER MINES

The economic importance of the Laurion mines

ἔστι δὲ καὶ γῆ ἡ σπειρομένη μὲν οὐ φέρει καρπόν, ὀρυττομένη δὲ πολλαπλασίους τρέφει ἢ εἰ σῖτον ἔφερε. καὶ μὴν ὑπάργυρός ἐστι σαφῶς θείᾳ μοίρᾳ (*Poroi* 1.5). Such is the view of Xenophon, about to launch a programme for the increased exploitation of the silver resources. Silver was certainly 'the most important Athenian resource, exported in substantial quantities', and it is arguable that it was the only significant Athenian export.[1] One measure of this is the interest which the Spartans were encouraged to show in the mines in the latter part of the Peloponnesian war; another, the number of people the mines were thought capable of providing employment for. The 20,000 slaves who deserted to the Spartans in the Dekeleian war have often been associated with the mines, and Xenophon proposes to employ 10,000 public slaves there. Conophagos, on the basis of a close survey of the archaeological remains, suggests 11,000 were employed there. On any reckoning of the total population of Athens any of these figures represents a substantial proportion of the working population of Attika.[2]

It is not clear precisely how the exploitation of the silver resources was organised, but they were certainly a source of individual fortunes, as well as important for the Athenian economy as a whole. Two of the men most famed for their wealth in the fifth century have been thought to have gained that wealth from the mines — Kallias, called Lakkoploutos, and the politician and general Nikias.[3]

The history of the exploitation of mines stretches ever further back: excavation of a gallery in the side of the hill Velatouri at Thorikos has revealed that silver was first mined there in the early Bronze Age, with two later peaks of activity in the late Bronze Age and the Protogeometric period.

111

If the development of the settlement at Thorikos is closely linked to mining activity then there seem to have been further particularly intense periods (or particularly profitable periods) of mining in the late sixth century, later fifth century, and the middle of the fourth century.[4] Further archaeological work elsewhere in the Laureotike, such as the two recent washery excavations, may give a further control over the present picture, which is all too largely derived from Thorikos in particular and from coastal sites in general.[5]

The combination of an extremely important but locationally limited economic resource, private exploitation, and considerable historical variability makes the Laurion silver mines a peculiar force within Athenian society. Coincidentally the very nature and peculiarity of the mines has meant that we are relatively well informed about them: continuous and coherent descriptions of classical mining are lacking, and for the fifth century we have little more than the odd allusion in Aristophanes, but from the fourth century we have both the tendentious discussions in the orators and the reticent factual records of the *poletai* who leased out the mines; something of a continuous overview is provided by the remarkable material remains, which have long been known but which are only now beginning to be adequately charted and published. Not unnaturally the mass of evidence of different sorts has led to massive controversy over its interpretation. This controversy centres on questions of toponymy and questions about the formal structure of the organisation of mining. Since the broad outlines of this organisation seem tolerably clear this study attempts to get within the framework and to observe the activities and interactions of the personnel who chose to involve themselves with this peculiar activity.[6]

Who owns and who leases what, where, and why?

The extant mining leases can be assumed to provide a more or less random sample of those involved in mining in the fourth century: that they cluster in the 40s of that century

112

may simply reflect the intensity of the mining.[7] The leases describe the position of a mine by naming the owner of the land on which it is situated and the names of the owners of one or more adjoining property. This system of reference gives the impression that the mining area was full of small properties, separately owned, but detailed analysis modifies this picture.

Table 8 gives the details provided by the leases. This shows that there is no case where different owners appear on all four sides of a plot. Only in two cases are four property owners recorded with reference to a single mine. In four cases there are three different owners. These six cases which do suggest a large degree of fragmentation are scattered about the mining area: one case comes from each of Anaphlystos, Nape, Sounion, Thorikos, and one unrecorded location. Much more common are the cases where all we know is that the land on which the mine is situated is in the hands of the same or a different owner from the owner of property on one side. That it was deemed sufficient to name the owner on just one side suggests that that man must have been particularly prominent there, but otherwise these cases are not very informative. Where the ownership of properties on two sides is known, the number of cases where one owner is in question is equal to the number where there are two. Some of the boundary items are *ergasteria* or *metalla*, which might be very small, but despite this the overall picture is that holdings were often relatively extensive, although no owner clearly held a large tract of land.[8]

Further information about the degree of fragmentation can be gained from examining the location at which known individuals held property. Some men certainly had property at more than one location: Meidias of Anagyrous has property at Sounion and Laureion, Diopeithes of Euonymon at Laureion (two items) and 'at Sounion at Thrasymos', Lysitheides of Kikynna at Thorikos and at Maroneia or Amphitrope, and Diophanes of Sounion at Sounion and Maroneia. In addition Aiskhines tells us that Timarkhos once had property at Aulon, Thrasymos and Amphitrope.[9] In six cases a man owns more than one item of property in the same general area: Lysitheides owns land on which the Artemisiaka mines at Thorikos stood and also land near them; Kallias of Lamptrai owns both an *ergasterion* and land with a mine on it at Besa.[10]

Where more than one member of a family is known to have property the pattern is mixed. There are some very clear local connections: Lysitheides' children share his heavy interest in the Thorikos area; Phanostratos seems to pass on his *ergasterion* at Thorikos to his son Arkhestratos, and the same may be the case in Laureion, where the *kaminos* owned by Demostratos of Kytherros may be included in the *ergasterion* of his son Aspetos (who also has property at Besa); Diokles of Pithos and his son Diokhares are recorded owning property at Nape and at Sounion, but we do not know if these were in the same area.[11] In other instances family interests were certainly spread around: of the brothers Thrasylokhos and Meidias of Anagyrous the former has an *ergasterion* at Thrasymos, while the latter has property both at Sounion and at Laureion. The most impressive family holding, however, is that of the family of Pheidippos of Pithos: Pheidippos had property at Thorikos, while his brother Phaullos (II) had property which was probably at Sounion, and his son Diphilos had land with a mine on it, and perhaps an *ergasterion* at Anaphlystos, as well as leasing a mine at Sounion.[12]

The pattern emerging is a somewhat 'bipolar' one: small and large property holdings exist side by side, men with strong local interests own property beside that of men with interests scattered all over the mining area, and no individual or family monopolises land ownership in any particular area. By contrast with the pattern of agricultural holdings (above chapter 3) a local focus cannot always be found for the scattered holdings.

Consideration of the owners of more than one item of property who also lease mines complicates the picture but also suggests a possible rationalisation of the pattern. Only one of the five men who own property at more than one location also leases a mine, but only one of the five who own more than one item of property at the same location does *not* lease a mine. The small sample precludes sure conclusions, but it is possible that those involved adopted one of two alternative strategies: spreading risks by owning land in more than one location, or spreading them by leasing as well as owning.

The pattern among the lessees is rather different. All but two of the 137 men who lease mines but are not recorded owning property lease at only one location, mainly on just one recorded occasion.[13] Moreover, there are only four cases of family links among the lessees — the families of Apolexis of Aithalidai, Kephisodoros and Euphemides of Athmonon (and Kephisodoros' mine is registered by the only other man of that deme to feature in the leases), Isandros and Stratokles of Sypalettos, and Epikles, who leases at Nape.[14]

The minimal number of family links and of multiple lessees both suggest that leasing mines was not the most profitable activity in the mining industry: either lessees became disenchanted with mining after their first experience as lessees, or else they sought to involve themselves more heavily by buying property.

Men who both own property and lease mines almost always lease mines on or near the land they own. Thus in the earliest and most complete of the mining leases (*SEG* 12.100) the seventeen leases are taken by thirteen men who also own property: Kallias of Sphettos has property at Nape and leases two mines there; Pheidippos takes neighbouring concessions; Kephisodotos who leases mines at Laureion and Besa owned a workshop and other property at Besa, where his son later takes a lease. Pheidippos' name occurs nine times in leases, but only two locations are certainly involved.[15]

The further interpretation of these trends demands an enquiry into who it was who made money out of the mines.

The distribution of rewards

Silver, in contrast to stone, seems to have been considered a national resource from an early date. The whole story of the great strike at Maroneia and the diversion of the ensuing funds by Themistokles to the building of triremes assumes that at least a proportion of the silver found its way directly into public funds.[16] The precise legal basis for this has been much discussed and remains unclear, but since the surface is known to have been in the hands of private individuals some, albeit not expressly formulated, notion of 'Bergroyal' must be assumed.

The Themistokles story gives us information on the total income to the polis from the mines, although it is not clear whether this is the income from a single year or has built up over some lengthy period, but it tells us nothing about the organisation of the exploitation. For the fourth century the leases and Aristotle's *Athenaion Politeia* tell us something about the organisation but nothing about the total income. More information on the organisation comes from the Souda A 345 s.v. ἀγράφου μετάλλου δίκη but there is no way of telling to which period it relates nor whether all mines had to pay this $\frac{1}{24}$ tax. That the detailed organisation of the mines was altered at various periods is certain — it is one such change that inaugurates the series of inscribed leases. It is equally certain that the polis directly benefited at all periods. It is not possible, however, to deduce exactly how the polis benefited, or how large its income was. The leases give figures for money paid to the polis, but there is no general agreement as to whether these payments represent a rent or just a registration fee, and none as to the frequency of the payment.[17]

Although the question of the overall organisation of leasing affects the possibility of calculating the particular profit an individual may have made out of a particular lease, the fact that individuals did profit remains indisputable. Which individuals profited will affect the local and the social distribution of wealth, and through that the whole structure of Athenian society, yet this is an angle of enquiry which has never been pursued.

Nikias, the most famous of all profiteers from mining, is said to have made his money by hiring out slaves and using an *epistatēs*, Sosias the Thracian, who appears to have been 'un concessionaire, et non plus seulement l'intendant de Nikias'. However, while there is no evidence for Nikias' own direct involvement in the mining area his descendants Nikias (II) and his son Nikeratos certainly owned property there.[18]

Xenophon also mentions one Hipponikos, probably the son of Kallias 'Lakkoploutos', as one who made money from hiring out slaves to work in the mines. Nepos says that Kallias (II) 'magnas pecunias ex metallis fecerat' and the early date to which this reputation for profitable mining interests reaches back makes it unlikely that all the money came from hiring out slaves. Another Kallias is found with property at Besa in the fourth century.[19]

The third individual named by Xenophon is one Philemonides, who may have given his name to the 'Philemoniakon' mine which figures in the leases, and if this is the case it is likely that he too owned property.[20]

The figures who appear in the orators because of their mining interests are of still greater interest. Demosthenes 37, entirely devoted to mining matters, concerns the ownership of an *ergasterion*. Meidias' mining interests are made a source of discredit by Demosthenes (21.167) and the leases show that he was an owner. Hypereides 4, *Against Euxenippos*, lists various mining cases in which dikasts have refused to listen to sycophantic accusations: the Teisias and Euthykrates of the first case may reflect the leasing of a mine by Euthykrates of Kropia next to a 'Teisiakon' mine which is recorded in the leases; Epikrates of Pallene, attacked in the second case, is known from leases to have property at Nape, Sounion, and a lost location.[21]

All of this indicates that men who where well known to have made large amounts of money from the mines generally owned property in the mining region. This is despite the fact that Xenophon is only listing men who made money from hiring out slaves. The conclusion raises certain problems: it is easy enough to see that a man might make money from capital invested in plant (*ergasterion*, furnace, or whatever), for those who mined the ore would have to secure the use of

117

such facilities. It is not so easy to see what was in it for the men who owned the land on which the mines stood. The leases concern the relations of the exploiter with the bureaucracy of the polis, and silver mining is often assumed to involve only the lessee and the public authorities.[22] In such a circumstance those owning the land on which the mines stood would only be able to make money by themselves leasing the mine on their land; if they did not they would actually lose out from the surface disruption caused by the mining works, access roads, and so on. That owners make the most money out of mining indicates that there is a missing link in the chain of silver production, and this suggestion is supported by the fact that the extraction and ventilation shafts represent an effort of construction which cannot have been accomplished within the duration of most leases, and hence must have been dug previously, either by or with the connivance of the land owner. In such circumstances it is scarcely conceivable that the lessee made no payment to the owner, and given the complications of working on a shares basis when the yield of ore was variable that payment must surely have been a ground rent.[23]

On this model the attractions of ownership are clear: shafts could be constructed with free slave labour at slack periods, and then the landowner could expect a steady income for as long as anyone thought the ore below worth exploiting. Building and running an *ergasterion* on his land would give a second bite at the cherry, leasing out slaves a third. Much of this is speculative, but the close connection of wealth and ownership does demand *some* explanation.

The local distribution of owners and lessees

The mining leases give the demotics of a large number of individuals involved in the mines. Previous attempts have been made to mine this information for regional bias, but these have been vitiated by idiosyncratic definitions of 'mining demes' and by lack of rigour.[24]

The raw data on owners and lessees are presented in tables

9 and 10. The mining demes are clearly over-represented among the owners: 15.8% of the demes giving 34% of the owners — and this despite the fact that two mining demes, Besa and Anaphlystos, are not in fact represented at all. Besa provides no lessees either, and seems odd, while Anaphlystos is on the edge of the mining district and all our information about its mines comes from a very small fragment of the leases. Despite the over-representation of the other mining demes natives are outnumbered by almost 2:1 by outsiders, whose land ownership was clearly extensive. It is not possible to tell how outsiders acquired this land, but some acquisition may have been at an early date, to judge by the holdings of the Nikias and Kallias families in the fourth century. A notably large number of the natives come from the deme of Sounion.

The mining demes are less over-represented amongst those who own and lease. Three mining demes produce five of the examples (19% of the demes, 23% of the individuals). It may be that the particular strategy of spreading one's risks by owning and leasing was one especially popular with outsiders, for of those who only lease 19.8% come from the mining demes although those are just under 9% of the demes represented (5/59).

The location of the property and of the mines leased is of interest in the case of natives: eight or nine of the thirty-three owners have property in their own deme; $\frac{2}{5}$ of those who own and lease lease in their own deme;[25] and just four (six if Thrasymos is considered part of Sounion) of the twenty-three lessees lease in their own deme. These exiguous figures do suggest that men were less bound to lease in their own deme than to own land there. The behaviour of men of Thorikos is of especial interest: there is no certain case of a man of Thorikos owning land in another mining deme, and two of the four cases of a man from a mining deme leasing in that deme concern Thorikioi; indeed only one man of Thorikos is known to take a lease in another deme, and he leases in Sounion. It may not be entirely fanciful to suggest that the different behaviour of Thorikioi and Sounieis correlates with the contrasting strengths of community in the two demes, as reflected in the settlement patterns (above chapter 2).

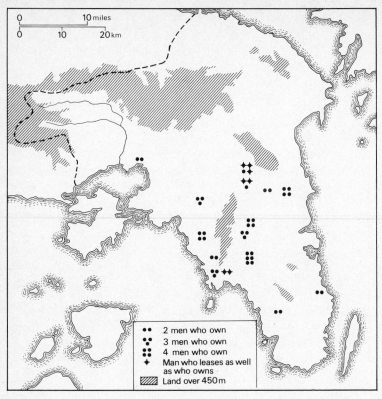

Map 7A. The origins of men owning property in the mining demes.

Chapter 3 has shown reason to believe that the majority of more or less wealthy men retained strong ties with their native deme even in the late fourth century, and since Davies (1981) has shown that those involved in mining are, not surprisingly, more or less wealthy, the local distribution of lessees and owners can be examined with profit. The resulting patterns are shown in maps 7A, 7B, 8A and 8B.[26] Not only are all the demes from which owners come (excepting only the uncertain Kopros[27]) south of the Pendele–Aigaleos line, but they form a pattern which is heavily influenced by the communications routes, with a result that the west coast is best represented north of the Koropi gap (Euonymon, Aixone, Halai, Anagyrous, all moderately wealthy demes),

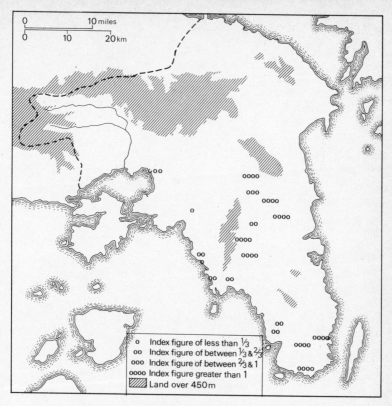

Map 7B. The origins of men owning property in the mining demes
(deme size discounted).

the Mesogaia is heavily represented (Gargettos, Kikynna, Kydantidai, Kytherros, Paiania, Sphettos, and cf. Pithos just to the north), but the east coast is only represented by Potamos and the city only by Alopeke – which had more than its share of prominent families.[28]

The pattern does not simply reflect increasing distance: the neighbouring demes of Atene, Thorai, and Kephale are unrepresented. Rather it reflects ease of communication, and of communication by land. The demes pick out the route northwards which splits to go round both sides of Hymettos. Travelling time seems more of a factor than absolute distance.

The pattern of lessees is more complex. Several demes

121

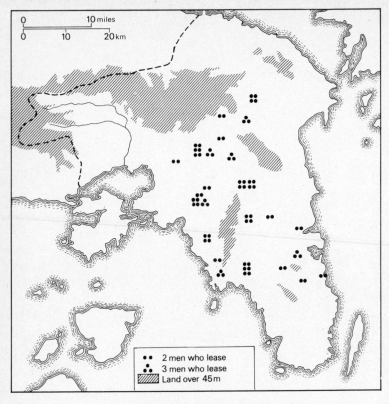

Map 8A. The origins of men leasing mines.

complement those already present: Deiradiotai, Prospalta, and Kephale are local additions; Myrrhinous, Erkhia and Philaidai fill out the Mesogaia, and Eleusis joins Kopros. The city representation now includes Melite, Kerameis, Kollytos and Kolonos. The Aigaleos–Pendele line is breached – but along a line of communication – with Pallene, Athmonon, Akharnai, Pergase, Dekeleia and Oion (if Oion Dekeleikon). Lessees plainly come from further afield than owners, but they do not come from simply anywhere: the east coast remains seriously under-represented. Moreover the very presence of a pattern clearly indicates that the owners and lessees were not simply based on Athens.

That lessees come from further afield than owners suggests

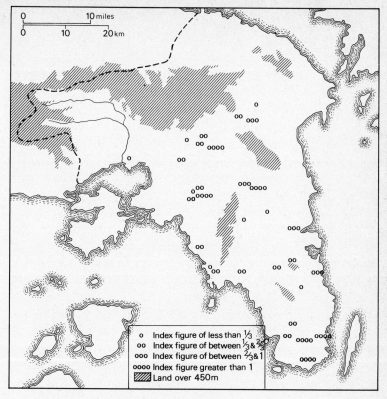

Map 8B. The origins of men leasing mines (deme size discounted).

that they took a less constant interest in what was actually happening in the mines than did those who owned, and no doubt liked to keep an eye on, property there. This may receive confirmation from some further epigraphic evidence. A decree of the deme of Gargettos survives, honouring one Epikydes; no demotic is given, and so this man may be a native of Gargettos, but the name is not common and the suggestion of Kotzias that this man be identified with the Epikydes son of Philokydes who leases a mine is attractive. If the identification is correct then Epikydes' deme was Akharnai, and his Gargettan connection may have come from that deme, providing him with a convenient half-way house for his journeys to and from the Laureotike.[29]

123

Mineral extraction and social disruption

From all this it emerges that there was a geographical as well as a social bias to the group of men who exploited the silver mines. A stake in the Laurion mines was clearly attractive to that part of the Athenian propertied class which had reasonably easy access to south Attika. The men and capital that the mines brought in disrupted the whole pattern of settlement in the area, and it also altered men's attitude to property ownership. Chapter 3 has shown how the ideology of the citizen landowner was to a large extent in fact an ideology of owning property and exploiting agricultural resources in and near one's own deme. But the great majority of those who bought themselves a stake in property that would yield a profit from mining activity were buying property outside their home area. This did not leave the local landowners unaffected: Thorikos, it is true, clung to the traditional values, and, helped by the presence of a strong community centre established before the main mining demand began, and by the possession of extensive agricultural resources of a high quality, the men of that deme remained loyal to the local resources; Sounion, on the other hand, was a deme whose very identity was already uncertain because of the rather separate identity established by the sanctuaries at the Cape already in the sixth century, and it crumbled before the pressure of the silver exploitation, with a complete breakdown in the pattern of settlement and no loyalty amongst the wealthy men of the deme to the local resources.

The effects on demes outside the mining region are more difficult to trace. Epikydes' honour, which he would never have received but for his wealth and his mobility, may be one sign of the increased interaction between demes that mining activities brought about. The relationship between mines and wealth is a complex one, for while in the mining demes the extraction of silver must surely have created wealth where there was none to speak of before, outside the area it was only men who were already wealthy, to a greater or less extent, who could create a niche for themselves, so that

124

here mining did not create wealth but reinforced existing affluence. The Laurion mines will have provided another forum in which the propertied class, or rather a geographically selected group from the propertied class, met together, and met with those local men with whom they now had a shared interest. This adjustment and reinforcing of existing links will have shaped and moulded the nature and effects of the power of wealth, and with it the detailed workings of both local and central political activity. Although these social effects are not dramatic, their contribution to the web of Athenian society should not be ignored.

Some broader effects are possible: Hopper argued that the intensity of mining was directly influenced by the 'agricultural cycle', while Lauffer suggested that the mines were particularly attractive to those who were anti-Macedonian in politics. Certainly the fairly direct way in which mining activity created wealth for individuals as well as for the public treasury will have meant that the ability of the citizens to satisfy the liturgical demands of the polis will have been directly related, in part at least, to the activities in the silver mines.[30]

The mines have a part to play in Athenian social, economic, and political life that strongly contrasts with that of the stone quarries: they are a revisionary force, undermining long established and deeply rooted values, while the exploitation of stone is limited and conservative. In both cases, however, an understanding of the overall impact of the particular ways in which particular minerals were exploited is only impeded by a viewpoint which sees the minerals as a resource outside the city which the city uses. The doggedly local exploitation of stone and the local pride in building work emphasises the peculiar rôle of discrete social units amongst the citizen body, and could hardly begin to be understood by any approach regarding οἱ Ἀθηναῖοι as an amorphous crowd. The rôle of the mines as an economic centre and focus for Attika only acquires its full social significance when the differential local effect of this is seen. Ties of neighbourhood do not work simply, however, and the full measure of their

125

importance is only drawn out when they are weighed against other social bonds, and in particular against the bonds created by kinship.

CHAPTER 7

KINSMEN AND NEIGHBOURS, CHOOSING AND USING

The previous chapters of this work have attempted to establish the nature and importance of the local base of Athenian citizens, and have begun to explore some factors which qualify that importance. This chapter looks at a factor which works alongside locality, and may compete with it or complement it: kinship.[1]

Did local links play any part in the formation of kinship ties?

Ties of kinship are formed in two ways: by marriage and by adoption. Adoption has left no trace in the epigraphic record, and our knowledge of it thus depends entirely upon the literary evidence. Adoption enables the continuation of the *oikos* of the party adopting. If the adopter is living, the adoption of a son gives all the advantages of having a natural child, in terms of care for old age and proper burial;[2] and, if the adopter has a daughter, adopting a son will avoid her becoming an *epiklēros*.[3] It is not the aim of adoption to take inheritance and the family name out of the ancestral line, but to strengthen that line. The speaker of Demosthenes 44 claims that it is because those themselves adopted so frequently fall out with the *oikeioi* of the family into which they are adopted, so that if they were themselves allowed to adopt they would turn outside the body of kin, that the law forbade those themselves adopted to adopt.[4]

The aim of adoption clearly affects the choice of who should be adopted. Given the centrality of the *oikos* in the ideology of adoption it is not surprising that there is a strong presumption that a kinsman should be adopted: thus the speaker of Isaios 2, justifying his own adoption, finds it necessary to point out that the adopter had συγγενῆ μηδέν᾽ ἄλλον αὐτῷ ὁπόθεν ἂν ἐποιήσατο υἱόν.[5] Most of the cases

127

we know of are cases of adoption of grandsons (daughter's sons), but there are also cases of the adoption of nephews/ nieces, cousins, wife's brother, and more dubiously of a wife's son by a previous marriage, and of a half-sister.[6] Adopting a kinsman might lead to the formation of links with another deme or might keep the links within the deme. In some cases all that is clear to us is that the adopted son came from the adopter's deme, and we cannot reconstruct any kinship between them.[7] The ranking of relationships is well brought out by Isaios 9.21 (although the argument is tendentious): εἰς τὰς θυσίας τοίνυν, ἐν αἷσπερ οἱ ἄλλοι Ἀθηναῖοι ἑστιῶνται, πρῶτον μὲν δημότην ὄντα, ἔπειτα δ' ἀνεψιόν, ἔτι δὲ τὸν υἱὸν τὸν τούτου μέλλοντα ποιεῖσθαι, εἰκὸς δήπου ἦν, ὁπότε περ ἐπιδημοίη, μηδὲ μεθ' ἑνὸς ἄλλου ἰέναι τὸν Ἀστύφιλον ἢ μετὰ Κλέωνος.

Residential propinquity did contribute to the attractiveness of adopting an individual, but it contributed in a rather secondary way; kinship was much the more important factor. In the determination of marriages, however, the situation is rather more open.

Marriage ties are both more and less important than adoption: more, because they are the norm, adoption the exception; less, because a family can expect to contract more than one marriage in every generation and can thus spread its duties and obligations in this regard, while there can only be a single adoption and the whole of the family line hangs on that connection. Although the questions of interest here are similar for marriage to those asked of adoption (e.g. where did marriage partners come from? were kin preferred? was there a tendency to local endogamy or local exogamy?[8]) the information available to answer them is rather different. We not only know of a lot more cases of marriage, but alongside the evidence of the orators, which remains important, we can put evidence from epigraphic sources, in particular from grave stelai. Grave stelai rarely provide us with long family trees, (cf. Humphreys (1980)), but they do give a lot of disjointed evidence of single marriage connections. Despite this additional source of information the data remain inadequate, both in quality and quantity, even to enable the ancient historian to do the sorts of analysis used in recent anthropology, for we have but a biased sample of actual marriages, and there is no way in which we can reconstract the universe of possible marriages.

The corpus of Attic grave stelai is large, and although the majority of the stelai are useless for present purposes because they only mention one name, the number that give evidence of marriages is large enough to invite at least a heuristic examination of the statistics. Even when stelai record more than one name, however, it may be impossible to use them, for the relation between the names is often not made clear, and it is not safe to conclude that the link is marriage just because it is apparently not filiation. Most useful are the stones that preserve the full name of the husband, with patronymic and demotic, the full name of the wife with patronymic and father's demotic, and a clear statement of the relationship between the two. Thus *SEG* 19.248:

Φιλη[σία Ν]ι[κ]ῶνος θυγάτηρ Παλλήνεως
Λυσιστράτου γυνὴ Θοραιέως
Λυσίστρατος Στρατοκλέους Θορα[ιεύς]

Such full information is relatively rare, and the absence of the man's patronymic is a common variation on the full form.[9] Most stelai are still more reticent, giving perhaps only a juxtaposition of male and female names, with no specification of relationship. These stones can only be used if the female name is accompanied by further information, for without it we cannot be sure that the tie is not filiation, and we have no sure information about locality. Even the presence of a demotic for the woman (which comes only with a patronymic) may not remove all doubts, for some principle of grouping other than marriage may be operative. Thus a large element of subjective judgment is involved in the exclusion or inclusion of such examples as cases of marriage links.

This is by no means the end of the problems, for a limitation to the more or less explicit cases may itself constitute a major bias: it is quite possible that the wives who appear with no demotic lack a demotic precisely because they are of the same deme as the husband. In one case from the second century it is more or less clear that this is the situation, and in no case does it seem to be ruled out.[10] But if this is true then the exclusion of these cases represents an exclusion of a large body of intra-deme marriages, making nonsense of all statistical comparison.

The fact that the evidence comes from grave stelai also limits its usefulness. Grave stelai, however mean, are indicative of wealth and pretensions. They come almost exclusively from the fourth century. Neither of these features is counteracted by the literary evidence, for this too is very largely fourth-century in date, and the large majority of the orations which supplement our information are orations concerned with inheritance or related issues, a concern that indicates that there is an inheritance worth worrying about. Since biographical sources concern themselves with major figures they are no more help. Where the literary sources do have a special value is in the way in which they give some context, for it is impossible to tell from stelai whether the marriage recorded is a first or a subsequent marriage. Remarriage was a far from infrequent practice, and comparative evidence suggests that different factors operate in determining the choice of a second spouse from those operative in the initial union.[11]

The upshot of all this is that it is difficult to reach any confident conclusions, and impossible to reach general ones. The bias towards wealth is especially difficult here, where social grouping and status affect marriage strategies. Nevertheless a show of figures can be made and a speculative discussion is possible. From the grave stelai the following data may be gleaned:

Inter-deme marriages
   Total no. of: 131
   Burial: virilocal 26; uxorilocal 13; known and neither viri- or uxorilocal: 39
   Demes neighbouring: 22; definitely not neighbouring 89

Intra-deme marriages
   Total no. of: 32 (add 80 if cases without demotic are intra-deme)
   Burial: local 13; definitely not local: 6.

Superficially the picture that these figures give is one of marriages outside the deme being more normal than marriages within it; of links with more distant demes being preferred to those with demes that are neighbouring; and of more people being buried in the deme in which they were born or into which they were married than were buried elsewhere. The virilocality is hardly surprising in a society where only the man has a public and political identity, and the prominence of home-deme burial is consistent with the persistence of land-holding in the native deme.

The overall statistics are somewhat undermined by some of the individual cases. That not all apparently inter-deme marriages are quite what they seem to be is shown by an inscription from Markopoulo in the Mesogaia.[12] This records a marriage between one Themullos son of Themullos of Oe, in the Thriasian plain, and Nausistrate daughter of Lykiskos of Hybadai. The position of Hybadai is not known, but its place in the lists of *prytaneis* suggests that it might belong to the inland *trittys* of Leontis, along with e.g. Eupyridai, and this would make it not far distant from Oe.[13] The stele also records the descendants of Themullos over three generations. His son Antiphanes married the daughter of Dionysios of Angele (Angelisi near Markopoulo), a deme without local or tribal connections with Oe or Hybadai.[14] He almost certainly became resident in his wife's family's deme, for his son, Themon, married a girl, Kleopasis, daughter of Kleokhares of that deme, and the final name on the stele is that of Arkhestrate, daughter of Meletos of Angele, with a space left on the stele which is almost certainly awaiting the name of Themon's son, husband to Arkhestrate. Because this stele, rather exceptionally, records a family's marriages over four generations it makes apparent, in a way that stelai recording a single link cannot, that not all inter-deme marriages, between demes which are not neighbours, are uninfluenced by local factors. Here it is only in the case of the marriage of

131

Antiphanes that we can be at all sure that locality was of small importance; in the first marriage locality may have had some influence, and in the last two cases it may have been the chief factor: neighbours are being preferred to fellow demesmen. Even here, however, we have no information to answer several crucial questions that arise: was Antiphanes a younger son? was there any earlier link with Angele in the family? were the wives taken from Angele related?

This may be an exceptional case, it certainly cannot be regarded as typical, but other cases where we can get behind the epigraphic information (which tend to be cases about propertied families) support the contention that locality had some rôle to play.

ii^2 5867 tells of the marriage of a son of Polyeuktos of Bate, a city deme possibly to be sited at Ambelokepoi, to Khrysogone, daughter of Xanthippos of Erkhia in the Mesogaia. The husband's family is the second branch of the Eteoboutadai, and it held the hereditary priesthood of Athena Polias. The family has marriage links with families of Phlya and Alopeke, but the interest of the connection with Erkhia is twofold: first Erkhia and Bate belong to the same tribe, Aigeis; secondly, if Davies' (admittedly speculative) reconstruction of the family is on the right lines then Khrysogone's father adopted her son, named Polyeuktos, who then married his parallel (FBD) cousin, Lysimakhe. The children of this union, Xanthippos and Drakontides, by their names, continue *both* the family lines. The stele comes from Erkhia.[15]

ii^2 6569 records the marriage of Dikaiogenes, son of Menexenos, of Kydathenaion, and Eukoline, daughter of Aristogeiton of Aphidna. This Aristogeiton is a descendant of the tyrannicide of that name, while the husband has connections with the family of the other tyrannicide, Harmodios. Harmodios also has connections with Aphidna, but these have been obscured by the fact that Dikaiogenes' grandfather was adopted by Dikaiogenes Menexenou of Kydathenaion. Extensive family lawsuits sprang from this adoption.[16] The marriage of Eukoline suggests that the adoption had not broken Dikogenes' links with the genetic family and the deme of Aphidna. Nevertheless it is only fair to note that locality seems of limited influence in determining the marriages in Aristogeiton's family: Eukoline's brother Thoutimos married Theosebeia, daughter of Kalliades of Anaphlystos (from ii^2 5752), while her aunt (or sister) seems to have married Androkles of Poros. That the names appear together on the stele seems an indication that the family remained close-knit despite marrying its daughters out.[17]

These examples of some local connections in inter-deme marriages do not seriously undermine their testimony that locality was not of the first importance in the choice of a spouse, but they do show that some tie of locality will often be revealed when there is detailed background evidence available. By contrast, when we have detailed information about intra-deme marriages, that can show a very high degree of marital solidarity within the deme. The extreme example of this is provided by the family of Meidon of Myrrhinous. Although not all the relations are transparent on the stele it appears that the three sons of Kalliteles of Myrrhinous all married girls from families in the deme: more than this, Meidon and Meidoteles married two sisters, daughters of Kallias of Myrrhinous, and Kallimedon married the offspring of Meidoteles' marriage, his niece Kleoptoleme (II). Meidoteles (II) and his son Kalliteles (II) were *manteis*, and this may have influenced the restricted connections of the family.[18] Certainly the family is remarkable for its *peribolos* with monuments to eighteen members of the family, and both the restriction of the marriage ties in terms of kinship and the restriction in terms of locality must have played a part in producing this situation.

More typical is perhaps the family of Epigenes of Kydathenaion. ii^2 6097 attests a link between Delias, daughter of Nikias, of this family, and a member of the family of Euaion of Erkhia. Her husband seems to have been Euaion's son Apolexis, and the stele comes from the Erkhia cemetery at Hagios Giorgios, Kokla. Phrasisthenes, their grandson, marries the daugher of Hierokles of Erkhia (ii^2 6135).[19]

From the same cemetery two monuments contribute to give a rare indication of a marriage which did not come off. This was to have been a marriage within the deme between Antikrates son of Kallikrates and Aristaikhme, daughter of Lysis, but the *loutrophoros* depicted in association with Antikrates indicates that he died unwedded.[20]

In one final example men linked through marriage are found in co-operation in another area: ii[2] 5525, found at Cape Zoster, records the death of Khairelea, daughter of Khaireas and wife of Eupolis; both Khaireas and Eupolis' father, Euthemon, are named in ii[2] 2820 as members of a commission responsible for having a statute of Aphrodite made, along with Eupolis himself and his brothers Euktemon and Theophilos.[21]

Of these examples of intra-deme marriages it is clear that in the case of the family of Meidon there is more to it than simply choosing marriage partners from the same deme because they are local girls. Meidon's family distinctly prefer to maintain a very closely knit kin group by a complex web of intermarriages. In other cases we simply do not have enough information to tell whether locality is a factor in its own right or a reflection of some other factor, such as existing ties of kinship. This remains a problem even in cases where much more information is available, for a preference for kin and a preference for locals may produce the same pattern of connections, so that it is a matter for debate which motive is prior.[22]

The literature has some advantages, in that at least on occasion it provides some context or a commentary in terms of the actor's or an observer's view. Examples of local influence on marriage ties are no more abundant here. The only family where marriage within the deme seems prominent is that of Euktemon of Kephisia, the object of Isaios 6. Euktemon's first marriage was to the daughter of Meixiades of Kephisia, and this union produced five children. Two daughters are known to have married, and the one for whom we have details married Phanostratos of Kephisia.

By contrast to this solitary and not very strong case the

orators furnish numerous examples of marriages between demes, with more or less disregard for locality. Thus the family whose affairs come under scrutiny in Demosthenes 44, as well as displaying a cynical manipulation of the tie of adoption, marries itself out widely: of the five children of Euthymakhos of Otryne, one, Arkhedike, marries into the deme of Eleusis (where her daughter does maintain the tie), and a second into the deme of Krioa. The daughter of this second marriage marries Aristoteles of Pallene.[23] The family of Euxitheos of Halimous provides a comparable example of out-marrying (see further below), and individual examples of inter-deme marriages are numerous.[24]

When the stemmata of the major Athenian families are examined it is the *lack* of marriages to fellow demesmen that is remarkable. Take the family of Andokides: Andokides' sister married Kallias son of Telekles, whose deme is not certain, but he was a member of the Pandionid tribe and thus may have been from the same deme, Kydathenaion. Kallias' sister, however, married Eukrates, half-brother of the general Nikias, of the deme of Kydantidai. We do not know the deme of Andokides' mother, but of her sisters one married Glaukon of Kerameis, and the other Xanthippos, son of Perikles, of Kholargos. Glaukon's aunt (his father's sister) had married Kritias, who was not of Kerameis since of the Erekhtheid tribe, and one of the sons of this marriage married the sister of Andokides' father's mother.[25] Despite our woefully incomplete information it is easier to find distant links of kinship between people of this stratum of society than it is to find examples of them choosing a spouse from their own deme. Locality is hardly a real factor in the choice.

Marriage determines kin, but in these examples it is also clear that, in part at least, kin determine marriage. Marriage is a bond that consolidates, it brings two groups into a strong moral link. The strategy employed in forming such a bond will depend on the particular circumstances, which themselves are not independent from the social status of the actors. The exchange of wives within the established kin

135

group both reinforces links and can prevent the dispersion of property. In a situation where local bonds are strong and are maintained by other means, marrying kin, especially if kin are not local, may be important to prevent the disintegration of the kin group. On the other hand marrying locally may be advisable as a means of creating or reinforcing sociable relations with neighbours. If a high preference is put on marrying within, or into, a certain social stratum this may force local exogamy, and equally marrying out may be a means of obtaining prestige. On another level, a man who brings in a wife from outside may be more free from the interference of the wife's family, and from the duties to the father-in-law which might otherwise accrue. In any real case the decision that is made is likely to be the result of the interplay between factors such as these, and the general principles espoused by the actor may not be practically reflected in his own actions.[26]

The literature reveals that there was some popular support for marriage to kin. An argument of rather curious logic at Isaios 7.11f. claims that not marrying one's daughters to a kinsman is a sign of standing hostility since marriages prevent any great variance, even among non-kin. Equally designed for its context is Andokides' allegation that he had a duty to marry the daughter of his kinsman Epilykos (1.119). More genuine seems to be the implied argument in Demosthenes 44.10, where Meidulides first offers his daughter to his brother to wed, and only marries her elsewhere when the brother has not only declined the offer but has agreed to leave the property undivided: marrying kin is motivated by material considerations.

In one instance the ideology of marrying kin was actually embodied in law: heiresses had to be married to next of kin, and this seems to combine the material interest and the sentimental interest in preserving the *oikos*.[27] That it is not unreasonable to talk of marriage strategies in an impersonal way emerges from the way brides are objects of exchange in archaic political marriages, and both oratorical texts such as Demosthenes 44.10, and such household discussions as

136

Xenophon's *Oikonomikos* confirm that parental calculation continued to be of paramount importance.[28] One way in which the positive value of marriage with kin is glossed is in terms of the importance of knowledge of the prospective spouse: it is thus that Isokrates (19.46) argues:

I have shown you that he made so much of our *oikeiotēs* that he married my father's sister and cousin. Yet to whom would one the more readily give one's daughter than to those from whom one has oneself thought it proper to take one's wife? From what house would one have more pleasure in seeing a son legally adopted to oneself than from that from which one has sought to acquire sons by natural procreation?

Kinship connections are rarely clear in the marriages attested epigraphically, but the literary evidence for the practice is abundant. The examples of first-cousin marriages have been collected by Thompson (1967, 1970 B); here it will suffice to draw attention to one, perhaps extreme, example: the Bouselids, whose affairs are known to us through the court cases to which the speeches preserved as Demosthenes 43 and Isaios 11 contributed, show five cases of marriage of cousins. Humphreys has noted that this family, like that of Meidon of Myrrhinous, has prominent religious interests.[29]

The prominence of virilocal marriages is in part connected with the preservation of property, for although dowries might consist of jewelry and linen or even a house, it does not seem to have been normal for them to have been of land (indeed the *horoi* show that amongst the wealthy, at least, land might be mortgaged to raise an appropriate cash sum); land remained in the male line, and would only leave it if the fortunes of the house came to rest on the shoulders of an heiress.[30] How many of the uxorilocal marriages are marriages to heiresses or in other exceptional family circumstances it is impossible to tell from the stelai.

The tension between the formation of marriage links as a matter of kinship and the rôle of the new household as part of the local community is brought out by the equivocation about what marriage actually is. In lawcourt speeches the stress is sometimes laid on the legal connection formed at marriage through the ritual of *enguē*. This ritual was a distinctly family act which relatives might be invited to attend, and it is the act of giving away by the father (or brother, grandfather, etc. who may be standing in for the father) which creates the legal bond.[31] At other times the emphasis in the orators is rather different: it is the public recognition by the local community of the offspring as legitimate that makes a marriage. This receives its most formal statement in the face of Neaira, at Demosthenes 59.122: τὸ γὰρ συνοικεῖν τοῦτ᾽ ἔστιν, ὃς ἂν παιδοποιῆται καὶ εἰσάγῃ εἴς τε τοὺς φράτερας καὶ δημότας τοὺς υἱεῖς, καὶ τὰς θυγατέρας ἐκδιδῷ ὡς αὐτοῦ οὔσας τοῖς ἀνδράσι. The failure to have one's offspring accepted as legitimate undermines the claim to have a legitimate marriage, as is brought out by the double argument at Isaios 3.76, where the failure to hold the *gamēlia* is linked to the failure to introduce the daughter to *phrateres*.[32]

The 'serious difficulty' in determining 'what constituted a valid marriage'[33] arises at least in part from this situation where marriage is one thing in the eyes of kin and another in the eyes of the community. Although not mutually exclusive there is little doubt that the contrasting claims of marriage according to the demands of kin and marriage according to the demands of the community could come into conflict — those who marry kin regardless of their local connections put kinship before local solidarity and introduce an alien element into the community; those who marry within the community with no regard to kinship links ask for trouble if the family line comes to some crisis. This tension is built into marriage, for marriage both creates kinship links and creates a community which must be part of a larger community,[34] but the particular marriage strategies pursued can exacerbate the degree of conflict involved.

The use of kinsmen and the use of neighbours

The social aspect

Marriage is not only the basic means of forming relations, of creating kin, it is also, and for that reason, an important way

138

in which existing relations, both genetic and local, can be used. The same was seen to be true of adoption and is true of the other major life-crises: birth/naming, initiation, and death.

Birth and marriage are closely linked: birth confirms and validates marriage. Peisistratos' care to avoid having children by Megakles' daughter is seen to invalidate the union (Hdt. 1.61), and Isaios gives a case of childlessness being a motivation for separation and the remarriage of the wife.[35] When a child is named, the *oikos* is visibly continued through the convention of reusing family names: it is quite regular for the first-born son to be named after the paternal grandfather, and other children are likely to be named after relatives.[36] The law case known to us from Demosthenes 39 (cf. 40) shows how important possession of the family name was to a claim to be fully a part of the family, and the failure to have any nomenclature overlapping with a family can be used as an argument against claims to inherit from that family (D. 43.48f.)

The actual process of naming, or rather the public recognition of the name, seems to have taken place at the festival of the Apatouria (D. 39.4). This is the most important male initiation festival and it marks, or at least foreshadows, the move of the boy out of the circle of close kin. At the Apatouria he is introduced into the *phrateres*, but through the aetiological myth for the festival he is also prepared for the *ephebia*, for fighting which is fighting for the community as a whole and fighting which is organised on a tribal basis. The boy is not just initiated into being a man but into being a citizen.[37]

At the other end of life the double connection with deme (*demos*) and with family comes out in the responsibilities for burial. Participation in the funerary rites of a man constituted an important way of both showing and claiming kinship, and hence a stake in the inheritance; helping non-kin with the expenses of burial, which could be considerable, is a demonstration of *philia*.[38] In the event of kinsmen failing to do their duty, however, the responsibility for action comes to rest on the local community (above p. 74).

In all these cases the nature of the event makes the involvement of kin inevitable. Nevertheless, the degree to which kin may be involved, and to which their involvement is publicised, does vary. Two short case studies will bear out this claim.

The account given above of the frequency of intra-deme marriages assumes that this frequency is uniform all over Attika. In fact, on the evidence that we have this is not so. Twenty-six demes yield examples of intra-deme marriages in the epigraphic sample; twenty-four give one example, Erkhia has two, and Sounion five. The prominence of Sounion cannot be explained by the nature of the finds. It is true that Sounion has a good marble source, but so do other areas of Attika, and it is not as if we have a fully excavated cemetery from this deme. Indeed one of the examples is furnished by a stele found in the Peiraieus. We cannot be sure, certainly, that the practice in Sounion was different from that in other parts of Attika, but the habit of inscribing certainly seems different for men of Sounion. Why are these men so keen to assert that they tend to local endogamy? Any answer must be speculative, but it is notable that Sounion is already known to be odd in other respects (above, chapter 2).

It has been argued above that the presence of important silver resources attracted a large number of men from other parts of Attika and disrupted the life, and even the settlement pattern, of Sounion. It is not true for Sounion, at least in the mining areas, as it is for other demes, that most of the land in a deme was owned and worked by men politically identified with that deme. In this way the visible identity of the deme of Sounion was undermined. Furthermore the fact that the temples at the Cape provided a focus for religious rituals and festivals involving men from many parts of Attika prevented religion providing a substitute way of asserting solidarity. Thus both the contracting of conjugal unions with other members of the deme and the public proclamation of these unions on stelai which give the full details of the deme of origin of both parties may have been a reaction to the forces eroding deme identity, a way of both maintaining and asserting the presence of a local community.[39]

Some support for this idea may come from a parallel phenomenon in the deme of Rhamnous. As far as funerary practice and the funerary record goes Rhamnous shows every sign of being an exceptional deme. While imposing marble funerary monuments are not common in Attika, and while large family *periboloi* are rare, Rhamnous can provide family monuments striking both in their physical and their genealogical extent.[40] These monuments do not share the Sounion virtue of making the nature of marriage ties explicit, indeed the only certain cases are of inter-deme marriage (although several cases of marriage within the deme can be suspected),[41] but their peculiar emphasis on giving long lines of Rhamnous families demands explanation. It is again true that Rhamnous had a ready source of marble (chapter 4 above) but this can hardly represent more than a necessary condition for these monuments, and it certainly does not determine their nature. More important are likely to be the presence of a major cult, that of Nemesis, which had very large cult funds, and, in the fourth century, that a garrison was permanently stationed there and even appears to have taken some part in the political decisions of the deme.[42] It is quite likely that the major settlement of Rhamnous was at some remove from the complex of fort, cemetery, and sanctuary (appendix B). Together these factors make it far from unlikely that the demesmen here, as at Sounion, saw themselves under threat. When the most prominent features of the deme — the sanctuary and akropolis site — were as much or more the preserves of strangers, the great line of tombs proclaiming the importance of the demesmen and the depth of local families and of their connection with the place will have served as a reassertion of the presence and solidarity of the men of the deme.[43]

Both these cases show the use of kin to express the identity of the local group: in the face of other forces kinship and neighbourhood join ranks, at Sounion to proclaim the identity of local and kin ties, at Rhamnous to reinforce the claim to the locality by the display of family lines.

An economic aspect

Agriculture was the economic base of Athenian society. Most Athenians, perhaps 85%,[44] were landowners and it has been argued above that they had a deme base from which they farmed fragmented holdings. The evidence for private leasing of agricultural land is exiguous and it has been argued in chapter 3 that the public land that was leased was taken up by the more wealthy. The exclusive identification of the landowner with the citizen gives the possession of land a positive valuation, and this extends also to the working of that land.[45] οἱ γεωργοῦντες may be aligned equally with the rich, as by [Xenophon] *Ath. Pol.* 2.14, or with the poor, as at Isokrates 7.44, so that the approval of the farmer is not just the approval of the wealthy.

This situation means that although Attika almost certainly remained an area of many small land-holders it is only misleading to treat these as peasants in any strong sense of that word. Certainly Athenian farmers shared a low level of technological development, the linking of farm with family (here, through inheritance, with the narrow family, the *ankhisteia*), the economic dependence upon agriculture, and probably the use of the immediate family for labour,[46] with the classic peasant; but it is far less clear that they were dominated by outsiders or exploited in any direct way by outsiders, and there is no evidence at all for their possessing a distinct cultural tradition.[47]

The two crucial factors which mark Athenian farmers out from peasants are the lack of a clear distinction between town and country (which is a general burden of this work, but see especially chapter 9), and the absence of a recognisable division separating small and large landowners. From the evidence that we have it emerges that landowners both small and large had scattered fragments of property and based themselves on their ancestral villages; the size of holdings and the number of fragments were no doubt extremely variable at both ends but there is no clear difference in kind between those of the rich and those of the poor, and no clear breakpoint separating them.[48]

The lack of distinctions among landowners is one of the things that emerges from a consideration of the labour force employed. Both the literary evidence and the arguments about strategies of intensification suggest that slaves were widely used in agriculture, by rich and poor alike, and of the agricultural use of slaves there should now be no doubt. However, the argument must not be taken too far. There were certainly farmers who had no slaves: Aristotle (*Pol*. 1252b 12) notes, albeit in a comment on a quotation from Hesiod, that the oxen takes the place of the slave for the poor. If this is an observation from life then these poor men cannot be men of *very* small land-holdings, for a very small holding would not justify the ownership of an ox; indeed, even to feed an ox requires a certain amount of land. However, once one is dealing with land-holdings that are of any size the problem of the labour force arises, for one man's labour will not be enough at peak moments in the agricultural year. This would leave a certain size of land-holder in a very difficult position — with less land than will justify a full-time slave, but more than he can cope with on his own.

The recent stress on the use of slaves may, therefore, have distorted the issue, for the use of slaves seems to be ruled out in just those circumstances (small property owners at the agricultural crises) which it was invoked to explain. Both the recent arguments turn on the cataloguing of alternative forms of agricultural labour and the dismissal of all but slavery as being of only marginal importance. The options are seen to be the use of hired labour or increasing the size of the immediate family and hence of the family workforce. Were the latter a course of action at all generally adopted the inheritance problems that would ensue could hardly fail to be visible in our sources. In fact the prospects of difficulties in the next generation seem to have ruled this choice out of court. The case with hired labour is not so clear-cut. There is no doubt that hired labour did exist and that it was of low status. Bands of hired labourers seem to have been available for seasonal work, and individuals also hired themselves out for specific tasks. Although the evidence is not large in quantity it leaves no doubt that hired labour was a familiar phenomenon, and was always available as an option to meet a crisis, and was used regularly by some landowners. Equally, however, it does not seem to have been the first or most common of the means of working land. It is worth noting that even a skeletal system of using hired labour in agriculture can only operate where the settlement pattern is nucleated and where there is a possibility of the labourers making themselves easily available at short notice to prospective hirers. We know that Kolonos Agoraios formed the 'labour exchange' for the *astu*; a similar, if less formal, labour market must have been a feature of many demes.[49]

Is it the case, however, that hired or family labour were the only possible sources of a farm workforce apart from slavery? Xenophon in the *Oikonomikos*, discussing the link between farming and being a soldier, makes a statement worth close scrutiny: συμπαιδεύει δὲ καὶ εἰς τὸ ἐπαρκεῖν ἀλλήλοις ἡ γεωργία ἐπὶ τε γὰρ τοὺς πολεμίους σὺν ἀνϑρώποις δεῖ ἰέναι, τῆς τε γῆς σὺν ἀνϑρώποις ἐστὶν ἡ ἐργασία (5.14). Since the whole point of the statement is the comparability of those one works with and those one fights with, those who share the farming here can hardly be slaves (or, given its slavish status, hired labourers). So who are these men?

The limitation of the options on who might have provided agricultural labour result from the constant parallel, more or less conscious, with peasant societies. Given that this parallel is not a strong one, however, comparative evidence from other situations may be more helpful. Xenophon is arguing in the passage quoted that farming be considered a social activity. The two prime factors in forming social groups have here been argued to be kinship and locality. Not only is there much good evidence for the execution of agricultural tasks by work groups formed on the basis of neighbourhood and kinship in such societies as that of the Ndendeuli of Tanzania, but even in the semi-modernised society of Panama work groups in agriculture are formed on lines of kinship and friendship on a one-for-one, tit-for-tat, basis.[50] Is there any evidence that such groups operated in Attika?

144

Although the amount of evidence is not large, some does exist. The most important piece of evidence comes in Menander. At lines 326—35 of the *Dyskolos* Gorgias is describing what a difficult man Knemon is. As one of the chief signs of this he points to the way that Knemon farms his large holding alone (329—31):

> μόνος, συνεργὸν δ᾽ οὐδέν᾽ ἀνθρώπων ἔχων,
> οὐκ οἰκέτην οἰκεῖον, οὐκ ἐκ τοῦ τόπου
> μισθωτόν, οὐχὶ γείτον᾽, ἀλλ᾽ αὐτὸς μόνος.

The first two options envisaged here for securing agricultural labour are the two envisaged in recent analyses — using one's house slaves or hiring labour; but the third option is surely that of entering a non-monetary agreement with a neighbour. Gorgias' advice to the smitten Sostratos is that the only way he has any hope of getting even a hearing from Knemon is to turn labourer: in particular (366f.)

δεῖ

> σκάπτειν μεθ᾽ ἡμῶν σ᾽.

Not only is Sostratos to show that he is a proper country-man, but he is to show himself the sort of man who will co-operate in agricultural labour.

The *Georgos* of Menander may have provided a further illustration of the theme. Here the brother of the girl whose pregnancy is the occasion for the plot is away in the country (18f.). He is working with Kleainetos who, although he has to be rich to satisfy the demands of the plot, is nevertheless a man who works his own land; indeed it is while digging that he breaks his leg. The brother then manages to distinguish himself in the care he takes of Kleainetos, and in this he stands out from οἱ μὲν οἰκέται καὶ βάρβαροι (56). Kleainetos does have slaves who presumably share in the agricultural tasks but he also has this lad working with him. The nature of the connection with the brother is never made clear in the extant lines of the play; there is certainly no indication that they are kinsmen of any degree and it cannot be ruled out that Kleainetos has hired the lad.[51] However, it is a slave, θεράπων, who brings back the news of what has happened,

145

and owning a slave and yet oneself working for another seem hardly compatible (though doubtless less unlikely in a drama than in reality). It is certainly possible that we have here another non-monetary working relationship.[52]

The 53rd speech of [Demosthenes] provides an example of agricultural co-operation between neighbours at a higher level: Apollodoros explains how he and Nikostratos grew up together and were neighbours in the country. This friendship continued into adult life and was used by Apollodoros to help him run his affairs: ὁπότε ἐγὼ ἀποδημοίην ἢ δημοσίᾳ τριηραρχῶν ἢ κατ᾿ ἄλλο τι, κύριον τῶν ἐν ἀγρῷ τοῦτον ἁπάντων κατέλειπον (53.4). Apollodoros and Nikostratos clearly felt obligations to each other, and exchanges of various kinds went on between them (cf. 53.5) but Nikostratos is very far from being either the slave or the hired workman of Apollodoros.

While little can be done in detail to trace how such relations with neighbours and more or less distant kin worked, there is at least a case to be heard for the existence of such a use of the social group. Non-monetary co-operation between kin and neighbours may well have been of considerable importance for precisely the smaller landowners who could not justify owning slaves and might not have the capital available to hire this labour. The shortage of evidence for this kind of labour exchange in the literature may be in part a product of the resolutely propertied bias of that evidence.

Not only do the strong bonds between kin and the strong bonds between demesmen form the essential background to the use of kin and neighbours respectively, but it is only the moral bond created by kinship that allows the use of the working relationship to create such a close tie with non-kin neighbours.[53] In this particular situation the stability of the deme enables these ties with neighbours to acquire some of the long-term advantages of kinship in less stable societies.

A political aspect

From all this it is at least arguable that men used their kin in matters of life and death, in birth, marriage, and burial, but preferred to use neighbours to supplement immediate kin in the economic sphere. This might be construed as a preference for kin in structured situations and for neighbours in less structured ones. Political relations are structured, but the structure is one that is artificial, where one structure was superimposed on another.[54] It is perhaps not surpising that it is in this area that there is some conflict between the use of kin and the use of neighbours, between local and genetic ties.

This clash of principles comes out most clearly from Demosthenes 57, the speech against Euboulides.[55] This speech, like the 12th speech of Isaios, is an appeal from a man who had been thrown out by his deme in the scrutiny of the middle of the fourth century.[56] What shows through the speech is a basic dispute about the criteria of citizenship. Euxitheos, the victim, has a very clear line to argue: he concentrates on establising that there is nothing wrong with his pedigree, that he is an Athenian of an Athenian father and an Athenian mother.

As far as Euxitheos is concerned, there are only two situations he can be in: he is either an Athenian of the deme of Halimous, or he is a *xenos*. At the start of the speech he makes it clear that he has no sympathy for *xenoi* who get themselves mixed up in affairs proper only for Athenians: ἐγὼ γὰρ οἶμαι δεῖν ὑμᾶς τοῖς μὲν ἐξελεγχομένοις ξένοις οὖσιν χαλεπαίνειν, εἰ μήτε πείσαντες μήτε δεηθέντες ὑμῶν λάθρᾳ καὶ βίᾳ τῶν ὑμετέρων ἱερῶν καὶ κοινῶν μετεῖχον (3). Later he raises what is surely a legal quibble to argue that his mother's activities selling ribbons in the agora exclude the possibility that she was a *xenē*, since the law prohibited *xenoi* from the agora (31f.).

The positive burden of proof as Euxitheos sees it lies in demonstrating that he is an Athenian by descent. To do this he has to make a split between being a demesman and being an Athenian. He urges the court not to take the decision of the deme into account, on the grounds that if the decision of the deme was important, provision for appeal would not have been made (6)! Since all the dikasts will have been members of one deme or another Euxitheos is on dangerous ground here, and so he tries to paint a picture of Halimous as anything but a typical deme, and at the end of the speech he repeats this ploy by claiming that ἐν οὐδενὶ τοίνυν εὑρήσετε τῶν δήμων δεινότερα γεγενημένα τῶν παρ᾽ ἡμῖν (58).

This case has a previous legal history which lies in the evidence which Euxitheos gave in defence of one Lakedai- monios in a (political?) trial for *asebeia* (8). Defeated there on that ground Euboulides has chosen this occasion for attacking Euxitheos with care: he tries Euxitheos before *demesmen* (9). Not the least of Euxitheos' complaints is that the way the meeting was conducted prevented him from calling up οἰκείους μάρτυρας (12), and he further complains that no witness τῶν μεν φιλων ἢ τῶν ἄλλων ᾽Αθηναίων was present (12). Behind this complaint surely lies the truth of his condition: his predicament is that his real support lies outside the deme (despite his complaint in 15, delay till the next day would not have helped him), and Euboulides has found one issue which gives the deme real judicial power.

True enough, there do seem to have been some kin who were prepared to support him: the cousins of his father (four cousins, but the children of just two of his father's uncles on the paternal side) must be men of Halimous (20f.), but it is notable that he tries to make a limited number of witnesses seem very important by the number of names mentioned in giving their genealogical connection, and by using men in more than one capacity: that he claims to be producing kin, demesmen, and *phrateres* as witnesses (23f.) but in his summary (29) mentions only the kin, and that he only names the kin suggests that he may have produced no demesmen or *phrateres* who were not also kin. The arguments that are brought to show connections with the deme, service as an office-holder in the deme and so on (26), are all circumstan- tial or a priori arguments.

Euxitheos' strength lies in his family. It is clear that his family is one with a high degree of solidarity:[57] he is able to refer to a family burial place (πατρῷα μνήματα, 28) and the strong and exclusive sense of belonging to the same *genos* associated with them. When he turns to his mother he first uses the quibble over the agora to turn an accusation which

148

implies at least acting like a woman of low, non-citizen, status, to a 'proof' of citizenship, and then parades his mother's family before the jury in confusing detail. He names a large number of kin on his mother's side, kin who extend through a number of different demes, yet at the end of section 38 he produces only two figures. When he produces *demotai* in section 40 these must be *demotai* of his mother's deme, that is, men of Melite, not men of Halimous.

The case that Euxitheos presents is made to turn wholly on kinship connections; he demonstrates family history and calls family witnesses. The nature of his mother's side of the family means that to do this is to call up men from quite distant demes: the man he calls up as believing that his mother is a citizen by his marriage to Euxitheos' half-sister is Eunikos of Kholargos (43). While blatantly turning this into a matter of establishing kinship links and genealogical descent (44) Euxitheos finds himself having to counter the accusation that the men he is producing are not genuine kin (52), and to resort to a claimed inconsistency to get rid of the charge. The final summary makes it clear that his claims to be recognised by kin and his claims to be recognised by demesmen rest on different bases: kin and their testimonies are actually produced in the court; demesmen's views have to be inferred from their reported actions (67).

The basis of Euboulides' case against Euxitheos can only be inferred from the report of his actions by Euxitheos and from the nature of the defence here presented. Both the handling of the deme meeting and Euxitheos' concentration on the question of descent strongly suggest that Euboulides' grounds for expelling Euxitheos were based on the position that he was not a person acceptable to the deme. Euxitheos' remarks about his own services to the deme reveal that there had been an earlier series of expulsions from the deme which followed the loss of the *lexiarkhikon grammateion* when Euboulides' father Antiphilos was demarch: that family evidently has a continued concern to keep membership of the deme under control and to assert the right of the deme to decide who should belong. It becomes clear not only that

149

there has been an old feud between the families of Euxitheos and Euboulides (47f.) but also that Euxitheos does not want to have to go into too great detail concerning his past relations with the deme: he deliberately does not give any account of his *demarkhia* on the grounds that that is outside the scope of the case (63). But it is precisely in his interests to limit the scope of the case, and it is as a further part of this strategy that he claims that Euboulides' remarks on the social standing of his family are not relevant (33). That it is conceivable that Euboulides attack the witnesses as not genuine kinsmen suggests that Euboulides is trying to put the authority of the deme first: the testimonies of those from outside the deme can be undermined.

Why was Euxitheos so vulnerable? The personal and family hostility of Euboulides will hardly provide a convincing explanation, for, however corrupt the meeting was, the very way in which Euxitheos presents his case suggests that he had little support among members of the deme. Part of the explanation may lie in the past history of Euxitheos himself — the way he exacted debts in his demarchy may not have won him many friends — but it is equally possible that his claims on that score present a specious reason covering up a real score and are an attempt to show that he is a responsible Athenian, not inclined to be unreasonably partial to his own deme. Part of the explanation, however, may be family: Euxitheos' father's side is slightly odd: the family endogamy whereby his grandfather married a half-sister reduces the extent of family on the paternal side; his mother's side, however, lies entirely outside the deme of Halimous and has no close connection with any particular deme — men of Kholargos, Halai, Melite and Plotheia are mentioned from this maternal line in the speech. Part again may be explained by a local factor: although Euxitheos has clearly been something of a local busybody, getting short-listed for a priesthood as well as serving as demarch (46), he may not live in the deme: it emerges that once the deme had voted Euxitheos out some men went and demolished the *oikidion* which he had *en agro* (65). It is not, of course, impossible that Euxitheos should have had some sort of shelter on his land even if he dwelt in the main deme settlement, but it is far from unlikely that this indicates that he did not have such a residence in the deme. Thus, in attacking Euxitheos, Euboulides is attacking the activities in the deme of a man whose most powerful family ties (his father died when he was relatively young) are outside the deme, and who does not reside locally; Euboulides' interests are not so much with the infiltration into the citizen body of foreigners, but with Athenian outsiders interfering in local affairs.

This case, which provides a clear, if hardly typical, display of the use of kin as witnesses, reveals the tension inherent in the identification of the citizen once recognition of descent was put into the hands of demesmen and thus coupled with a local basis. Is a citizen one who is born from two citizen parents, or is he the man who is recognised as a fellow demes-man by other members of the deme? Generally the two coincide, but kinship and locality could operate independently, and could bring about conflicting obligations.

Progressive deracination or stable equilibrium?

This chapter has investigated the rôle played by kin and by locality in the formation of bonds in Athenian society, and the use that is made of kinship and local connections in particular social circumstances. An attempt has been made to show how when *oikos* integrity is at stake men turn first to kin and only indirectly or secondarily to those who live near them, while for short-term assistance which has little in the way of moral obligations attached, and where the chief alternative is to bring in men who as slaves are outsiders in many senses, neighbours may be found to be an important resource. In both these cases the reserves of family and demesmen are more or less complementary, and the strength of each has an important part to play in enhancing the other, so that when, as at Sounion and Rhamnous, the local identity

151

is menaced, it is the rooting of that identity in the bonds of kinship (horizontally at Sounion, vertically at Rhamnous) that is paraded. Kinship and propinquity are the two stable feet maintaining the equilibrium of the social body.

Silverman (1968), working with data from central and southern Italy, has noted a correlation between agricultural organisation and social structure, and the picture created here of Attika is consistent with those findings. Here are neither the isolated farms that give rise to 'amoral familism', nor the 'agro-towns' where residence has little local connection with land-holding and where there is little sense of local identity. The Attic pattern has more similarities with the position in central Italy, marked by co-operation between informal neighbourhood groups, but it lacks the strong class structure or the strong division between landowners and landless. Rather, Attika provides a situation where both local and family bonds are strong, but where most commonly they are not equivalent alternatives (i.e. the family and the local group are not identical), and this leads to a situation where kinship and locality are more often complementary factors than in direct competition. One important factor in preventing direct competition is that in agriculture a source of labour was available which was neither local nor akin — slaves.

The complementary and the competitive cannot, however, be so easily separated out: in the end a man may have to make the choice as to whether his interests are best served by marrying his daughter to a local man or to a kinsman who lives elsewhere, and any decision that he makes will be open to criticism. It is thus that a basic tension is found between principles based on kinship and those rooted in local solidarity, in the very definition of what a citizen is, and the case of Euxitheos can show the potentially disastrous effect that this tension might have on individuals. Given the strength of local solidarity in the fourth century, as manifested by the insistence on using local stone resources and by the very peculiarities of Sounion and Rhamnous, a solidarity enabled by the village pattern of settlement, that clash with the deeply rooted solidarity of kin was almost inevitable. That the clash is most visible in the political sphere is a sign of just how completely, whether intentionally or not, Kleisthenes had revolutionised the basis for political activity.

CHAPTER 8

THE RELIGIOUS FACTOR: CONFIRMATION OR ALTERNATIVE?

Cult activities involve groups of people; the groups may be large or small, created by the cult or taken over from some other area of society. The cult activity is a way in which the group defines itself, and thus reveals the sorts of self-definitions the society makes. As the clientele of a cult varies so does the place which it occupies in society, the degree and nature of its influence. Religious activities aim to affect the natural course of events — even if only to secure the status quo — and the same cult may be thought to have different aims by different members of its clientele, albeit within certain limits. This chapter aims to reveal something of this 'multivocality' in action in classical Attika.

Artemis Brauronia

The archaeological history of the cult

Artemis Brauronia was the only divinity whose cult was founded on a rural sanctuary in Attika who also had a sanctuary on the Akropolis in Athens. Pausanias refers to the Akropolis sanctuary as a *hieron* containing a statue by Praxiteles;[1] the building was in fact a stoa and stood on the south side of the Akropolis, between the Khalkotheke and the Propylaia. This side of the Akropolis appears to have been largely uncontaminated by early religious associations, and the way in which it was possible to level off the site of the Parthenon contrasts strongly with the way that the Erekhtheion respects natural levels and former cult associations. This may go some way to explaining why a non-religious building, the Khalkotheke, and a stoa associated with a divinity with no traditional ties with the Akropolis could be built here. The exiguous physical remains of the stoa have recently been examined in detail and three phases

154

of building have been distinguished, but none of the phases can be closely dated, and now that it is established that the stoa was not bonded into the Kimonian or Periklean akropolis walls it is even possible that the earliest building was of the fourth century.[2]

There are no epigraphic dedications to Artemis from the Akropolis in the period down to the Persian Wars, and at most one dedication on a vase. It is now recognised, however, that a particular shape of vessel, the *krateriskos*, is found almost exclusively at shrines of Artemis. The shape of the vessel seems to have protogeometric progenitors, and the association may be of some antiquity. Significant numbers of such vessels have been found at the Artemis shrines at Mounykhia, Brauron, Halai Araphenides (Loutsa), and Melite, and at the Cave of Pan at Eleusis. *Krateriskos* fragments are also known from the Akropolis and these date from the late sixth century. They are not, however, good evidence for any cult of Artemis there in that period, for all the fragments may come from a single vessel, and the case of the Cave of Pan warns that they may be found even where Artemis is not the main deity worshipped. Artemis and Athena can be shown to have a close relationship in the sixth century and it is certainly not out of the question that the *krateriskos* was dedicated at the shrine of Athena.[3]

Evidence for cult activity is lacking even from the later period after the construction of the stoa, and indeed the building of a stoa rather than a temple is unlikely to promote active cult. The Praxitelean statue is more likely to have been a dedication than a cult statue. The only further items known to have been in the Artemis sanctuary are the treasury records of Artemis Brauronia found there. The earliest dates to *c*. 416 BC although the bulk come from the latter part of the fourth century. These records from the Akropolis seem to be, at least in the fourth century, duplicates of records kept at Brauron, and to record objects that were at Brauron. Since the earliest dated record of all from Brauron, of the year 416/15, records the removal of objects to the Akropolis it is possible that some of the items recorded in the early

155

Akropolis lists were on the Akropolis, although the presence of items from Brauron in the records of objects in the Hekatompedon and the Opisthodomos (below p. 160) may indicate that those objects that were removed were stored there, and not in the Brauronion. If this is the case it is possible that the stoa simply housed the records, and was built for that purpose.[4]

The history of the Brauron sanctuary is better known. The site was occupied in prehistoric times, but the santuary first used in the Geometric period. From the beginning the use seems exclusively religious, and the presence of *krateriskoi* on the site from the sixth century is some indication that there were links between this and other Artemis sanctuaries. This is further supported by the peculiar form of temple (probably late sixth-century or early fifth-century in its extant form) which shares with the Artemis shrines at Loutsa and Aulis the presence of an *adyton*. The *krateriskoi* seem to be of local manufacture, although the other pottery includes some of high quality and by known Athenian potters.[5]

East of the main temple is a second, smaller one, again originating in the sixth century and probably to be associated with Iphigeneia. There may have been further building to the east, but the next major monument known fully is the Pi Stoa. This stoa too housed treasure records, and a date of *c*. 420 for its construction has been thought consistent both with the earliest of these records and with the style of the architecture. Euripides' *Iphigeneia in Tauris* suggests that there was general interest in the cult in the late fifth century, and this must make it not unlikely that there was 'Periklean' monumentalising here, particularly in view of the building activity at other Attic sanctuaries in this period. The construction of buildings of a similar type (stoai) on the Akropolis and at Brauron might suggest a similar rôle for both, but it is notable that the Akropolis stoa lacked the back rooms with couches present at Brauron and plausibly used for dining. In any case the decision to build up Brauron at the same time as creating a niche for Artemis Brauronia on the Akropolis suggests that, far from there being a political

156

move to take over the Brauronian cult, the vital importance of the rural sanctuary was recognised.[6]

The history of the destruction of the santuary is little clearer than that of its construction. An inscription, apparently of mid-third-century date, has been found in the sanctuary: it refers to repairs to various buildings, although it is not clear whether these are routine or more serious, and we do not know whether they were even carried out. The archaeological record suggests that there was little subsequent activity on the site. Nor does cult evidence from the Akropolis improve, and there is no sign that the city sanctuary ever took over any of the functions of that at Brauron.[7]

Myth, ritual, and the nature of the cult

The Brauron sanctuary lies in the Erasinos valley, near the mouth of the river, a site comparable to the Attic shrines of Dionysos *en limnais*, Herakles at Marathon, and Artemis by the Ilissos. Artemis is frequently associated with water, coasts, and marshes, and in Attic literature this is stressed by Euripides in the *Hippolytos*. Water in general, promoting growth, seems important, rather than fresh or salt water in particular. Nilsson's characterisation of Artemis sanctuaries as situated 'wo die Vegetation üppig war und nicht von der Sonne verbrannt wurde' fits the site well. Such a habitat is natural enough for a goddess associated with hunting and wildlife, but there may be more to it than this. The placing of Artemis' sanctuaries on the edge of cultivation, on the coast or the wild margins of rivers, is demanded by the association with young human life, green, flourishing and indeterminate, with the human life cycle as it develops through birth and puberty into marriage and birth. In Attika shrines of Artemis are coastal at Loutsa, Vouliagmeni, and the Peiraieus, and fluvial at the Ilissos and Oinoe.[8]

Our information about the rites at Brauron comes from a variety of sources: we have statements that are, or purport to be, historical records; we have two clusters of myth, one aetiological and one pseudo-historical; and we have some

157

iconographical information from pottery and sculpture found on the site, which may relate to the myth, the history, or both, or neither. Any attempt to comprehend the cult must make use of all of this.

The surest information comes from the epigraphic record, and from this it is clear that Artemis received a large number of dedications, and that these dedications were recorded and annually checked and re-recorded. Most the dedications are of clothes of one sort or another, many of them are of ordinary clothes, in particular χιτωνίσκοι, but some are quite exotic pieces and there are others that are not clothing at all but objects of precious metal or other objects of value. It is once observed that a coverlet that is dedicated is new, and this may imply that the other dedications were of clothes that had been worn. The Hippokratic *Peri Partheniōn* 13 ridicules the practice of dedicating costly garments by girls recovered from the delirium produced by the inability of menstrual blood to escape.[9]

Publication of the better preserved lists of dedications from Brauron itself will considerably assist our understanding of what is going on here, but with the 125 names provided by the Akropolis duplicates a limited analysis can be done. Many of the names are a single woman's name, possibly indicative of the activity of women in their own right in the sanctuary, but some have husband's or father's name added. We know too few female names from Athens to push the analysis of these very far, although some names do look 'aristocratic' (e.g. the various names ending in *-ippē*) while others might even fit slaves (e.g. Pheidulē). Sixteen cases gives husband's/father's demotic as well as name, and these can be analysed. It is striking that only three of the sixteen come from the Mesogaia (from Teithras, Paiania, and Halai (if Araphenides)). None come from Philaidai or the neighbouring rich deme of Angele. Two demes are represented by more than one woman: Akharnai (2), and Phrearrhioi (3). Out-marriage and the maintenance of the religious ties of the genetic family may explain part of the pattern, but they hardly provide a complete account.[10]

Social factors may be important. Seven of these sixteen women belong to known families. In one case the family is only known from a grave stele of a daughter, but in the rest we know rather more. Diophante, dedicant of a κάνδυν . . . πασμάτια ἔχοντα χρυσᾶ ῥάκος (ii² 1524.180) was wife of the wealthy Hieronymos of Akharnai, trierarch in 337/6, whose family is well known. Three husbands have political connections: Xenariste (ii² 1514.44 a dedicant in 345/4) was wife of Antiphon of Perithoidai, *prytanis* in 360/59; the wife of Kallistratos of Oe (ii² 1523, 1524) was of the family of the general of 418/17 (cf. *ML* 77.21, Paus. 7.16.4, Plut. *Mor.* 844b) and mother of the Philemon responsible for ii² 381; the third is the wife of the prominent politician Kallistratos of Aphidna (ii² 1523.18). Perhaps the most interesting, however, are the women of Phrearrhioi: one is the wife of Epeukhes (ii² 1517.214) a doctor from a family of doctors, son of the famous Dieukhes (Galen IX p. 163.795, Athenaios 1.5a) who figures in a dedication of a college of doctors, found in the Asklepieion (ii² 4359), and brother of Diakritos, doctor, and *prytanis* in the middle of the fourth century (ii² 1744) beside one Lysanias Lysikratous, who must be related to the Lysikrates whose wife is the second lady in question here.[11]

This sample is clearly ridiculously small, but some comments are possible. All the known women come from the more distant of the demes represented. Two of the families were certainly wealthy (those of Kallistratos of Aphidna and Hieronymos of Akharnai) and all were of high status. However, the links between the women from Phrearrhioi suggest that this is no random cross-section of Brauron dedicants. While these cases make it clear that fourth-century Brauron was an attractive place in the eyes of the wealthy and prominent at which to make a dedication, there is a strong possibility that it is precisely those whose family connections are worth showing off, and who want to be recognised, who identify themselves by giving the name of the husband or father along with his demotic. For the wealthy there may well be special motives for dedicating to Artemis: Epeukhes' family seems to be inclined to dedicate to divinities relevant to health, as befits a medical family. The very fact that the bulk of the dedicants do not identify themselves clearly either to us or to their contemporaries suggests that for them it was the making of the dedication and not the being seen to have made it that is important.

No dedications are known to have been made to Artemis Brauronia outside Brauron. Some objects dedicated at Brauron seem to have been removed to the Akropolis for safe-keeping, however. The records of the Akropolis treasuries first record them in 401/0 and they are then found repeatedly through the fourth century. It seems that items of small value stayed at Brauron while objects of large value, and particularly of precious metal, tended to be transferred to the Akropolis: thus from 371/0 on 'seven silver hydriae' repeatedly figure in the records. There seems to be no hard and fast rule about what is transferred, but something of the mechanism emerges from the presence in the accounts from the Akropolis of a 'box from Brauron'. The name given to this box makes it likely that the Brauron authorities had landed the Akropolis with it. It contained horse-trappings dedicated by Xenotimos Karkinou of a propertied family of Thorikos. Although the third-century repair inscription mentions *hippōnes* at Brauron, and the dedication is in line with the aristocratic interests in the cult, its form is unexampled and may have been of some embarrassment to those in charge. Religious officials, including priests, seem to have been liable to examination at the completion of their term of office, and so the transfer of responsibility for items whose loss might be distressing can be seen as a natural policy.[12]

The dangers involved in handling dedications are revealed by the hypothesis to Demosthenes 25, which may relate to this very sanctuary. Hierokles, son of the priestess, was charged with *hierosulia* after he had been seen with clothes that had been dedicated, and were marked with the names of the dedicators in gold letters, outside the sanctuary. Hierokles claimed, and his mother supported the claim, that he was removing them for use in τὸ ἱερὸν κυνηγέσιον. *Hierosulia* was a capital charge, and the danger from such accusations as this would make sanctuary administrators very keen to get valuable items off their hands.[13]

Two further priestesses of Artemis at Brauron are known, but neither is named. One seems to be mentioned in connection with another errant child, while the other is used to identify a husband punished for inciting another to violence. These cases, and particularly the latter, suggest that the priestess of Artemis Brauronia was sufficiently well known for any close relative to be more likely to be mentioned for the connection with her than by his own name.[14]

While the ἱερὸν κυνηγέσιον seems to have been under the control of the priestess, the major festival of the Brauronia was controlled by the ten ἱεροποιοὶ κατ᾽ ἐνιαυτόν appointed by the *boule*, οἲ θυσίας τέ τίνας θύουσι καὶ τὰς πεντετηρίδας ἁπάσας διοικοῦσιν πλὴν Παναθηναίων ([Arist.] *Ath. Pol.* 54.7). ii[2] 1480.12–16 records dedications by these *hieropoioi*, and the festival is the butt of jokes in Aristophanes' *Peace*. Although the Aristophanes passage is full of *double entendre* and although Θεωρία appears for the sake of the comic mileage she offers and cannot be considered a technical term, this passage seems solid enough evidence that the four-yearly festival of the Brauronia involved some sort of a procession to Brauron. Hesykhios has picked up from somewhere the detail, again presumably to be associated with this festival, that there were rhapsodes at Brauron, and there may also have been *kanēphoroi*. None of this, however, gives a very clear picture of what actually went on at the sanctuary.[15]

The two myths associated with Brauron have something more to offer. The main authority for the story of the rape of Athenian women celebrating a festival at Brauron by Lemnians is Herodotos. Having referred to the episode in book 4, as if it would already be familiar to readers, Herodotos tells the full story in book 6 in connection with the trial of Miltiades. The essence of Herodotos' tale is that after the Athenians had expelled the Pelasgians they settled on Lemnos. To get their own back on the Athenians they raided Brauron when they knew the festival was on, kidnapped a

161

whole lot of women and took them away to be their παλλακάς (mistresses). The women, however, did not integrate with the Lemnians and brought up their children as Athenians. In fear at the outcome of this the Lemnians murder all these children and their mothers. Lemnos is then hit by a complete failure of crops, and on the advice of the Pythia the islanders go to Athens to accept just punishment for their crime. However, when the Athenians demand that they hand over their land to them they say they will only do so when a ship sails in one day with a north wind from the land of the Athenians to their own land. Miltiades' raid on Lemnos from Athenian-held territory in the Chersonese fulfils this condition, this *adunaton*. That the story had political overtones is clear: 'nobody has ever denied that [the Brauron rape story] is meant to justify the Athenian conquest of Lemnos and the expulsion of its inhabitants. That dates its origin in the last decade of the sixth century BC' (Jacoby). As far as the Brauron sanctuary is concerned, the story at least means that a purely female festival was an established part of Athenian religious activity in the late sixth century. The story gains in richness, however, when read beside the myth of the establishment of the *arkteia*.[16]

In the literary tradition as we have it the aetiological myth for the presence of *arktoi* (bears) at Brauron is closely bound up with the explanation of the phrase Ἐμβαρός εἰμι and the aetiology of goat sacrifices for Artemis Mounykhia at the Peiraieus. There may have been *arktoi* in the Peiraieus sanctuary, but it is clear that two separate clusters of myth have become loosely intertwined. With the single exception of the *Lexeōn Khresimōn* s.v. *arkteusai* (Bekker, *Anec. Graec.* 1.444f.) the two aetiologies are never mixed. The myth that concerns Artemis Mounykhia is marked out by its mention of the Peiraieus and/or Embaros; this leaves just two main sources for the particularly Brauronian version: the scholiast on Aristophanes' *Lysistrata* 645, and the Souda s.v. *arktos*, and these almost certainly have a source in common.[17]

The stories which concern the Peiraieus focus on the explanation of goat sacrifices, those concerning Brauron on the 'bears'. The structure of the stories is very similar but the details specific to each are consistently different. In the Peiraieus versions a wild bear 'appears', harms many (where these details are specified at all), and is killed by 'the Athenians', or 'certain young men'. Plague/famine results and an oracle orders that someone should sacrifice his daughter to stop it. Embaros then does a bargain that he will sacrifice his daughter in exchange for the possession of the priesthood in perpetuity, only to substitute a goat for the daughter in the actual sacrifice. In the Brauron version the bear is tame: ἄρκτος τις δοθεῖσα εἰς τὸ ἱερὸν . . . ἡμερώθη in the scholiast, ἡμερωθεῖσαν αὐτὴν τοῖς ἀνθρώποις σύντροφον γενέσθαι in the Souda. It also 'belongs' either to the sanctuary or the settlement. It plays with a maiden and, under provocation in the Souda, hurts her; it is killed by one or more brothers, who hunt it down. Plague results, and Artemis orders that girls become bears before they can marry in expiation.

This comparison should make it clear that although the stories concerning the Peiraieus and Brauron have some similarities — both concern the death of a bear and its aftermath — they are essentially different. Bears are powerful mythical creatures because of the peculiar position they occupy: they are certainly *not* the type of animal which it is pemissible to sacrifice; and they are animals which have disturbingly human characteristics. The Peiraieus story 'explains' the sacrifice of goats to Artemis (a common feature of Artemis cults, including that at Brauron, and not limited to the Peiraieus) by making their problematic sacrifice a substitute for the still more problematic killing of a bear. The Brauron story exploits instead the ways in which bears are like men as part of a structure where men appear like bears.[18] That two separate aetiologies developed, each accounting not just for a separate aspect of the ritual but for a different sanctuary's practices implies that the stories were independent to a late stage. Since both sites produce similar ceramic finds by the sixth century this further implies that that late stage had been reached by then — i.e. that both cults were of very considerable antiquity.

The scholiast on *Lysistrata* 645 offers more than one explanation of the *arkteia* and his other main account cannot be ignored. This connects the 'bears' with the slaughter of Iphigeneia, which is said to have occurred at Brauron rather than at Aulis. Euphorion is quoted as the authority for this, and the claim is further made that it was a bear and not a deer that was sacrificed in Iphigeneia's stead. Two factors suggest that this version was already important by the classical period. One is the archaeological evidence for a temple of Iphigeneia at Brauron, already reviewed, and the other is the literary evidence of Euripides and Aristophanes. Euripides' *Iphigeneia in Tauris* simply has Athena tell of the place that Iphigeneia will occupy at Brauron, but the Aristophanic evidence is more complex. The passage of the *Lysistrata* which the scholiast is commenting on is a claim by the *choros* that their Athenian blood ensures that their advice is good for the polis (643–5):

ἑπτὰ μὲν ἔτη γεγῶς᾽ εὐθὺς ἠρρηφόρουν·
εἶτ᾽ ἀλετρὶς ἦ δεκέτις οὖσα τἀρχηγέτι,
καὶ χέουσα τὸν κροκωτὸν ἄρκτος ἦ Βραυρωνίοις.

Aiskhylos in the *Agamemnon* (239) describes Iphigeneia as

κρόκου βαφὰς δ᾽ ἐς πέδον χέουσα . . .

and the coincidence of phraseology can hardly be coincidental, thus establishing that a link between the *arktoi* and Iphigeneia was perceived in the late fifth century.[19]

The final source of information about events at Brauron is the iconography of various vases, and in particular of the *krateriskoi* found in the sanctuary. These show not only Artemis with a bow, but also processions of relatively mature women, dances or races of small girls, naked or dressed in short chitons, an actual bear and a figure with a bear mask. Unlike the majority of the *krateriskoi*, Kahil claims that those with these scenes are of central Athenian and not local production.[20]

None of this information allows us to reconstruct a day in the life of the Brauron sanctuary but all of it together does enable a certain comprehension of the place of the cult in Athenian society. The explicit literary references make it clear that the cult was and was recognised to be initiatory in nature: the Lysistrata scholiast describes it as a μυστήριον; ἀρκτεῦσαι is glossed as δεκατεῦσαι, a term explained by Harpokration as meaning μνῆσαι; and Diphilos (2.549 Kock) used the term ἐποπτεύειν, normally associated with the Mysteries, with reference to Brauron.

The myth of the *arkteia* is insistent that service as a 'bear' is necessary before an Athenian girl can get married. Physically the necessary condition for marriage is the arrival of puberty. Greek medical writers consistently, although perhaps traditionally, ascribe the onset of menstruation to the fourteenth year of life, i.e. to girls aged thirteen. *Arktoi*, however, had to be between the ages of five and ten. That the *arrephoroi* had to be between seven and eleven indicates the ritual significance of this age group, and the age range allowed for *arktoi* may be connected with the fact that the major, if not the only, celebration of the Brauronia was once every four years. Girls of ten will not have reached menarche even in exceptional cases, but puberty rituals in other cultures may anticipate menarche, and signs of pubescence, including the growth spurt, precede menstruation. Aristotle notes that the breasts are considerably developed before menarche, and it seems clear that the *arkteia* is a puberty ritual, but one that puts the stress on the emergence of sexual difference rather than on the arrival of the final confirmation of maturity. Greek medical writers noted that menstruation often began during illness, and modern evidence supports the idea that a change in life-style or a shock may be triggering factors, so the ritual events at Brauron may even have played a limited rôle in inducing menarche.[21]

One of the images recurrent in literature to describe marriage is the image of taming,[22] and it is upon the interaction of the wild and the tamed that the *arkteia* aetiology is built. The bear is a creature of the wild, but it has not only come to be in a human context, the sanctuary at Brauron or the settlement of Philaidai, it has also come to share men's food. Since the bear has also been given to the goddess it occupies a position between human and divine control, as well as between men and beasts. The girl who plays with the bear is a *parthenos*, a wild human, not yet yoked, and the very fact that she plays is a sign that she is not where she should be, is not under the control of the women's quarters: it is hardly surprising that her actions become improper. The Souda passage makes the impropriety clear with the phrase ἀσελγαινούσης τῆς παιδίσκης, where ἀσελγαίνω has overtones of licentious action and παιδίσκη is a regular term for a prostitute. By moving in the same sentence from *parthenos* to *paidiskē* the text makes the dangerous state of the girl clear.

Thus enraged ('sharpened', παροξύνεσθαι) the bear attacks the girl, and tears out her eyes. In view of the fate of Teiresias the localisation of the injury here needs little explication, but the issue of what it is or is not right to see is linked with the motif of dressing up that is basic to the ritual. It is kin that come to the girl's defence; they take back the girl into her proper domestic environment, but they do so by hunting the bear, by categorising it as wild. The problematic nature of the killing is again brought out by the language of the Souda: τοὺς ἀδελφοὺς αὐτῆς κατακοντίσαι τὴν ἄρκτον. κατακοντίζειν is a good classical verb, but not one that is used very frequently; it is never used of killing animals but always of killing men, and of killing them in a situation where trickery is involved and the odds are not equal. To kill in this way is to kill in a way that brings only discredit. The killing of the bear by the brother(s) is unacceptable because they kill it not as a wild animal should be killed, but in a way which recognises that the bear is not wild. They confuse what should be distinct, thereby reinforcing the distinction. The bear is wild and tame, human and not-human. The girl is tame yet wild, human and yet . . . When plague results and all Athenian girls are ordered to play the bear in order to restore the natural order before they can marry, the punishment fits the crime: those who though tame proved wild must be wild in order to be tamed. The kin who chose the wild παρθένος and killed the tame bear asserted that the girl was important to the family, ready for taming and ready for taming in marriage. Now kin have to recognise that the tame must have been wild to have become tame.[23]

The rôle of the bear in the myth is illustrated by the way in which Aristotle sees bears. Bears are discussed at several places in the *Historia Animalium* and a major stress is on features of bears that are like those of men. Thus we are told that they copulate lying down, not standing up, that they have one or two offspring and never more than five, that the young when first born are hairless and helpless, that bears are omnivorous, eating fruit, pulses, honey, ants, and flesh and attacking wild boar as well as deer and bulls, that they can walk on two feet, that they have just one stomach, though a large one, that they drink by gulping rather than by lapping or sucking. Aristotle is also interested in their winter semi-hibernation and notes that the young are born then and the female keeps both them and herself in seclusion for some considerable period. Aristotle is well aware of the particular ferocity of the pregnant bear, and of bears in general if the cubs are stolen; and later writers note in addition that bears can never be completely tamed but are liable to turn on apparent 'friends'. From all this it is clear enough that bears are a difficult animal: on the one hand they are very domesticated, with a strong sense of family and the 'home', yet on the other they are incorrigibly wild. They are not men, yet they are very close to men, and the female bear bringing up her young in her lair is like the good Athenian woman bringing up children in the seclusion of the women's quarters. In the light of all this, the problem of the wild and the tame, and of the ever-fluctuating boundary between them in the myth stands out even more clearly.[24]

The rôle of Artemis in the myth will also stand further examination from this point of view. Artemis' connections with the wild are of course strong, and at Brauron they are stressed by the ἱερὸν κυνηγέσιον, an occasion when, if dedications of clothes were really taken out of the sanctuary for it, the part of the Brauronian ritual in the recognition of

167

the wildness of the domestic will have been made explict. One notable feature of the myth is the general statement of the intention of the *arkteia* given by the *Lysistrata* scholiast: ἐκμειλισσόμεναι τὴν θεόν. The ritual which makes play with the wild and the tame in men itself 'tames' the goddess. The story of Kallisto is relevant here: a companion of Artemis, Kallisto was raped by Zeus, and, according to one version, it was Artemis who, when Zeus had turned Kallisto into a bear so that she should escape the notice of Hera, shot her because she had lost her virginity. Here Zeus' action in raping Kallisto, an action which might tame her (had it been marriage), makes her wild because it is done precisely outside the context of marriage. Rape defies the rigid order of categorisation: Kallisto must be made a bear and must be shot by Artemis. For Kallisto the virgin was wild and needed taming, she was the companion of Artemis; now she has lost her virginity and at the same time is and is not wild, is and is not a bear.[25]

Through the case of Kallisto the link between the myth of the *arkteia* and the myth of the rape by the Lemnians becomes clear. The Brauron ritual represents a crisis point for the girls taking part. On the verge between the wild and the tame they need to be guided into the taming of marriage, but they are susceptible to being drawn into the wild, to the dangers of the outside. The Lemnians come in from outside, find women in a public space, outside the domestic context, and take them away to become concubines, to remain outside the domestic context, untamed by marriage. As concubines these women are in a particularly problematic position, wives and yet not wives, and as such they are particularly dangerous. Their existence outside accepted categories puts the Lemnians — husbands and not-husbands — and the children — Lemnians and not-Lemnians — in an equally problematic situation. The killing by the Lemnians is a result and a reflection of the breakdown of the distinctions which constitute civilised life. The plague which results is but a further manifestation of that on a cosmic scale. That the end of the story has an *adunaton* fulfilled is inevitable in such circumstances.

The ritual and the parallel with Iphigeneia enact and control the critical position of the girls. The girls put on and put off the bear, they relate as bears to men and as men to bears. They are and are not bears at every stage of the ritual. They can only become tame through the death of the bear, and it is thus that they are found in the position of Iphigeneia: they must strip for sacrifice, but what is sacrificed is precisely what they have stripped off, the wild. Becoming Iphigeneia in ritual tames, for it is the necessary precondition for a strong birth, for Iphigeneia. But the assumption of the rôle of Iphigeneia also stresses the relation with society as a whole: the sacrifice that is vital to social reproduction is the sacrifice of a girl, a girl that is a bear. There is a pain and loss here which leaves a question-mark over the status of the gain.

Ritual nakedness is not common in Athenian ritual, it is only otherwise attested in the birth ceremony of the Amphidromia. The nakedness here is not only one side of the dressing up, it is in itself basic to the change that is created and reflected in the action. The nakedness here is the nakedness of birth: this is the last occasion on which girls appear in the state of their birth, in the state of minimum sexual difference before the onset of puberty. Here, as the companions of Artemis the huntress, the wild girls appear in the condition of wild nature, and their nakedness is the condition that they must give up if they are to grow up. Once they can see, they mask the fact that they are *paidiskai* with the appearance of the *parthenos*, they can no longer remain naked, they must be unseen or else unseeing.[26]

Artemis is strongly associated with the dance, and it is clear that it was in a dance, or at least a controlled ritual sequence, that bears and girls interacted in the *arkteia*. Dances rely on rhythm and music, they not only create a context that is not the context of everyday life and a time that is outside time, but there is little doubt that they induce a particular neurobiological condition: 'the rhythmic quality in and of itself produces positive limbic discharges resulting in decreased distances and increased social cohesion'. The girls are literally not the same at the end of the ritual as they were at the beginning, and it is the ritual that has both produced and controlled the change. Through the ritual the course of the wildness of the girls is controlled, their passage through a life crisis is governed, and that they will be ready for taming and will not turn wild, will express their emergent sexuality in socially acceptable ways, is ensured.[27]

Many of the dedications in the Brauron inventories seem to have marked childbirth. Childbirth (abortion/miscarriage) and menstruation are conditions that render unclean, and the dedication of worn clothes marks the end of a dangerous condition, dangerous physically and ritually. These dangerous conditions are at the same time necessary conditions of the good wife, and this critical importance necessitates ritual control. Brauron provides the structure within which adolescent sexuality can be comprehended; the festival of the Thesmophoria comprehends the activities of the Athenian after marriage.

The sanctuary at Brauron is divorced from the settlement of Philaidai, and was not used for the display of decrees of that deme as other sanctuaries were. With its position on the east coast of Attika it is at an extreme remove from the city. The girls grow up by being bears but they do not grow into citizens, they do not acquire any civic rôle, they remain essential to but at the margins of political society. The geographic position of Brauron is the social position of women. The position which the *arkteia* prepares Athenian girls for is the delicate position controlled by the Thesmophoria.

The Thesmophoria did not start in Athens at all; it started in a sanctuary on the west coast of Attika, at Halimous, from which the women processed to the city: the women are both pushed to the margins and central to the city. This point is further confirmed by the problematic recognition of the day at Halimous as part of the festival: only by both counting and not counting this day can the third day and the middle day of the festival be equated (Ar. *Thesm*. 80 and schol.). The Thesmophoria brings the women in from outside to create an alternative political society in a way that the festival at Brauron does not. This is brought out clearly by two features: women organise themselves to celebrate the Thesmophoria in demes, that is in the political units of their husbands; and Halimous has its own rape myth that contrasts with that of Brauron. The Halimous rape is again bound up with politics and (pseudo-) history: Plutarch tells how Solon tricked the Megarians by sending a message pointing out that all the Athenian women, including the most noble, were gathered alone at Halimous, and could be captured for political use. The Megarians were taken in, and when they landed they found that the women were men — Solon had sent the women away and dressed up soldiers as women. Once more the historical rôle of the story does not exhaust its interest, for it is basic and essential to the whole of the Thesmophoria that these women are men, an alternative city within the city. The procession from Halimous to Athens is a physical manifestation of that assertion: this is a procession that is 'symbolic anti-structure' indeed.[28]

The festival at Brauron too had an associated procession, but this is a rather different affair. Religious processions feature in many Athenian rituals and festivals, but they come in very various forms, from the relatively small processions involving only small numbers of priests and acolytes as part of the ritual of sacrifice, to such public carnivals as the Panathenaia. The Panathenaic procession is an act of almost overt political identification and self-assertion, but the long-distance procession to Brauron is hardly of that order and may more reasonably be compared with the procession to Eleusis. How far this latter served to break down normal social barriers and achieve an alternative community is indicated by the institution of abusing the 'pilgrims', and apparently particularly leading citizens, as the procession crossed the Kephisos bridge.[29]

The festival at Brauron shared with that at Eleusis the element of initiation, although it can hardly have been just the initiates who made the journey to Brauron. Those who went were those interested in what would happen at the other end, and what would happen was a matter of becoming a mature human being, not a matter of becoming a citizen.

Those who process do not process as Athenians, and their procession is a recognition of the distance separating the cult from the city, and all that the city stood for, it is even a celebration of that social distance which the festival serves to reinforce. The procession is itself part of the ritual which is socially conservative but politically independent, and it occupies a space, a space begrudged to those excluded from politics by sex as well as age, which is not susceptible to the concerns of public civic life.

The Brauronia in the classical period was clearly much more than simply a female puberty ritual, for while the *krateriskoi* suggest that the *kanēphoroi* and the bone *aulos* from the sanctuary site can be associated with that, the rhapsodes and stables do not fit so well. There is little doubt that in giving an opportunity for display, whether to prominent women, prominent horsemen, or prominent *hieropoioi* the Brauronia was open to manipulation which could not but have political overtones. But the *arktoi* remained central, and the majority of women who made dedications chose not to identify themselves clearly. While birth and growth and features of the female nature structured the life of the sanctuary, social differentiation and political manipulation could only appear as ephemeral irrelevances in a cult whose myths could establish history.[30]

The Mysteries of politics

The study of the Brauronia has shown that not only is there no evidence for any transfer of the cult from Brauron to the Athenian acropolis, but that it was inconceivable that such a transfer could occur. The location of the sanctuary at Brauron is itself part of the essential nature of the cult. The sanctuary there was well established by the beginning of the fifth century and received considerable attention throughout the classical period. By contrast the *hieron* on the Akropolis probably did not exist until the late fith century, had no temple, no dedications, and apparently no ritual. It was a

172

reminder of the rural sanctuary, not a competitor for its clientele or prestige.

People, some at least of high status, came from quite distant parts of Attika to make dedications at Brauron. The rites were initiatory and the opposition which they set up was between those who could be and were initiated, Athenian women, and those excluded. This was not a local opposition, and that eighty of the 125 names of dedicators occur only once seems an indication that there was no concentrated interest from any group, local or otherwise. To have been *arktos* strengthened one's claim to be an Athenian, but it did not define one more precisely.[31] The girls did not set themselves apart from others, rather they shared the common pain of growing up.

It was not simply girls who featured in the clientele of the Brauronia; the penteteric celebration did not only focus on a particular repressed portion of the community and smooth its passage from one social context to another, it actually, not least through the procession, lifted the participants out of all practical social contexts, out of normal constraints, and briefly offered the experience of being part of a community that was literally utopia, even if still firmly Athenian and overseen and policed by *hieropoioi* appointed by the *boule*.

None of the dedicants at Brauron is known to come from Philaidai, although some surely did, and this neighbouring deme has left no trace that it used the sanctuary for its own purposes at all. The natural locality of the sanctuary was certainly very important, but the political locality was not. By contrast the political as well as religious context provided for the *hieron* of Artemis Brauronia in Athens by the Akropolis was important, if only in a crucially limited way. The Akropolis sanctuary represents one side and only one side of the cult — part of the public aspect, the dedications. This limitation is itself a recognition of the fact that the sanctuary at Brauron could not be reproduced; by recording the dedications on the Akropolis the tangible manifestation of the cult activity is recreated, and a single feature of the cult is emphasised. This feature is one that acknowledges the centrality of the female to the polis, for the dedications mark childbirth. Thus the women, banished to the margins, are allowed back to the centre in as far as they are essential to male continuity. There is an element of control present in the establishment of a Brauronian presence on the Akropolis, but it is a control over the female, a recognition that the cult at Brauron successfully performs an essential task, not a control over the running of the sanctuary of Brauron.[32] The politics are the politics of sex.

Not all cults, however, are cults of women, and not all share, and must share, the Brauronian feature of being physically outside a politically recognised centre.[33] While the political isolation of Brauron is an essential part of its very nature as a sanctuary it does not follow that sanctuaries which do belong to settlements are any the more open to political use or manipulation. One of the clearest demonstrations of this is given by the cult of the Mysteries at Eleusis.[34]

We have practically no evidence for the institutional development of the Mysteries prior to the classical period, but this has not prevented modern scholars from reading the variety of institutions associated with the Mysteries in the classical period in an evolutionary mode. The methodological problems with this approach hardly need to be detailed here, and no attempt will be made to combat such speculations. This brief examination is limited to an attempt to suggest how it is that the features of the cult found in the classical period continue to co-exist: that is, to understand some institutional aspects of how the cult works.

It is basic to the myth of the foundation of the Eleusinian Mysteries that the cult is an open one, not restricted to the members of any single social or political group.[35] We know that in the classical period slaves might be initiated (e.g. ii² 1672.207) and the only two demands that were made were that the initiate spoke Greek and was pure of the shedding of human blood. The rôle that the Lesser Mysteries at Agrai perform for Herakles is one of purification from blood; they cannot and do not make him an Athenian. We do not know when the Lesser Mysteries were established, nor how early they had any close connection with the Mysteries at Eleusis, but we have no reason to invent a late creation for 'political' motives.[36]

Upon this crowd of miscellaneous devotees order is imposed in various ways. Priestly authority is limited to two families, the Eumolpidai and the Kerykes. The Kerykes go unmentioned in the *Homeric Hymn to Demeter*, but the significance of this is something that it is impossible to assess. It has been claimed that the Kerykes are a late addition and mark the take-over of the cult by the Athenians on the grounds that no member of the Kerykes is known who belongs to the deme of Eleusis, but this argument has no force since demotics only measure local affiliations at the end of the sixth century, and there is only a single Eumolpid who is *Eleusinios*. If anything is to be deduced from this shortage of Eleusinians it is surely that by the end of the sixth century the Mysteries did not rely, even at the upper levels, upon people tied by locality.[37]

The more routine and administrative tasks connected with the Mysteries fall outside priestly responsibility. Just as in the cult of Herakles in Akris the deme of Eleusis shares responsibility with cult officials, the *hieromnemones*, so in the Mysteries, where the clientele was vastly greater than simply the members of the deme, the larger political body gives assistance. *Hieropoioi* of one sort or another are found from an early date: in i³ 6 of the early fifth century they and the Athenian assembly share financial control; i³ 5, which may relate to the Mysteries, has a body of ἱεροποιοὶ Ἐλευσινίον, who should be '*hieropoioi* of the Eleusinians', while inscriptions of the later fifth century have ἱεροποιοὶ Ἐλευσινόθεν (*ML* 73), ἱεροποιοὶ Ἐλευσῖνι (i³ 391), and the ἱεροποιοὶ κατ' ἐνιαυτόν also in Aristotle (*ML* 84, *Ath. Pol.* 54.7). This variety of names may be simply a result of casual and inconsistent terminology, but the title 'of the Eleusinians' ought to indicate a close connection with the men of the deme of Eleusis, and not just with the place Eleusis. In the fourth century there are certainly two separate boards of *hieropoioi*

175

concerning themselves with Eleusis at the same time, and both are central appointments: ii² 1672.252 and 303 has 'annual *hieropoioi*', while ii² 250 and 299 have '*hieropoioi* from the *boule*'. These are in addition to the *hieropoioi* appointed from the members of the prytany in charge when the Mysteries were celebrated (ii² 1749.80—4). There seems little system or structure to all of this; rather, when something needed to be done relative to the Mysteries an interested party would propose that some official be created to do it. It is to be noted that when a revision of the *aparkhe* regulations takes place in the fourth century it is on the proposal of a man from Eleusis.[38]

Which political body took responsibility for cult administration depended on which was informed of the problem, and since more adherents came from outside Eleusis this body was more often the assembly. That there is a chance factor in the division of responsibility is brought out by the coincidence that two similar pontifical exercises separated by a century of time are known from inscriptions. In i³ 79 the *boule* and *demos* concern themselves with the bridging of the Rheitoi, while in ii² 1191 (cf. *Anth. Pal.* 9.147) the deme and resident garrison honour one Xenokles for the construction of a bridge while '*epimeletes* of the Mysteries'. These bridges vital to the ritual are the legitimate interest of either local or central political bodies.

The Eleusinian Mysteries created a body of initiates linked not by locality or citizenship but by a common religious experience. This experience did involve their all being together in one place at one time, and the *Homeric Hymn to Demeter* makes clear how important it became that that place was Eleusis. Both deme and central organisation in Athens take, as a matter of course, decisions relevant to the Mysteries because they were each organs through which those involved could take decisions relevant to their own religious activities.

By contrast with the token presence of Artemis Brauronia on the Akropolis, the Mysteries did have a fully-fledged sanctuary in the city which was, in the classical period, part of the rites. But this city sanctuary was far from being the only one outside Eleusis. There were Eleusinia for certain at Paiania (i³ 250) and in the Tetrapolis (ii² 1358), and the document recently published as 'A lex sacra of the Attic deme Phrearrhioi' (Vanderpool (1970)) not only mentions an Eleusinion with altar and court but may well be a set of regulations for a local Eleusinion and not a deme decree at all. If the identification of the puzzling building of the Periklean period at Thorikos, a structure with a peristyle of 7 x 14 columns with large gaps in the centre of the flanks, which is certainly not a regular temple, as an Eleusinion is correct, then Thorikos had a very large investment in the cult. Certainly a dedication τοῖν θεοῖν is known from Thorikos, and the Thorikioi sacrificed to Demeter at least twice a year, on one occasion possibly as Demeter Eleusinia (*SEG* 26.136. 21,38).[39] Most interesting of all is perhaps the Eleusinion at Phaleron, apparently the half-burnt temple of Demeter, for this features with the shrines at Eleusis and in Athens in a decree from the middle of the fifth century (i³ 32) which puts all their finances under the same board of *logistai*.

It is tolerably clear from all this that the Eleusinion in Athens can only be understood in the framework of all these other Attic Eleusinia. All are dependent upon the sanctuary at Eleusis for their very identity, and one may suspect that it is initiates from Eleusis who form their clientele. Unlike the Brauron rites the Eleusinian mysteries are not linked to any particular physiological change or state of life, and, while there are particular ceremonies which are experienced in a special way the first time, the tie with the cult does not end there. It becomes clear from the fourth-century regulations (Clinton (1980)) that the logistics of the Mysteries became of considerable concern, and the local Eleusinia represent the other side of this, for they enable a continued link with the cult both at times of the year when there are not major ceremonies at Eleusis and for those unable to make the trip even for the festivals. Thus it is that the Erkhians combine with other religious activities in the city and use the Athens Eleusinion for a sacrifice on 12 Metageitnion, the eve of the Eleusinia.[40]

There are clearly some political overtones to all this: that a community has its own Eleusinion or that a deme makes its own private sacrifice to Eleusinian deities sets up differences and asserts identity. At the same time, however, the very act of calling it an Eleusinion or noting that the sacrifice is to Demeter Eleusinia recognises the dependence upon what happens at Eleusis. All these commemorations outside Eleusis can only be alternatives by also being confirmations. Far from establishing the city shrine as a rival with that at Eleusis, the processions associated with the Mysteries assert the dependence upon the shrine outside the city, and in fact recognise, by the abusive community they set up, that there is a lack of fit between 'Athenian citizen' and initiate and that procession and initiation occur outside the political space. While it is central to the Thesmophoria that it must happen at the Eleusinion in the *city*, it is as vital for the Mysteries as for the Brauronia that the crucial events take place outside the city.[41]

A festival with no political definition of participants, controlled by priests very largely not members of the local community and by officials created *ad hoc* to deal with administrative problems as they arose, begun by a departure and continued by the creation of a community with no local identity that refused normal social order and control, the Mysteries rely at every stage on their separation from temporal organisations of any kind. Once this is recognised it becomes clear that the confusions and seeming contradictions that mark the festival are not to be explained by an evolutionary approach which looks for political take-over by Peisistratos or by the Athenian *demos*; they are features which are integral to the nature of the cult.

The cult of the deme

The Brauronia and the Eleusinian mysteries both depend upon locality, but in both cases it is natural locality and a peripheral relation to the political unit that is important. Both exploit the fact of being outside Athens the political centre, and the Brauronia exploits the fact of being outside any deme. It is likewise the case with many local cults, such as hero cults, that they are tightly bound to the natural but independent of the political locality.

It is also the case, however, that both the polis and the demes could and did act as sacrificing groups. By doing so a group which was primarily defined as a political unit asserted that it had a common religious interest. The nature of the interest might vary from festival to festival, but it could be precisely a shared political interest which produced the religious activity. This is most clearly and most extremely the case with the Great Panathenaia, which is not only a common celebration of political identity but a means of controlling the constituents of that identity − the demes. The demarchs played a part here and it was as demesmen that Athenians received meat from the sacrifices. This is the only festival where demes seem to have been involved as demes, and that the festival could be a means of controlling subject allies is but an extension of its rôle in limiting Athenian demesmen.[42]

The activities of the demes as sacrificing groups are as various as those of the polis as a whole. There are, again, cases where sacrificial activity is directly used to strengthen the political identity. This is most clear with the Peiraieus, where in the third century, at least, there were sacrifices limited to demesmen (ii[2] 1214). Given the cosmopolitan nature of the Peiraieus, it is possible that religious activities were a necessary bolster to, and almost the sole manifestation of, the social constitution of the political community. But it is important to note that the limitation to demesmen does not correspond with worship of any particular divinity, there is no attempt here of a community to monopolise a god, and no community is known to have done so.

As has already been noted in the cases of Halai Aixonides and Sounion, demes make sparing use of local sanctuaries. Thus the Thorikioi make little use of the Eleusinion, and the Phrearrhioi certainly share their local Eleusinion with other groups. This is despite the fact that the sanctuary was often the focal point in a locality, and that the demesmen of Halai Araphenides made use of the publicity offered by the festival of the Tauropolia by displaying deme decrees in the sanctuary of Artemis Tauropolos.[43] Nor do demes concentrate on local heroes; these usually receive some recognition but not a lot. At Thorikos Kephalos and Prokris are remembered but once a year, and Thorikos himself and his heroines two or three times; Erkhia has some anonymous Numphai and the curious import Leukaspis but no clearly localised deity of its own; the demes of the Tetrapolis can only manage Hero in Arasileia between them.[44]

The bulk of worship in demes falls into one of two categories: worship of life-crisis divinities, notably Kourotrophos, and worship of appropriate divinities when there is a major festival in the city. Both Erkhia and Thorikos worship the divinities of the Arrephoria at the time of that festival in Athens, those of the Diasia at the Diasia, and at least Hera at the Theogamia, while Thorikos also observes the festival of Artemis Mounykhia, the Dionysia, the Plynteria, the Pyanopsia and the Proerosia; Erkhia the Genesia with holocausts; and the Tetrapolis the Skira, the Mysteries, and, by appropriate sacrifices, the Lesser Mysteries and Eleusinia.[45] By choosing to recognise a major festival a deme exerts a control; on the one hand the correspondence indicates a dependence upon what is happening centrally, while on the other hand the provision of a separate local sacrifice establishes independence. But not only are the sacrifices in the deme not the same as the festival in the polis: they are not substitutes but additions, for they do not exclude demesmen from the festival, and the clientele of the deme sacrifice is itself part of the festive polis. The Plotheia financial decree from the late fifth century makes it clear that the demesmen might see their action as relevant to the deme even if it in fact occurred outside the deme context: financial subsidies are to be given for religious activities ὅποι ἂν δέ[ηι Π]|λωθέας ὅπαντας τελε͂ν ἀργύριω[ν ἐς | ἱ]ερά, ἢ ἐς Πλωθέας ἢ ἐς Ἐπακρέα[ς ἢ ἐς Ἀ]θηναίος ... (i³ 258). Different demes mark out different selections of festivals, and which they mark out seems dependent on the particular interests of the demesmen. Thus we have several decrees from demes which seem to reflect moves by individuals or groups of demesmen to get the deme to interact more actively with a particular divinity: ii^2 1184 concerns Kholargos and the Thesmophoria, i^3 250 Paiania and the Eleusinian deities, i^3 256 Lamptrai and the local Numphai.

Any cult where demesmen are conscious that they are taking part as demesmen acquires a political dimension, for it contributes to the self-definition of a political group. The range of deme interests in religious cults reflects the multi-faceted nature of the deme. In particular it reflects the difference between a deme and a locality: the deme is made up of Athenians, and the religious activities of the deme use the religious framework of the Athenian polis. Cults celebrated in this way are often totally independent of the precise locality of the deme. At the same time there are local cults, heroes named and unnamed, which are also recognised by the deme and which are part of the distinction between deme and polis, part of the inalienable location of the deme.

The location of cult

This chapter has looked at two cases of cults of which it has traditionally been claimed that 'the state' took them over and attempted to use and control them for political ends, and in particular for the domination of the city of Athens over any and every other possible centre of power. It need hardly be said that this view does no justice to the nature of religious power, for in assuming that the power that accrues from cult can simply be annexed it overlooks the fact that such power is embedded in the cult and is closely defined and limited by it. Both the Brauronia and the Mysteries at Eleusis are essentially localised, and extra-Athenian, the power that they possess is in an important way constituted by the structure of the cult, a structure built on the locality.

Cults in the demes are significant as indications of the self-definition of the demesmen. It is therefore notable that the

181

demesmen join in cult activities which join them with the community outside the deme, they do not assert their own independence with cults peculiar to their deme alone. The cults do not limit the deme, they enlarge it. The cults recognise the dependence of the deme on the polis and assert a claim to be constituent of the polis. At the same time the attention afforded to the Kourotrophoi links the demesman with the apolitical elements of the polis, with the women and children vital to his own and the deme's reproduction. In both of these areas any given individual's activities as member of a deme will be complemented by his activities as an individual, where he might himself take part in the great festivals in Athens or outside. The deme group is one that is necessary for the political identity of an individual, but the deme as such is not necessary for an individual's religious identity or activity.

Cult activity is vital to the relations between city and countryside, but not because the countryside exercises its political voice by religious activity. It is vital because through cult the separation of city and country is comprehended: physical separateness and the differences in physical characteristics become recognised as themselves integral features of human society and social life. The rural cults do not control the rural inhabitants, they control the experiences which the polis, and particularly the public, political, face of the polis, does not and cannot control. By providing the space in which the polis can be reconciled to the non-political, the country, because it is country, puts itself at the centre of the polis in which city and country must be complementary partners.[46] The religious structure of the countryside thus does offer an alternative construction to that constituted by the political organisation, but this alternative itself functions as a confirmation.

CONCLUSION

CHAPTER 9

THE REPLACEMENT OF ATHENS

Within the Greek world as a whole a man was categorised by his name, his patronymic and his ethnic; all Athenians were Ἀθηναῖοι. Thus from the outside Athens was given primacy over Attika, and reference to the polis or to its citizens involved reference to the city. From the inside matters looked rather different. Ἀθηναῖος was no part of a citizen's nomenclature at home, rather he was identified by his name, patronymic and demotic. By this means the identity of the Athenian was firmly rooted in the deme from which his family came, and the membership of which was an essential part of his political status. Thus although the city was the political centre of Athens, the place at which the Athenians took all their political decisions,[1] no Athenian was singled out as coming from the city, no one had his claim to be a *politēs* privileged by his name.

That the links with the city established by the name Ἀθηναῖος only exist because of the political function of the city becomes clear from the case of Athenian women. αἱ Ἀθηναῖαι is not a possible form of reference to the wives of Athenian citizens, rather they are Ἀττικαὶ γυναῖκες.[2] Women have no political rights and hence they have no special connection with the city, indeed they are excluded from just those areas which distinguish city life. The women do not even belong to demes, they are located more precisely by the demotic of their father and then their husband but in their own right they are residents in settlements whose political status is irrelevant: thus it is that Lysistrata refers to Kalonike at the opening of the *Lysistrata* as ἥ γ᾽ ἐμὴ κωμῆτις (line 5), one who lives in the same village, rather than as one who lives in the same deme.

Demes do vary in size, and certain large or otherwise

important demes had the *trittys* to which they belonged named after them, but *de iure* all demes are of equivalent status and there is no hierarchy of demes. Although demes are divided into three regional groups, the city, the coast and the inland region, it is part of the ideology that each group is equal, and the division meant to manifest and ensure equality rather than to establish a hierarchy. Wherever their deme of origin is, the citizens cannot afford to ignore it if they wish to exercise their political rights, for it is the deme that first recognises them as citizens and it is through the deme that men enter the running for office as *bouleutes*. Effectively this means that residence in the deme is essential for any man who wishes to enjoy a full political life, or the social life that depends on it. At the same time since Athens *is* the political centre, where the assembly meets and where all officials have to perform the bulk of their duties, anyone who desires to participate actively in as many political activities as possible needs to reside in the *astu*. This clash of demands can be met by the rich, for they can maintain a base in their deme and a base in the city, but the less rich are restricted by the contradiction unless they live nearby. If a man stays in his deme his appearances in the assembly will be correspondingly fleeting, but if he moves from his deme to the city he risks exclusion from local political life, and this can lead to an equal exclusion from central politics. The suggestion has been made above (pp. 147–51) that Demosthenes 57 marks a move in precisely this direction — to stifle the political voice of a man who had left the deme.

It follows from this situation that the democracy which gave political status to the villages also built a safeguard to the settlement pattern, for a man could not abandon his deme without risking his political life. At the same time, however, the settlement pattern restricts access to central politics, for location is important as a determinant of political activity, as chapter 4 tried to show. As a result of this the democracy which is based upon equality produces an inequality precisely by its refusal to recognise the unavoidable physical inequality between parts of Attika. The rich can

184

overcome the local constraints to an extent that the less rich cannot; they keep their local base (as Philokrates at Hagnous) but they also cultivate the *astu* (where Philokrates' interests are manifested by his *ergasteria*).

It is not the case, however, that less well-off Athenians had no contacts outside their deme. While there are indications that it is precisely these men who throw themselves most whole-heartedly into local politics there are also plentiful indications of contact and co-operation between men of different demes, contact which the web of kinship (above chapter 7) made unavoidable. It is in this light that the distinction between the *asteios* and the *agroikos* must be seen. This is not a distinction between the man who lives inside the walls of the city and the man who lives outside, it is a distinction based on behaviour, and in particular on political behaviour. Aristophanes' title character in the *Georgoi* tries to buy himself out of a political office, while some character in Menander's *Georgos* claimed that he had no experience of τῶν κατ᾽ ἄστυ πραγμάτων (F. 5 Sandbach). Theophrastos' Agroikos (*Char.* 4) does appear in the assembly, but in a state that shows that he is not used to such company. Living in the country certainly may make it more difficult to be urbane — Strepsiades excuses his ignorance of what happens in the Phrontisterion on the grounds that he lives far off in the country, although he only comes from Kikynna[3] — but it does not produce the boor. Comedy laughs at both the *agroikos* and the *asteios*, and they can be ridiculed because they are both extreme examples of what may happen if one lives exclusively in either an urban or a rural environment.

Rural residence was not only encouraged by the democratic system, it was both conducive to and partly a product of the particular status of land-holding. The strong ideology of land ownership that goes with its restriction to Athenian citizens militated against the abandonment of ancestral property, and hence also encouraged a continuing link with the ancestral deme. Although slaves were used in agricultural work it is notable that in this area, and perhaps only in this area, neighbours might also be used; the land has a political status, and is appropriately worked with the assistance of citizens.

One feature of agricultural activity is that it is common to all demes. While the proportion of land devoted to any particular agricultural pursuit undoubtedly did vary from deme to deme, and some demes were particularly well known for a specific crop,[4] all demes and the vast majority of demesmen had a major stake in the land. The other natural resources were not so evenly distributed through Attika, but various factors combine to ensure that no single deme or group of demes had any monopoly of a particular resource. In the case of quarrystone the doggedly local demand for most stones meant that control over extraction did not become a matter of economic significance. The only stones which did find a wider market seem not only to have been in demand only erratically and on a relatively small scale, they seem to have been largely exploited by the use of slave and metic labour. That there was little political or social clout to be gained by a deme in the vicinity of which quarries were worked is indicated by the ancient practice of identifying marble as 'from Pendele' and 'from Hymettos' — places which are not demes. Silver, by contrast with stone, is a resource which is locationally concentrated and of great economic significance, yet it does little more to single out particular demes. There are two aspects to this: in the first place the labour force in the mines was almost exclusively servile, and hence without any political affiliations; in the second the exploitation of the silver demanded previous capital and this made it unavoidable that the men who bought mining land or leased the rights to mine should come from all over Attika. Place of origin did have some influence upon who took advantage of the mining possibilities, but it did not introduce sufficient bias to make any particular region of Attika clearly economically superior simply because it had access to the silver mines.

Not only is it the case that no area of Attika had a distinctive economic base, neither did the city itself. Many men who resided for part of the time in the *astu* will have had land in

186

their own deme somewhere outside, and many who belonged to urban demes will have themselves had land either adjacent to the *astu* or further away. The city is a service centre, but many of the distinctly urban services are wholly or largely in the hands of slaves or metics and do not produce citizens with economic interests. This lack of a distinctly urban productive system is no encouragement to a distinctly urban social organisation,[5] and there is never any suggestion that there is any urban challenge to, or alternative for, an ideology of citizen land ownership. The city is distinguished by its political, and to some extent also its religious, rôle, not by its economic status or services.

One aspect of Athenian religious life is the interconnection of religious festivals and political units: for both the city as a whole and for the deme the fact of political identity encourages religious sacrifices and festivals. It is thus that religion mediates the political relationships − strengthening the bonds between citizens and between demesmen but also questioning the status of the bonds between deme and polis, deme and deme − in a more or less direct way. Against this, however, religious festivals also constitute a totally separate geography of Attika, which is a geography of the society outside politics. This is most clearly seen in the women's festivals at Brauron and of the Thesmophoria, which explore and control the social and the physiological condition of women, and do so in a way that questions and yet also reinforces their lack of political position. In the processions that were such a marked feature of the Eleusinian Mysteries there is an almost total escape from any political aspect: Eleusis made citizenship unimportant and the procession destroyed temporal physical ties as it moved, outside the bonds of social conventions to a place that had to be Eleusis, but had to be not because Eleusis was a deme but because Eleusis was Eleusis. Here again, however, the alternative was also a confirmation, was yet another feature of the complex Athenian political identity.

In Athens the polis, the *astu*, does not exploit the country-side either politically, economically, or socially. Politically the distinction between *astu* and country is not only ignored, it is effaced. The assertion that all Athenians are equal regardless of place of origin within Attika is an assertion that denies the real differences in access to politics which did exist, and it is an assertion that actually helps to maintain the differential geography of Attika. The insistence on the small geographical divisions, the division into demes, prevents the emergence of large geographical blocks. By turning the social interest in on the small group it also discourages the emergence of distinct economic groups and maintains the communications between the rich and the poor by making them an essential channel of political communication and activity. Town and country fail to be important blocks either to act in or to think with precisely because locality is made so important. It is a further effect of the way in which politics is submerged in the local community that the political aspects of society are embedded irretrievably in the social relations of the local group and in its religious and economic manifestations. It remains one of the paradoxes of this study that Athens, thought of as a mass democracy and one with a strong city base, should emerge as a polis with no abiding city, where 'true' democracy is only found on the small scale of the deme.

Although there is no indication that relations between town and country change to any degree over time, it is clear that the system *was* capable of malfunctioning under stress. The evidence for this takes us back to a deme which featured in earlier pages, Akharnai. At the beginning of the Peloponnesian War, when the Spartans first invaded Attika, the men of the deme of Akharnai show themselves peculiarly keen to respond with armed aggression. Thucydides notes some of the peculiar features of the position: this is the first invasion of the war; by coming right up to Akharnai Arkhidamos has disappointed expectations that he will go away again as Pleistoanax had done; Akharnai is a particularly big deme with a large number of hoplites;[6] the Athenians have been forced into the walled area for the first time ever. Not only can we add further details to this — e.g. that

Akharnai, forming a whole *trittys*, had more institutionalised power than simply a large deme; and incalculable factors such as the experience of seeing the recently built temple of Ares, the local equivalent of the Parthenon, abandoned before the enemy; but Aristophanes' choice of Akharnians as the aggressive chorus in the play named after them and his later references to Akharnian aggression in the *Lysistrata* of 411 (l.62) indicate the marked local feeling. As if all these factors were not enough we might also note that Aristophanes' jokes about the Arkharnians being charcoal-burners may further indicate that Akharnai did have something of a different economic base.[7] Only under such a combination of exceptional factors does a local interest emerge in Athenian politics.

Kleisthenes' reforms politicised the Attic countryside and rooted political identity there. Those local political roots continue to be the basis for political activity throughout the classical period, and just as it becomes the mark of a conservative to defend Athenian democracy so the democracy itself conserves a settlement pattern which displays little or no change during the whole of the next two centuries. For all who would be Athenians the deme group had to be the primary group, a group which both catered for the non-political expression of local identity and which was strong enough in itself to accommodate the interests of members in other, extra-local, groups, whether the product of kinship ties, associates in wealth and in service to the polis, or religious activity. The abiding importance of the deme tie prevents any of those other groups becoming exclusive, and always provides the unavoidable channel for political activity. The contradiction that the basic public body was a group restricted in its local ties actually serves to keep private interests public and check any tendency towards the separation of town and country. Wherever it is found, the δῆμος is the δῆμος.

APPENDICES

A: Isolated farms in classical and hellenistic Attika

The following aims to be a complete list of those sites which have been, or can be, seriously claimed to be isolated farms of the classical or hellenistic periods, other than those of the Vari—Vouliagmeni and Sounion—Thorikos areas discussed in the text.

ANO LIOSSIA: (1) Dema House: excavated because of its proximity to the Dema Wall this house was thought by the excavators to be 'probably a farmhouse' despite the lack of direct evidence for this. The house was large and well-equipped with fine pottery, and the excavators regard the wealth which produced these remains as a product of the surrounding countryside. However, the house seems to have been occupied for at most a decade in the fifth century, and in a reduced way for a short time in the fourth century. The immediately surrounding land is not good, and whatever caused this attempt to settle in comparative isolation it is clear that it proved an abortive attempt. This house is hardly good evidence for active agricultural activities based on isolated residences. *ABSA* 57 (1962) 75—114.

(2) 'Grosses Haus': noted on the *Karten* Blatt VI, this building received a surface investigation from the excavators of the Dema House. As planned it is large but with few internal divisions. Surface finds were few but indicate residence and a classical date, possibly contemporary with the Dema House. A conduit system appears to serve both buildings and some close connection between the two cannot be excluded. *ABSA* 57 (1962) 83, Boersma (1970) 244 no. 142.

LIMIKO (east of Markopoulo): a free-standing tower, previously connected by scholars with the road to Steiria, has been claimed by Langdon as a farm. The construction appears to be classical/hellenistic Greek, but the only sherds locally are medieval and Roman. Langdon's interpretation has only the negative support of his exclusion of the military option. *Hesperia* suppl. 19 (1982) 97f.

LIMIKO (south of Rhamnous): substantial remains of a round tower, now literally cut in half by a modern house plot (autopsy 23 May 1981), once interpreted as a watch-tower. Discovery of an olive press nearby suggests that this might be a farm. Chandler (1926) 4, Kahrstedt (1932) 22–3, Vanderpool (1978) 240f.

MERENDA: *AAA* 1 (1968) 31f. records a farm building, but this can hardly be regarded as isolated in view of its proximity to the known cemeteries. More isolated but less certainly a farm is the site on the west of the hill (425 m) which has yielded domestic pottery of the archaic period. Smith and Lowry (1954) 28f.

PAIANIA: a house at Karella, excavated but not published, apparently dated to the fifth century BC. Nothing marks this out clearly as a farm. *Praktika* (1919) 32, *ABSA* 57 (1962) 102 n. 29

PENDELE: on Mavrinora a square structure tentatively suggested by Langdon to be a farm if not a grave enclosure. Possible classical terracing nearby. *Hesperia* suppl. 19 (1982) 92ff., cf. Langdon (1976) 102.

PSYKHIKO: on the hill of the college of Athens a farm dated to the Roman period with hellenistic sherds also associated. *AAA* 2 (1969) 142 n. 1.

STAMATA: 'traces of what may have been a farmstead' on the slopes of Stamatavouni. No date suggested. Langdon (1976) 104.

VARNAVA: an oil press was found with building remains (not dated), but the presence of substantial graves suggests that this might not be an isolated site. *AM* 12 (1887) 318, Milchhoeffer (1900) 12.

VOURVA: remains of an olive/grape press associated with sherds of hellenistic and Roman date. Possible village site to south and west. *BCH* 89 (1965) 24–6.

Considering the area of Attika and the number of known village sites this is an extremely short list. Even then the number of these sites which are certainly (a) classical, (b) isolated, and (c) farms in a very low proportion. The Dema House may well be part of a ribbon development, given the known settlement nearby at Ag. Soter (appendix B) and the odd 'Lager' site. For the latter see Milchhoeffer (1883) 45, *ABSA* 52 (1957) 172f. and McCredie (1966) 67, 71. The Limiko (Rhamnous) tower is certainly within half a kilometre of a settlement (appendix B), and the same is probably true of the Merenda non-hillside site and the Vourva farm. Of the remaining sites only in the cases at Varnava (not dated and possibly not entirely isolated) and Psykhiko is there any evidence that we are dealing with farms, and the Psykhiko evidence is certainly post-classical.

B. Remains of nucleated settlement in Attika

This is a conservative list of archaeological remains indicative of extensive settlement. Only sites where a considerable amount of surface material has been found are included, and those where the material is likely to have come from a cemetery or religious site are excluded. Sites recorded by investigators prior to the middle of this century are only included when particularly convincing or confirmed by later investigation or personal autopsy.

Settlement remains can plausibly be associated with the following demes.

Aigilia: Eliot (1962) 106f., *Hesperia* 39 (1970) 50–3, but compare the arguments of Lauter (1980B) 243 n. 10. See also *ADelt* 21B (1966) 97f., 29B1 (1974) 108–10; *AAA* 7 (1974) 219ff.

Aixone: Eliot (1962) 6–24; *ADelt* 25B (1970) 125f., 27B1 (1972) 159f., 29B1 (1974) 55–8, 30A (1975) 309–21.

Anagyrous: see text above pp. 26ff.

Anaphlystos: Eliot (1962) 75–109, Pritchett (1965) 135ff.

Angele: Milchhoeffer (1889) 11, cf. *AM* 62 (1937) 9 no. 7. Autopsy of 21.6.81 revealed that there is indeed a very substantial scatter of ancient sherd material in this area.

Aphidna: Milchhoeffer (1889) 60. This is something of a problem deme, and the existence of local toponyms in the classical period make it likely that in this case the deme consisted of more than one nucleation. Examination on the ground on 11.4.81 did reveal that to the south-east of the akropolis of Kotroni, in the vicinity of Agioi Saranda, there is a heavy scatter of ancient sherd material.

Besa: Eliot (1962) 121f.

Eleusis: cf. e.g. Travlos (1949), Mylonas (1961).

Elaious: Milchhoeffer (1895) 23, *ADelt* 23A (1968) 6f.

Erkhia: *BCH* 89 (1965) 21–6. Examination of the area on 18 April 1981 revealed a block dressed with pointed work, and a triglyph block measuring 0.4 × 0.4 × 0.57 m. It is unclear whether or not this is to be associated with the Doric capital, apparently of the early fifth century, previously found on this site.

Hagnous: see chapter 3 n. 26.

Halai Aixonides: see text pp. 22ff.

Hekale: Milchhoeffer (1889) 58, *AJA* 5 (1889) 162f., *ASCS Papers* 6 (1890–7) 374ff. Lewis has argued that the Koukounari site be considered simply that of a religious sanctuary (1963, 31f.) but this claim has been countered by Bicknell (1978) 372 n. 17. Examination of the Koukounari valley on 3 June 1981 confirmed that there is a good deal of ancient material built into the church of Agia Paraskeue and the ruined monastic buildings around it (pl. 11); in addition the general vicinity has a notable scatter of sherds. This would seem to suit a settlement site rather better than simply a 'cult spot'.

Kephale: *AA* (1963) 455—98.

Kholleidai: *Kharisterion Orlandou 1* (1965) 174f.

Kikynna: Milchhoeffer (1883) 32. The identification of the remains at Khalidou is not certain, but investigation on 12 May 1981 showed that there is certainly a heavy scatter of sherds in this area.

Kothokidai: Milchhoeffer (1895) 23.

Coastal Lamptrai: Eliot (1962) 47—61, Pritchett (1965) 138—40.

Upper Lamptrai: Eliot (1962) 47—61, Pritchett (1965) 139, Themelis, *AAA* 8 (1975) 275—91.

Peiraieus.

Phegaia: *BCH* 89 (1965) 26 n. 1, Vanderpool (1974).

Philaidai: *Praktika* (1956) 80, *ADelt* 21B (1966) 106. A visit to the area west of the Basilika on 21 May 1981 revealed that a strip of land had been deep-ploughed, and that this had brought up at least three sizeable stone blocks, a quantity of the tile in large pieces, and large fragments of at least one combed *kalathos* beehive and its extension ring, pl. 12.

Phrearrhioi: cf. under Aigilia, with Eliot (1962) 91 and n. 58.

Phyle: Petropoulakou and Pentazos (1973) X6 Y6 4 and X6 Y6 6, BSA sherds A31 (with sketch), ASCS sherds A12. Colin Edmonson tells me that in recent years the American school expedition has found Geometric sherds here.

Probalinthos: Milchhoeffer (1889) 40, Soteriades, *Praktika* (1932) 221, cf. *AJA* 70 (1966) 321 n. 7 and Vanderpool (1974). A visit to the area on 10 June 1981 showed that there was a very extensive scatter of sherds along the ridge up to the Moni tis Theotokou, spread over a distance of at least 400 m. To the south-east, between this site and the probable site of Phegaia, are possible traces of an ancient road.

Prospalta: Petrou, *Hellenika* (1935), esp. 228, *AM* 12 (1887) 281—6, Milchhoeffer (1889) 12. On the ridge just north-west of Agios Petros (Petrou's 'Gkourimpim'?) there is a definite scatter of ancient sherd material, which can be traced for some distance. (Seen 6 May 1981.)

Sphettos: *BCH* 93 (1969) 56—71.

Thorai: Eliot (1962) 65—8, 47—51; *AAA* 7 (1974) 224 and fig. 11.

Thorikos: cf. especially the summary of Mussche in *MIGRA* 1 (1975) 44ff.

Archaeological remains indicative of nucleated settlement but which cannot be surely identified with any ancient deme are known from the following modern locations.

Aigaleos: an area with a lot of ancient blocks, carving and bricks on the north-eastern slopes towards Kamatero: Gardikas, *Praktika* (1920) 66.

Akharnai: Yerobouno hill: extensive classical—early hellenistic pot and tile scatter: *Kharisterion Orlandou* 1 (1965) 172 n. 9, *Hesperia* 35 (1966) 282, McCredie (1966) 61f., cf. *ABSA* 53/4 (1958—9) 292—4.

Anavyssos: Ari: Houses and buildings connected with mining activities: Milchhoeffer (1889) 25, Eliot (1962) 90, 100, 107. Cf. *Hesperia* 39 (1980) 49ff.

Ano Liossia: Agios Soter: traces of walls and much sherd material around the church: *Praktika* (1920) 64f., BSA sherds A55 with plan.

Kharbati (now Pallene): Matringou: west of Kharbati and north of the main road at the 17 km post, on and around the ridge (spot heights of 181 and 185 on *Karten* Blatt XII) remains of walls were visible in the nineteenth century. Now (visit of 2 June 1981) there is an extensive and locally very heavy sherd scatter visible (cf. *BCH* 89 (1965) 24, and for another identification Bicknell (1978)). It is uncertain whether the extensive remains also reported to the south at Vlikhos represent a totally separate settlement or are from a cemetery for the Matringou site. See Milchhoeffer (1889) 3, 37, Löper, *AM* 17 (1892) 353f., *Praktika* (1920) 58, *ADelt* 29A (1974) 194—225 (esp. 196 and n. 9), *AA* 41 (1926) 400.

Kioupia: an extensive but otherwise apparently unrecorded scatter of classical sherds was seen at this site on 16 June 1981. The site lies north-west of Raphina and about $\frac{1}{2}$ km east of the claimed Neolithic site at Kasarma (*AM* 71 (1956) 1). It should be pointed out here that the remains of substantial structures which have generally been associated with the site of the deme of Araphen, and which Eliot (in *PECS* s.v.) is wrong in claiming to be not now visible, are certainly post-classical in date, since they make widespread use of mortar.

Kokkini: ancient remains around the chapel of Panagia: Milchhoeffer (1895) 18, Vanderpool (1978) 245 n. 26.

Koundoura: 1 km east of hill (506 m) an extensive scatter of sherds: Edmonson (1966) 70. West of this, at Agios Giorgios, a site sometimes identified as Ereneia: Edmonson (1966) 152f., McCredie (1966) 85—7, *ABSA* 49 (1954) 108, *AEph* (1910) 151f., Sakellariou and Pharaklas (1972) 13, 23, 26, 33, and Epimetro 2 par. 5.

Limiko (South of Rhamnous): area of walls (now cut through by the motor road to Rhamnous) and sherds, from which a number of grave stelai have been rocovered: *AM* 4 (1879) 278, 12 (1887) 317; *ADelt* 21 (1966) B107, autopsy of 23 May 1981. See also above appendix A.

Merkouri: Milchhoeffer (1889) 6.

Metropisi: Lulje Kouki: Eliot (1962) 113, Milchhoeffer (1889) 24, Crosby (1950) 189f.

Mpogiati: Milchhoeffer (1889) 58f.

Ntraphi: Milchhoeffer (1889) 37; *BCH* 80 (1956) 246f., 81 (1957) 519ff., 82 (1958) 681; *AM* 5 (1880) 346, 12 (1887) 305; Boersma (1970) 254; *AJA* 61 (1957) 282.

Pendele: Ag. Trias: Milchhoeffer (1889) 33—5. Slopes of Mt Aphorismos: Smith and Lowry (1954) 35f.

Peristeri: Philippson (1952) vol. 1, part 3, p. 857 n. 1.

Polydendri: Milchhoeffer (1900) 15.

Sounion: see text.

Spata: Vathy Pegadi: various archaic grave monuments have been found in this area and it has been suggested that it might be the site of a small deme (*BCH* 89 (1965) 24—6, *Mnemosyne* 28 (1975) 60). Since this might simply be an extension of the certain nearby cemetery (cf. *ADelt* 6 (1920—1) 133f) and since the whole area is now being churned over in the construction work for the new airport, and apparently producing more finds (cf. *Vima* for 30 June 1981, and 3 June 1981, p. 8) it seems prudent to reserve judgement.

Stamata: Panagia tis Myrtidiotissas: Petropoulakou and Pentazos (1973) X8 Y6 40.

Voula: see text pp. 24—6.

Vourva: *BCH* 89 (1965) 24—6. Cf. *Hesperia* 39 (1970) 46, *ADelt* 6 (1890) 105—12, *AM* 15 (1890) 318—29, *ABSA* 57 (1952) 137.

Table 1. *Probable age structure of the population of classical Athens (based on UN model life tables for under-developed nations).*

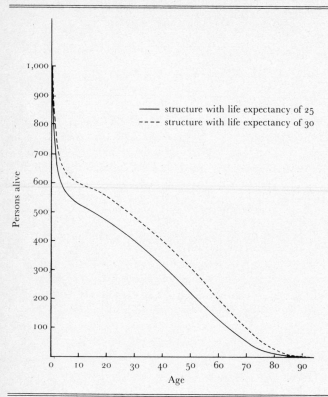

Table 2 (a). *The local distribution of propertied families*

Deme	*Bouleutai*	Men of property	Wealth index
North-east Attika			
Ionidai	2	0	0
Ikaria	5	4	0.8
Dekeleia	4	4	1
Oinoe	4	4	1
Oion Dekeleikon	3	3	1
Rhamnous	8	8	1
Semakhidai	1	1	1
Trikorynthos	3	3	1
Aphidna	16	19	1.19
Kolonai (both)	4	5	1.25

Table 2 (a) (continued)

Deme	*Bouleutai*	Men of property	Wealth index
Hekale	1	2	2
Plotheia	1	2	2
Cf. Phyle	2	2	1
	54	57	1.05
East coast			
Araphen	2	1	0.5
Probalinthos	5	3	0.6
Philaidai	3	2	0.666
Marathon	10	7	0.7
Halai Araph.	5	4	0.8
Deiradiotai	2	2	1
Phegaia	3	4	1.333
Prasiai	3	6	2
Steiria	3	8	2.666
	36	37	1.03
Mesogaia			
Konthyle	1	0	0
Myrrhinoutta	1	0	0
Teithras	4	1	0.25
Oa	4	2	0.5
Hagnous	5	7	1.4
Myrrhinous	6	10	1.666
Kikynna	2	4	2
Pallene	6	12	2
Sphettos	5	11	2.2
Erkhia	7	16	2.29
Paianiai	12	28	2.333
Gargettos	4	7	2.75
Kytherros	2	6	3
Angele	2	8	4
Kydantidai	2	10	5
	63	122	1.94
South-east Attika			
Besa	2	1	0.5
Prospalta	5	3	0.6
Atene	1	1	1
Kephale	9	11	1.22
Sounion	4	6	1.5

Table 2 (a) (continued)

Deme	*Bouleutai*	Men of property	Wealth index
Thorikos	5	8	1.6
Amphitrope	2	6	3
	28	36	1.28
South-west Attika			
Aigilia	6	1	0.166
Thorai	4	1	0.25
Anaphlystos	10	8	0.8
Phrearrhioi	9	9	1
Lamptrai (both)	14	24	1.785
Anagyrous	6	18	3
	49	61	1.24
Coastal plane South of Athens			
Halai Aix.	6	4	0.666
Halimous	3	2	0.666
Phaleron	9	4	0.44
Aixone	8	11	1.38
Euonymon	10	20	2
Cf. Themakos	1	1	1
	37	42	1.13
Within walls of *astu*			
Koile	3	2	0.666
Melite	7	9	1.28
Kydathenaion	12	24	2
Skambonidai	3	6	2
Kollytos	3	7	2.333
	28	48	1.71
Closely adjacent to the *astu*			
Keiradai	2	1	0.5
Agrylai (both)	5	2	0.4
Daidalidai	1	1	1
Boutadai	1	1	1
Ankyle	2	2	1
Diomeia	1	2	2
Alopeke	10	21	2.1
Kerameis	6	13	2.166
Oion Kerameikon	1	4	4
	29	47	1.62

Table 2 (a) (continued)

Deme	Bouleutai	Men of property	Wealth index
Lower plain of Athens			
Korydallos	1	0	0
Eiresidai	1	0	0
Epikephisia	1	0	0
Erikeia	1	0	0
Kolonos	2	1	0.5
Hermos	2	1	0.5
Peiraieus	9	5	0.56
Xypete	7	6	0.86
Hestiaia	1	1	1
Ptelea	1	1	1
Thymaitadai	2	3	1.5
Kholargos	4	10	2.5
Bate	1	3	3
Lousia	1	3	3
Lakiadai	2	9	4.5
	36	43	1.2
Upper plain of Athens			
Iphistiadai	1	0	0
Eupyridai	2	0	0
Sypalettos	2	1	0.5
Paionidai	3	2	0.666
Phlya	7	7	1
Potamoi	3	3	1
Pergase	4	5	1.25
Perithoidai	3	4	1.333
Kholleidai	2	3	1.5
Akharnai	22	37	1.68
Athmonon	6	12	2
Pithos	2	7	3.5
Kephisia	6	22	3.666
	63	103	1.64
Plain of Eleusis/Thria			
Pelekes	2	0	0
Thria	7	4	0.57
Elaious	1	1	1
Kropidai	1	1	1
Oe	6	7	1.17

Table 2 (a) (continued)

Deme	Bouleutai	Men of property	Wealth index
Eleusis	11	14	1.27
Kopros	2	4	2
Kothokidai	2	4	2
Cf. Oinoe (Hipp.)	2	2	1
	34	37	1.09
Demes of uncertain location			
Aithalidai	2	0	0
Pambotadai	1	0	0
Hippotomadai	1	0	0
Epieikadai	1	0	0
Anakaia	3	0	0
Kettos	3	1	0.333
Azenia	2	1	0.5
Phegous	1	1	1
Sybridai	1	1	1
Otryne	1	1	1
Poros	3	3	1
Tyrmeidai	1	1	1
Akherdous	1	1	1
Hybadai	2	3	1.5
Hamaxanteia	2	3	1.5
Auridai	1	2	2
Krioa	1	2	2
Eroiadai (both)	2	6	3
·Kedoi	2	7	3.5
Leukonoion	3	18	6
	34	51	1.5
Overall	491	683	1.39

Note: The Eiteai, Trinemeia, and Potamos Deiradiotes have been omitted from these calculations. In the first and last cases this is because of the difficulty of dividing up the propertied men from homonymous demes — by including the other Potamoi I have slightly distorted the evidence. In the case of Trinemeia it is because although the general location is known Traill's exact location must be wrong, and it is uncertain whether the deme should go with the north-eastern group or that of the Upper plain of Athens.

Table 2 (b). *The distribution of wealth by tribe and* trittys.

Tribe	*Trittys*	Deme(s)	Deme index	*Trittys* index	Tribe index
Erekhtheis	City	Agrylai	0.4		
		Euonymon	2		
		Themakos	1	1.44	
	Coast	Anagyrous	3		
		Kedoi	3.5		
		? Lamptrai	1.785		
		Pambotadai	0	2.15	
	Inland	Kephisia	3.666		
		Pergasai	1.25		
		? Phegous	1		
		? Sybridai	1	2.42	1.98
Aigeis	City	Ankylai	1		
		Bate	3		
		Diomeia	2		
		? Erikeia	0		
		Hestiaia	1		
		Kollytos	2.333		
		Kolonos	0.5	1.6	
	Coast	Araphen	0.5		
		Halia Araph.	0.8		
		Otryne	1		
		Phegaia	1.333		
		Philaidai	0.666	0.86	
	Inland	Erkhia	2.29		
		Gargettos	2.75		
		Ikarion	0.8		
		? Ionidai	0		
		? Kydantidai	5		
		? Myrrhinoutta	0		
		Plotheia	2		
		Teithras	0.25	1.54	1.36
Pandionis	City	Kydathenaion	2	2	
	Coast	Angele	4		
		Myrrhinous	1.666		
		Prasiai	2		
		Probalinthos	0.6		
		Steiria	2.666	1.84	
	Inland	Konthyle	0		
		Kytherros	3		

Table 2 (b) (continued)

Tribe	Trittys	Deme(s)	Deme index	Trittys index	Tribe index
		Oa	0.5		
		Paianiai	2.333	1.9	1.9
Leontis	City	Halimous	0.666		
		?Kettos	0.333		
		?Leukonoion	6		
		Oion Ker.	4		
		Skambonidai	2	2.38	
	Coast	Deiradiotai	1		
		Potamos Deir.			
		et al.	0.6		
		Phrearrioi	1		
		Sounion	1.5	1.0	
	Inland	?Aithalidai	0		
		Kholleidai	1.5		
		Eupyridai	0		
		Hekale	2		
		?Hybadai	1.5		
		?Kolonai	1.25		
		Kropidai	1		
		Paionidai	0.666		
		Pelekes	0	0.795	1.29
Akamantis	City	Kholargos	2.5		
		Eiresidai	0		
		Hermos	0.5		
		Iphistiadai	0		
		Kerameis	2.166	1.71	
	Coast	Kephale	1.22		
		?Poros	1		
		Thorikos	1.6	1.29	
	Inland	?Eitea	?0.25		
		Hagnous	1.4		
		Kikynna	2		
		Prospalta	0.6		
		Sphettos	2.2	1.34	1.43
Oineis	City	Boutadai	1		
		Epikephisia	0		
		?Hippotomadai	0		
		Lakiadai	4.5		

Table 2 (b) (continued)

Tribe	Trittys	Deme(s)	Deme index	Trittys index	Tribe index
		Lousia	3		
		Perithoidai	1.333		
		Ptelea	1		
		? Tyrmeidai	1	1.73	
	Coast	Kothokidai	2		
		Oe	1.17		
		Phyle	1		
		Thria	0.57	1.0	
	Inland	Akharnai	1.68	1.68	1.46
Kekropis	City	Daidalidai	1		
		Melite	1.29		
		Xypete	0.86	1.07	
	Coast	Aixone	1.38		
		Halai Aix.	0.67	1.07	
	Inland	Athmonon	2		
		? Epieikidai	0		
		Phlya	1		
		Pithos	3.5		
		Sypalettos	0.5		
		Trinemeia	0	1.35	1.18
Hippothontis	City	? Hamaxantheia	1.5		
		Keiriadai	0.5		
		Koile	0.666		
		Korydallos	0		
		Peiraieus	0.555		
		Thymaitadai	1.5	0.74	
	Coast	? Akherdous	1		
		? Auridai	2		
		? Azenia	0.5		
		? Elaious	1		
		Eleusis	1.27		
		Kopros	2		
		Oinoe	1	1.25	
	Inland	? Anakaia	0.333		
		? Eroiadai	3		
		Dekeleia	1		
		Oion			
		Dekeleikon	1	1.0	1.0

Table 2 (b) (continued)

Tribe	*Trittys*	Deme(s)	Deme index	*Trittys* index	Tribe index
Aiantis	City	Phaleron	0.445	0.445	
	Coast	Marathon	0.7		
		Oinoe	1		
		Rhamnous	1		
		Trikorynthos	1	0.88	
	Inland	Aphidna	1.19	1.19	0.9
Antiokhis	City	Alopeke	2.1	2.1	
	Coast	Aigilia	0.166		
		Amphitrope	3		
		Anaphlystos	0.8		
		Atene	1		
		Besa	0.5		
		Thorai	0.25	0.74	
	Inland	Eitea	?0.25		
		?Eroiadai	3		
		Kolonai	1.25		
		?Krioa	2		
		Pallene	2		
		Semakhidai	1	1.62	1.24

Table 3. *Attic leases*

	All leases	Leases by demes	Type of property leased	
Lessee from deme in which property is located	12[1]	10	4 *khōria* 2 *phelleis* 2 *oikiai*	1 quarry 1 theatre
Lessee from neighbouring deme	1	0	1 garden (with religious connections)	
Lessee with no apparent local links	12	3	1 *phelleus* 3 *oikiai* 4 properties with religious connections 1 *ergasterion*	1 garden 1 theatre

[1] The lst decree from Teithras almost certainly provides a 13th example but this cannot be formally proved. It is a lease by the deme of a *khōrion* in the vicinity of some religious properties (*AM* 49 (1924) p. 3 no. 1).

204

Table 4. *The* hekatostai *inscriptions*

	Deme leasing	Territorial body leasing	Religious body leasing
Lessee from deme in which property is located	15 certain, 8 probable	0	7 certain, 3 probable
Lessee from neighbouring deme	1	3	3
Non-local lessee	3 probable	4	4
Multiple leasing	all properties in own deme, 6	in neighbouring deme, 1	in non-local deme, 3

Note: With one possible exception all the properties leased by one man are in a single deme.

Table 5. *The* horoi

	Type of property		
	House(s)	Land and house(s)	Land (*khōrion*)
Location			
In *astu*	32	13	17
Outside *astu*	5	31	27
	(3 Peiraieus 2 Eleusis)	(9 Mesogaia 8 Plain of Athens 5 North-east Attika 2 West coast 1 Plain of Eleusis 1 Peiraieus)	(6 Plain of Eleusis 6 Mesogaia 5 Plain of Athens 3 North-east Attika 3 South Attika 3 Peiraieus 1 Rhamnous)
Creditors			
Local	2 (out of 2)	11 (out of 25)	$1\frac{1}{2}$ (out of 12; also one vague local connection, *SEG* 21.653)

Table 6. *The subject matter of deme decrees down to the end of the fourth century*

Honorific	42
Religious	11 (6 of these are calendars)
Financial	11
Leases	10
?Victor list	1

Table 7. *Known individuals in local and central political activity*

Rôle	No.	No. otherwise known
Demarch	42[1]	16 (39%)
Proposer of deme decree	33	20 (61%)
Honoured in deme decree[3]	20	13 (65%)
Proposer of central decree 352–318	57[2]	33 (58%)

[1] Four of the names are seriously fragmentary. Adjusted figure: 42%.
[2] Thirteen names are seriously fragmentary. Adjusted figure: 75%.
[3] Only men honoured by their own deme are counted.

Table 8. *Property ownership in the mining leases*

Same owner of	
property on all sides (? and *edaphos*)	3 cases
edaphos and property on 2 sides	7
property on 2 sides	11
edaphos and property on 1 side	15
Joint owners holding property on 3 sides	1
Different owners of	
property on each of 3 sides and of *edaphos*	2
property on each of 3 sides (1 owning *edaphos*)	2
property on each of 3 sides	2
property on each of 2 sides and of *edaphos*	7
property on each of 2 sides (1 owning *edaphos*)	5
property on each of 2 sides	11
property on one side and of *edaphos*	17

Table 9. *Men leasing mines*

No. of lessees with demotics attested in the leases	161
No. of demes attested	61
No. of men who only lease and do not own property	139
No. of demes attested as origin of such men[2]	59
No. of men who both own and lease	22
No. of demes from which men who own and lease come	17
No. of men who only lease who come from mining demes	23
from Amphitrope (no name complete)	3 (1.5)[1]
from Anaphlystos (2 without full name)	4 (0.4)
from Phrearrhioi (1 without name)	4 (0.56)
from Sounion (1 without name)	6 (1.75)
from Thorikos (2 without names)	6 (1.2)
No. of such men who lease a mine in their own deme[3]	4
No. of lessees who come from outside the mining demes	116

Outside demes producing 2 lessees

Aixone	(0.25)	Kerameis	(0.33)
Deiradiotai	(1)	Kolonos	(0.5)
Dekeleia	(0.5)	Oe	(0.33)
Eleusis	(0.18)	Pergase	(0.5)
Erkhia	(0.29)	Philaidai	(0.67)
Kephale	(0.22)	Prospalta	(0.4)

Outside demes producing 3 lessees

Athmonon[4]	(0.5)	Oion	(0.75)
Halai Aix.[5]	(0.5)	Sybridai	(3)
Kollytos	(1)	Sypalettos	(1.5)
Myrrhinous	(0.5)		

Outside demes producing 4 or more lessees

four:	Aphidna	(0.25)	Melite	(0.57)
	Euonymon	(0.4)	Paiania	(0.33)
	Gargettos	(1)	Pallene	(0.67)
six:	Akharnai	(0.27)		
	Lamptrai[6]	(0.43)		

[1] The figures in brackets are an index figure calculated to remove the factor of deme size from the calculations. The index is the result of dividing the number of lessees from a deme by the bouleutic quota for that deme. The results are plotted on maps 8A and 8B.

[2] Reading Φαυλλος at Crosby (1950) 13.64, 71, to give a lessee from Pithos.

[3] Total will be 6 if Thrasymos is in Sounion.

[4] These three are an interesting group: Kephisodoros and Euphemides are father and son (Crosby (1950) 9.9, ii^2 1587.17–19), and the mine leased by Kephisodoros is registered by the third man of Athmonon attested in the leases.

[5] Two might be identical.

[6] Four of these lack names and may not all be distinct individuals.

Table 10. *Property owners in the mining demes*

No. of owners with demotics attested in the leases	100
No. owning *edaphē*	27
ergasteria	30
khōria	11
kaminos	1
No. of demes attested	38
No. of men from mining demes	33
from Phrearrhioi (two names not preserved)	4 (0.44)[1]
from Amphitrope	3 (1.5)
from Thorikos	7 (1.4)
from Sounion (eight names not preserved)	19 (4.75)
No. of these owning property	
only in their own deme[2]	8
partly in own deme	1
Types of property in hands of owners from mining demes	
edaphē	7
khōria	6
ergasteria	6
lophos	1
No. of men from mining demes who both own land and lease mines	5
No. of men from outside mining demes owning property in mines	67

Outside demes from which two or more property owners
in the mining demes come

Demes producing two owners

Aigilia	(0.33)	Kopros	(1.0)
Aixone	(0.25)	Kydantidai[3]	(1.5)
Anagyrous	(0.33)	?Potamos	(1.0)

Demes producing three owners

Alopeke	(0.3)	Halai Aix.	(0.5)
Gargettos	(1.0)	Kikynna[4]	(1.5)

Demes producing four owners

Euonymon	(0.4)	Paiania	(0.33)
Kytherros	(2.0)	Pithos	(1.33)

Deme producing more than four

Sphettos (6)	(1.2)

[1] The figures in brackets are an index figure calculated as in table 9
For the mapping of the results see maps 7A and 7B.
[2] Nape is considered part of Sounion.
[3] The two are related.
[4] All three are from the same family.

1. View east from the Cliff Top Tower showing the variation of vegetation with underlying rock type: foreground is on marble, land immediately beside the road crossing the picture is on mica schists, the maquis of the middle ground is on marble, the cultivated land beyond is on mica schists, the further maquis beyond is again on marble, and the denser scrub vegetation in the far distance is on upper schists.

2. View of the deme site of Halai Aixonides at Ano Voula.

3. Rubble walling of the Khremonidean war fort (?) at Ano Voula.

4. The quarry road leading down from the Spelia quarry, Pendele.

5. Terracing for the quarry road on the Dragon House slope of Hymettos.

6. Cutting for a column drum, Cliff Top Tower quarry, Agrileza valley.

7. Cuttings in the Stephani quarry, Thorikos.

8. Quarry face, Perati.

213

9. Quarry face, Brauron quarry.

10. 'Tomb of Sophokles', Dekeleia.

214

11. Ancient blocks built into monastic buildings, Koukounari valley.

12. Philaidai deme site after deep ploughing.

215

NOTES

1. *The polis and its* politai

1. For the date see Meritt's commentary, *Hesperia* 5 (1936) 412. The court is referred to as τὸ δικαστήριον τὸ μέσον τῶν καινῶν, but this seems to refer to the building ('the middle one of the new court-rooms') rather than to some 'Middle Court' which specialised in hearing 'New Cases' (see Wycherley (1957) 147–8). Euthykles son of Euthykles, the *kurōtēs para prytaneōn* (1.127f.) is of known family (Davies (1971) 12444). The exact function of the *kurōtēs* is not clear, although the term occurs in a similar context at ii² 1678 A 27. For the translation of *apographein* as 'denounce' see Finley (1952B) 474–5 and n. 3.
2. For the quarry lease see chapter 5.
3. By Meritt in *Hesperia* 5 (1936) 393ff. It is a further part of ii² 1582.
4. Cf. e.g. Rhodes (1981A) 559; Harrison (1971) 293 n. 1; MacDowell (1978) 167 n. 380.
5. The records of *apographe* cases follow no regular formula. In this case the name of the debtor appears after the description of the property, in the following case it appears before it; only in the case of Philistides' first contract here is the date of the contract recorded; the phrase *metaskhonta telous* (with genitive) is omitted for Philistides' part in the 5-dr. tax in the mines although included with all the other similar contracts; Meixidemos is said to be in debt to τῶι δημοσίωι τῶι Ἀθηναίων, Nikodemos in the following case simply τῶι δημοσίωι. All of these little variations indicate that the stone records the cases more or less in the form in which those involved presented them. This is still more clear in the earlier case, which preserves elements of direct speech: see Finley (1952B) 478 and n. 9.
6. *Amphiktyon, BCH* 8 (1884) 295; *tamias:* ii² 1627.73.
7. The *amphiktyons* may have been elected partly by tribe, see Arist. *Ath. Pol.* 62.2 with Rhodes (1981) ad loc. It is not clear how the *tamias* of the *trieropoïka* was chosen, see D. 22.17, 20 and Rhodes (1972) 121–2.
8. He might be related to Meixias the *antigrapheus* in the deme decree of the middle of the fourth century (ii² 1182.24).
9. ii² 2385 col. 1 10.
10. Mining lease: Crosby (1950) no. 14.15

11. A stone reading Σίμος κατέλαβε Ἀσκαληπιακόν was discovered in a room in the complex in the Soureza valley recently excavated by Conophagos. See Lauffer in Conophagos (1980) 388 no. 1 and *AAA* 12 (1979) 15–23.
12. See Judeich (1931) 441 nn. 3–4; the relevant inscriptions are ii² 47 (see chapter 5 for the quarry involved), ii² 4962 and ii² 4453.
13. *ADelt* 28B1 (1973) 46–8, and chapter 5.
14. Cf. ii² 2498.
15. Hypothesis to D. 25. M.H. Hansen, *Apagoge, endeixis and epheaesis* (Odense, 1976) 144ff. has argued that this speech is genuinely Demosthenic.
16. The accepted text of D. 53.2 declares that men who denounced property for confiscation received three-quarters of something. Harrison (1971) 212 and MacDowell (1978) 166 assume that they get three-quarters of the price fetched by the property, Finley (1952B) 478 is more doubtful. Osborne (forthcoming) argues, partly on the basis of this case, that those who made denunciations frequently received nothing, and never received more than one-third.
17. D. 53.2 (to the public treasury); ii² 1631.365–8 (to victim).
18. Comparison with the known value of *sunoikiai* is not very helpful: in D. 45.28 a *sunoikia* is stated to be worth 10,000 dr., while in D. 53.13 another supports a mortgage of 1,600 dr. (it may have been worth much more). The restoration of συνοικία καὶ ἐσχατιά in line 9 of the preceding inscription in *Hesperia* 5 must be considered doubtful, see Pritchett, *CPh.* 51 (1956) 102 n. 9.
19. ii² 360 (*SIG*³ 304), on which see chapter 4.
20. ii² 3207.25f. with Kirchner ad loc.
21. See Osborne (1983), on Athen. 407d–408a.
22. ii² 4355, 4960–1.
23. If Hermolokhos was a wandering metic then the *Odyssey* might have provided the name for his son.
24. This case is complicated by the fact that not only are Aphidna, Oinoe and Rhamnous all demes in the same area of Attika but all are in the tribe Aiantis, and it is against the tribe that Nikodemos has committed his offence. It is not possible to distinguish between tribal solidarity and local factors as motivating forces for the actors. The only figure otherwise known is Nikokrates, the purchaser, who belongs to a family with prominent grave monuments at Rhamnous (*Praktika* (1978) 9–15).
25. Note that the property of Theosebes is next to a Daidaleion. The other neighbour is Philippos of the deme Agryle which adjoined Alopeke. Of the two *klētēres* one, Diogeiton, is from Alopeke, and the other, Philoitios from Ionidai, the deme of Theomnestos. Two

217

of the creditors have no local connection (Smikythos of Teithras (cf. Lykomedes Smikythou of Teithras, *Hesperia* 33 (1964) 209.9), and Diogeiton of Gargettos with the Medontidai), a third, who claims the expense of burying Theosebes' father, is a demesman of Xypete, and the fourth, Aiskhines of Melite and the *koinon* of the *orgeones* may or may not have a local link. The purchaser comes from Lakiadai, a deme on the other side of the city.

26. ii² 1631.288–325 (cf. ii² 1623.218–33, 1628.620–41, 1629.1088–1132), with Davies (1971) 3568.
27. See Harrison (1971) 74ff.
28. *The Greek gift: politics in a Cypriot village* (1975).
29. Cf. Radcliffe-Brown (1940). The idea is incorporated into Cherry's complex definition (1978, 411) and perhaps stems from Weber.
30. Note that the prosecutor in cases of violence had a say in the assessment of the penalty. In the context of such a situation talk of the 'legal supremacy of the state' (cf. Ehrenberg (1969) 21) is at least misleading.
31. Cf. Finley (1963) 37, Starr (1965) 208.
32. E.g. it seriously obscures the fact that the majority of Athenians lived outside the *astu*, and that it was important that they did so.
33. Cf. Murray (1980) where 'the city of Athens' is used on p. 176 of the *astu*, but on p. 261, 'the Peisistratidai left in the city were suspect', 'city' is used for the polis as a whole, and 'in Athens itself the victory gave the democracy a new self-confidence' uses 'Athens itself' of the whole polis.
34. Cf. Geertz (1980) 121. For the importance that is attached to the equation of polis and state cf. Renfrew in Renfrew and Wagstaff (1982) 280 'there is no reason to doubt that these cities of the classical Aegean were indeed states'; and compare the evolutionism inherent in talk of 'The rise of the Greek state' (cf. Snodgrass (1977)), and in the statements of Ehrenberg (1969) 19, 21. For a critique of such evolutionism see Clastres (1977).
35. Cf. Soph. *OT* 50ff., Thuc. 7.77.
36. Loraux (1981A).
37. Cf. Cherry (1978) 411.
38. Skinner (1978) 254. The idea of separation is fundamental not only to early modern political theory but also to much recent sociopolitical theory.
39. Cf. the criticisms of Robinson (1962) 9–10.
40. Aristotle himself was certainly aware of the gap between theory and practice: see *Pol.* 1292b11ff., and chapter 4.
41. For the importance of *euthunai* see chapter 4, and Arist. *Pol.* 1298a–b.
42. The commentary of Friis Johansen and Whittle (1980) vol. 3, 60 on this passage reveals how difficult it is to conceive of

Aiskhylos' point: 'By the addition of *arkha* . . . it becomes clear that by *to demion* one should, at least mainly, think of the executive power in Argos . . . '
43. On this law see Manville (1980).
44. For the terminology here cf. Skinner (1978) 352.
45. Cf. Ehrenberg (1969) 75—6 on religion: 'Religion was not independent of the state, but neither was the state independent of religion . . . Between the Polis and its god there was a definite legal relationship, which imposed serious obligations on the state.'
46. Cf. Xen. *Poroi* 1.
47. For the gradual adoption of the demotic see Raubitschek (1949) 474—6.
48. For the practical reality of these ties even in the late fourth century see chapter 3.
49. See Davies (1971). Without Davies' work in this field this work would not have been a practical proposition.
50. Cf. especially Traill (1975). For the degree of debate remaining in this field cf. Siewert (1982).
51. Haussoullier (1884).
52. Compare the conclusions of chapter 4 with Haussoullier's claims that (a) the rich ran the demes; and (b) the demes were the schools in which those intending to be active in the assembly and in central offices learnt their trade.
53. Compare the work of Eliot, Traill, McCredie and the other pupils of Vanderpool represented in Vanderpool (1982). A quite separate school of investigation of Attika centres on Professor Hans Lauter of the University of Bochum.
54. See chapter 2.
55. Cf. Humphreys (1978) 134: 'Classical Athens and Hellenistic Alexandria — cities comparable in size, density and level of economic specialization — may serve to represent the ideal types of urban—rural continuum and urban—rural dichotomy'; Snodgrass (1977) 18 'In a successful polis, town and country were equal and complementary partners in the state. It is the failure to match this achievement which has bedevilled almost all advanced cultures before and since, including our own.'

2. The pattern of settlement of classical Attika

1. Thuc. 2.15; Philokh. *FGH* 328 F 94; Arist. *Pol.* 1252b17. On Attic *sunoikismos* see chapter 4.
2. Detienne (1963) 20, cf. 27.
3. Hes. *Works* 639f., cf. 493f. On the site of Askra see *AR* (1981—2) 27, Snodgrass (forthcoming).

4. Grote (1851) vol. 3, 93; vol. 6, 172; Murray (1980) 183f.; Snodgrass (1980) 144 but cf. 34.

5. Scattered settlement: Kotzias (1925) 172, Kondis (1967) 163; villages: Bradford (1956) 180, Kirsten (1952) 1002, Eliot (1962) 75; villages and farms: Jones (1975) 100, Lauter (1980) 279, Lauter (1982) 313. Compare also the cautious remarks of Pečirka (1973) 121.

6. (1973) 133 with n. 1.

7. Thuc. 2.14—16; Arist. *Ath. Pol.* 24.1.

8. Cf. section 41.

9. D. 53.4, 16, 15. Paley and Sandys ad loc. regard the nursery and rose garden as a commercial venture, but there is no positive evidence either way.

10. D. 55.23f. If the barley was for human consumption it would feed a family for no more than a month (Kuenen-Janssens (1941), Forbes and Foxhall (1982)). The offending wall is said to have been built to prevent trespassers grazing their animals on the *khōrion* (55.11, 23), which would hardly be a problem if there were a residence on the land.

11. Lys. 17.8. For discussions of the *poletai* inscriptions see chapters 1 and 3; for mining see chapter 5.

12. The Platonic easements are closely modelled on those ascribed to Solon by Plutarch (Plut. *Solon* 23.5f.). That the latter are genuinely Solonic, or at least archaic, is suggested by their use of the otherwise unattested *hippikon* as a unit of measurement. The Solonic regulations about getting water from neighbours seem to be designed to *enable* isolated land to be farmed, although the low limit on the amount of water that can be claimed from a neighbour would seem to preclude permanent isolated residence. See further below p. 38.

13. On this aspect see Dover (1975) 112—14 and Humphreys (1978) 133, who give further references.

14. Laertes' dwelling in isolation seems to mark the way in which he has become a social outcast. In the idealised landscapes of Phaeacia and of the shield of Akhilleus there seem to be no isolated farms, and creatures which do live in isolation (the Kyklops, Kirke) are inhuman and antisocial.

15. Xen. *Oik.* 11.15f.; Higgins (1977) 36.

16. See Finley (1952A) 60 and n. 45.

17. i^3 427.70.

18. Ar. *Pol.* 1258b 18, D. 20.115; i^3 427.72.

19. Bad for hunting: Xen. *Kyn.* 5.18, Arr. *Kyn.* 17.4; grazed: Ar. *Clouds* 71.

20. (1973) 210—12.

21. *Hesperia* 5 (1936) no. 10 p. 403 lines 186—8.

22. Antiphanes fr. 21 Kock; Lys. 12.18; D. 18.129.

23. Other terms are from time to time translated 'farm' but none of these prove any more attractive as isolated farmsteads. E.g. LSJ gives 'farm' as a meaning of *katoikia* in Polybius, but in fact he seems always to use the term of villages (cf. Walbank (1957) 605).

24. The *Heros* is set at Ptelea, the *Sikyonios* at Eleusis, and the *Epitrepontes* in an unknown deme (for which see Gomme and Sandbach (1973) 290.

25. The archaeological evidence for isolated farms has been reviewed by the investigators of the Dema House (*ABSA* 57 (1962) 102 n. 29) and by Pečirka (1973) 133f. Appendix A aims to give a complete list of classical isolated farms that have appeared in published accounts.

26. Eliot (1962) 25–46; Lauter (1982) 311–13.

27. In the literature the names Mikro and Megalo Kavouri have sometimes been confused. The correct current usage applies Mikro Kavouri to the narrow peninsula projecting south, and Megalo Kavouri to the more substantial promontory jutting out west.

28. *ADelt* 11 (1927/8) 9–53, *AEph* (1938) 1–31, *ADelt* 16B (1960) 40.

29. *AEph* (1938) 1ff., esp. 6 n. 1.

30. *AEph.* (1953/4) C. 327, 341, 343.

31. J.N. Coldstream, *Greek geometric pottery: a survey of ten local styles and their chronology* (London, 1968) 399–403; BSA Sherd Collection A15 (3).

32. *ADelt* 19B1 (1964) 72

33. Eliot (1962) 32ff., *AA* 58 (1943) 804f., *Polemon* 1 (1929) 172, 4 (1949) 138, *ADelt* 22B (1967) 134f.; *ADelt* 24B1 (1969) 89f.; *ADelt* 29B1 (1974) 60ff., 105f., 158ff.; *AR* (1979–80) 14f.; Lauter (1982) 313.

34. Papagiannopoulos, *Polemon* 4 (1949–50) 138; Eliot (1962) 32

35. BSA Sherd collection A15 (2). These sherds include the handle and rim of a Koan amphora; part of a fish-plate close to Sparkes and Talcott (1970) no. 1072 (dated by them to 350–25) (cf. *ABSA* 68 (1973) 380 no. 43); part of a plate close to Sparkes and Talcott (1970) no. 1060 (dated by them to 350–25, and part of Thompson's Group A); and a foot not closely parallel to anything in Sparkes and Talcott (1970) but more similar to no. 445 (dated by them to early fifth century) than to anything else. The measurements were made on visits to the site on 29 May and 22 June 1981. The site has been separately discovered by the Lauters, whose publication has been held up by the Greek Archaeological Service investigation. They agree with my dating (*per epist.*, Lauter (1982) 311).

36. See table 2, below.

37. See in general Eliot (1962) 37–46. For the tombs: Wrede (1933) 36, 98f., *ADelt* 7 (1891) 28ff., 21B (1966) 95f., 29B1 (1974) 108; *Praktika* (1920) 38–43; *AM* 13 (1888) 360ff.

38. Wrede (1933) 36f.; *AA* 52 (1937) 122, 50 (1935) 172–5, 51 (1936) 123f., 54 (1939) 224f., 55 (1940) 126f., 175f.; *BCH* 61 (1937) 450f., 82 (1958) 672; Karouzou (1963); *ADelt* 17B (1961) 37, 18A (1963) 115f., 20B1 (1965) 112f., 21B (1966) 106; Humphreys (1980) 108f.

39. McCredie (1966) 29, *AM* 94 (1979) 161–92, *AA* 55 (1940) 177f., *Praktika* (1920) 41, Lauter (1982) 312 and n. 67.

40. The remains on the summit seem insufficiently monumental to mark a Peloponnesian War refuge (as Eliot (1962) 42 and Lauter-Bufé (1979) suggest). There seems nothing distinctly out of keeping with a religious site.

41. Milchhoeffer (1889) 15, *AEph* (1965) 163–7, *ADelt* 19B1 (1964) 72, Lauter (1982) 313 n. 71, autopsy 22 June 1981.

42. *ADelt* 22B (1967) 136f., *ABSA* 68 (1973) 355–452, Eliot (1962) 43f., Lauter (1980A) 279–86.

43. *ABSA* 68 (1973) 397–414; to Jones' list of find-spots of coarse *kalathoi* should be added the Philaidai deme site (appendix B) where a number of fragments (including an extension ring) were ploughed up.

44. Lauter (1982) 282. Lauter does not illustrate the material, and does not cite parallel pieces.

45. Eliot (1962) 43f., and figs. 3D and E.

46. Lauter (1982) for the inscription. For the idea that this *horos* marks the boundary of the deme see below p. 41f.: it is not impossible in the hellenistic period, but highly improbable in the classical. ii^2 2617–19, *horoi* of the Kerameikos, are hardly boundaries of the deme, which was called Kerameis (ii^2 2362.58, Harpokration s.v.). On all this see Wycherley (1957) 221–3. Lauter's interpretation of the Thiti inscriptions is very close to that given independently by Traill in Vanderpool (1982) 162–71, but that does not make it any more likely to be correct. For hellenistic farmsteads see below p. 31 (Poundazesa) and appendix A.

47. *MIGRA* 1 (1975) 45–54; *Thorikos* I–VII passim.; *BCH* 85 (1961) 176ff.; *Hesperia* 29 (1960) 339–43, 371–3, 30 (1961) 299–304; Dilettanti (1817) 57–9; *ADelt* 6 (1890) 159–61, 8 (1892) 27, 19B1 (1964) 80–6; *AEph* (1895) 221ff.; *Praktika* (1897) 12ff.

48. Milchhoeffer (1889) 28, *Hesperia* 10 (1941) 168, *ADelt* 19B1 (1964) 73, *AAA* 9 (1976) 24–43.

49. Milchhoeffer (1889) 28; *Hesperia* 10 (1941) 168f., 178f., 171f., 190; *PAA* (1959) 259–63; *Ann. Géol. Pays Hell.* (1959) 137–49; *Hesperia* suppl. 19 (1982) 193–8. Remains indicative of a temple suggested to Young (1941) 163–91 that this is the Porthmos of the Salaminioi inscription, *SEG* 21.527.

50. Milchhoeffer (1889) 28; *Hesperia* 10 (1941) 167, 171, 181; *AM* 62 (1937) 6; *ADelt* 17B (1961) 35, 19B1 (1964) 73; Conophagos (1980) 398.
51. In general: Oikonomides (1957), Dinsmoor (1971); fort: *BCH* 88 (1964) 423–32; *heroon*: Picard (1940) 5–28, Abramson (1980); ship-sheds: *ABSA* 42 (1947) 196ff., *ADelt* 24B1 (1969) 89–91.
52. Conophagos (1980) is the latest survey of the mining remains and of the processes involved. It includes a report on his own washery excavation. For the other washery excavation see *Ant. Class.* 45 (1976) 149ff.; *AR* (1977–8) 13–15, (1978–9) 6–7, (1979–80) 17–19, (1981–2) 12–13.
53. Young (1956) 122–46.
54. *ABSA* 68 (1973) 448f., *MIGRA* 1 (1973) 136.
55. *Hesperia* 46 (1977) 162–77, Waelkens (1982), Wickens (1983). This is the only fully published field wall from Attika and is of little use for calculation of agricultural potential. Lauter (1981) claims firm farm boundaries on a site in the Kharaka valley.
56. Young provides a modern equivalent of Timesios in the Laurion butcher Tsimboukis, who owned some land in the Sounion area but 'the stones so discouraged Tsimboukis that he no longer lives there; the farm is left in charge of the guardian-shepherd, Yorgis, . . . ' (1941) 174 n. 31.
57. See pl. 1, which presents the view east from the Cliff Top Tower.
58. Above n. 55. Note that the property in D. 55 is walled (its location within Attika is unknown).
59. The quotations are from Young (1956) 142.
60. The inscription was found in the upper Agrileza valley and since it was to be set up in the (new) agora the presumption is that that agora was in the upper Agrileza valley. This assumption is strengthened by the fact that the land for the agora is given by one Leukios, known from mining leases to have had land in Nape, Nape being plausibly sited in the Agrileza valley (*SEG* 12.100.46,80). However, the stone might have been moved from its original location by the nineteenth-century mining railway which passed close to the find-spot. Close and reliable dating for all the agora remains in Sounion would throw much light on the development of the deme.
61. Kakovogiannis (1982).
62. *SEG* 26.136
63. Dinsmoor (1971).
64. Cf. (with Lewis) i³ 130, 133. For the festival cf. Herodotos 6.87.
65. *Hesperia* 7 (1938) 1–74, 10 (1941) 163–91.
66. The geography of the area produced several different havens for shipping. For Sounion as harbour cf. Thuc. 8.4, Xen. *Hell.* 5.1.23, as well as i³ 8.
67. Cf. Eliot (1962) 75, Traill (1975) 73f., 101f.
68. *Hesperia* 5 (1936) no. 10 p. 402 line 155.

69. Smith in Ucko, Tringham and Dimbleby (1972) 409f., Wagstaff (1965).
70. Pečirka (1970), (1973) 140–7, Pečirka and Dufkova (1970) for the area of the Black Sea; Adamesteanu in Finley (1973A) 49–61 and Carter (1981) for Metaponto.
71. For Argolid and Karystos: oral communications from Curtis Runnels and Donald Keller at the Conference on Archaeological Survey in the Mediterranean, Athens, June 1981; Boiotia: Cambridge and Bradford Boiotia survey.
72. Gallant (1982).
73. For the easements see above n. 12. For a discussion of water resources and their effect on settlement pattern see Pečirka (1973) 116ff., and now also J.M. Wagstaff, *The development of rural settlement: a study of the Helos Plain in southern Greece* (1982) ch. 1.
74. The only soil map of Attika is that of Zvorykin and Saul (1948), and this analysis perforce uses the somewhat dated soil categories which that employs. Geological maps are only available for the southern tip: Marinos and Petrascheck (1956), reprinted in Conophagos (1980) and modified by the Thorikos team (*Thorikos* IV, 7–53 (with maps), VI, 73–127).
75. Deme locations here generally follow Traill (1975) 37–53, but Araphen has been considered unknown (cf. appendix B s.v. Kioupia). Moving Hekale would not affect the soil issue.
76. Johnson (1977) 490.
77. Amphitrope, Besa, Deiradiotai, Eitea (whichever was at Grammatiko, see *ADelt* 25A (1970) 204–16, Bicknell (1978)), Eupyridai, Hekale, Korydallos, Kolonai, Pelekes, Phyle, Rhamnous, Sounion.
78. For the importance of the sea cf. Xen. *Poroi* 1.3, and the presence of fishing boats off the west coast of Attika in Xen. *Hell.* 5.1.19–24, Polyain. *Strat.* 6.2.2. For a modern discussion see Hopper (1961) 202. The importance of fishing is never likely to have been more than marginal: see Gallant (1981).
79. For this location: Thompson (1970A) 64f.; against it: Bicknell (1978).
80. The deme is located on the evidence of Milchhoeffer (1883) 11f., and I have not been able to check the nature of the remains or the reliability of the evidence.
81. Xen. *Oik.* 20.12. Theophrastus not only has a rich vocabulary of terms for the saltiness of soils (ἁλμή/ἁλμῶδης. ἁλμυρά/ ἁλμυρώδης), but he shows a specific concern with how to overcome the problems that a salty soil can bring: cf. e.g. *CP* 3.6.3.
82. The remote Skourta plain was pasture for Athenian as well as Boiotian shepherds, Thuc. 5.42.1; D. 47. 52f. implies pasturing off a man's own land; ii^2 2498 suggests that some coastal areas near

the Peiraieus were pasture. In 1961 some 400 square kilometres of Attika were classified as pasture, but it is not at all unlikely that much of this land was cultivated in the classical period, when up to about 50% of Attika might conceivably have been under some sort of cultivation.

83. Cf. Chisholm (1962) for a classic statement of the position.

84. See Davis (1969); Finley (1973B) 127 claims that peasants are ruled by the principle of least effort, but Garner (in Chorley and Haggett (1967)), whom he quotes as authority for this, knows that the situation is more complex.

85. E.g. Eretria had a system of demes and districts, but the demes do not seem to have been fundamental to a man's identity: only one demotic appears on a grave stele. See Wallace (1947).

86. See the review of the evidence in Raubitschek (1949) 467–79, with Bicknell (1972) for city demes.

87. Cf. also the fact that non-demesmen holding land in a deme were taxed: ii^2 1214.26.

88. Military recruits: Lys. 31.15, cf. 20.23, 16.13; court: D. 52.28; loans: D. 35.6, 10. Such examples could be considerably multiplied.

89. For the fifth-century evidence see Davies (1979); for the fourth century see Meritt and Traill (1974), Traill (1975).

90. For an argument that most Athenians retained a strong tie with the ancestral village even in the fourth century see chapter 3. It is arguable that the Kleisthenic system would have become unworkable if any substantial number of demesmen had severed their ties with their deme of origin.

91. The model populations used have not always been well chosen. Gomme (1933) appears to use a model based on recent, post-industrial, European demography (see his appendix C), while Ruschenbusch (1979A, B, 1981) and Rhodes (1980) both adopt one based on European statistics from 1750 to 1880. Patterson (1981) uses the same model as that adopted here, but weakens her case (a) by errors (e.g. taking over Gomme's figure of $\frac{1}{7}$ of the population being urban, a figure based on bouleutic quotas and including such demes as Piraieus and Phaleron, and using it to calculate the density of population within the Themistoklean wall . . .) and (b) by some far-fetched demography (especially her basic idea that a population growth of 1% per annum would not be possible naturally, which should be contrasted with Snodgrass (1977, 1980) postulating an annual growth of 4% in the archaic period).

92. Hopkins (1966).

93. There also seem to have been some 250 'alternates' available each year (Traill (1981)), but since there is no evidence that a man who was an *epilakhōn* but not called on to serve could not

subsequently still do his two full terms these men do not affect the calculations.

94. 15,300 are required if a life expectancy of thirty is assumed.
95. Rhodes (1972, 1980).
96. Lewis (1955) makes the quoted remark in a discussion of *diaitetai*.
97. Reinmuth's claim (1971, 126) that Aristotle says that all citizens had to have been ephebes seems to be based on an insufficiently close reading of the text.
98. See Rhodes (1972, 1980, 1981B) for the known examples.
99. Phythian-Adams (1979) 9.
100. For subjective judgments cf. Day (1942) 12f. Thompson's calculations (1970C) are vitiated by the dubious nature of his criterion of wealth, and his failure to take population into account.
101. Counting on this basis seems to be justified by Davies' findings on the mobility of wealth (1981, 73–88).

3. The pattern of land-holding in classical Attika

1. See Johnson in Lechtman and Merrill (1977).
2. Cf. Salviat and Vatin (1974) for the Larissa area in the hellenistic period (with V. Milojoic and D. Theocharis, eds., *Demetrias I* (1976) 157–73.)
3. For a general account of Attic property-holding drawn from literary sources see Davies (1981). Confiscated property lists: Attic Stelai, see Pritchett (1953, 1956), Amyx (1958) and Lewis (1966); property confiscated from the Thirty, Walbank (1982). For the *hekatostai* inscriptions see Andreyev (1960, 1967, 1974) and Lewis (1973). For the *horoi* see Fine (1951), Finley (1952) and Millett (1982).
4. On the Cliff Top Tower see above chapter 2 (p. 32 with n. 56). The extensive Hymettos terraces seen by Bradford (1956; 1957, 29–34) do not enable any conclusions to be drawn about size of holding.
5. This is brought out by the case of Alkibiades' land: on the basis of Plato, *1 Alk.* 123c Alkibiades would be though to have only a large estate at Erkhia, on that of Lysias 19.52 property worth 100 talents; the Attic Stelai show that he also had land in his own deme, Skambonidai (stele 4 (i³ 424) 24–30).
6. Two *oikiai* (Is. 10.23; D. 41.6, 16, 19), a *sunoikia* (D. 53. 15) and an *oikidion* (D. 59. 39) are the most likely.
7. For Dikaiogenes see Is. 5. 11, 29. For Lysimakhos see Davies (1971) 51. The other two owners are the Bouselids (Is. 11) and Timotheos (D. 49. 6, 11, 26).
8. For Kikynna and the slightly problematic Sphettos see appendix B.

9. Aiskh. 1. 97f. The house ὄπισθεν τῆς πόλεως is later described as ἐν ἄστει, and polis is presumably being used here of the akropolis (cf. Thuc. 2.15.6 and Gomme (1956) ad loc.).
10. Thompson's rather speculative reconstruction is at (1976) 47–52.
11. Stratokles' property includes *oikiai* at Eleusis and Melite; Euktemon and Dikaiogenes both have one house, and Kiron two houses, in the *astu*. Timarkhos has the house by the akropolis and Timotheos a house in the Peiraieus.
12. In the plain of Athens: Euktemon at Athmonon, Kiron at Phlya, Timarkhos at Kephisia and Alopeke, Timotheos 'in the plain'. In the Mesogaia: the speaker of Lys. 17 at Kikynna and Sphettos, Timarkhos at Sphettos. Compare the estate of Alkibiades at Erkhia (n. 5).
13. For deme liturgies see Wyse (1904) 267, Davies (1971) xxiii; for Aristophanes see Lys. 19, and for the wealthy family into which he married Davies (1971) 200f.
14. See Lewis (1966).
15. We know that Pherekles of Themakos owned a house there since this is where the profanation of the Mysteries took place (Andok. 1.13) but this does not figure in the Attic Stelai as extant. This is one of a handful of cases where we know of an individual's property from more than one source, and where the method adopted here is slightly misleading (cf. n. 5). Besides his house at Ankyle Polystratos has others in Kydathenaion and at Mounykhia, and half a *gēpedon* by the walls (stele 4 (i³ 424) 5ff.).
16. Stele 10 (i³ 430) 14–19, stele 6. (i³ 426) 88: houses at Semakhidai and an unknown location, *khōria* at Gargettos and Aphidna, and a *khōrion*, *kēpos* and *oikia* at Myrrhinoutta. For the location of Myrrhinoutta see Vanderpool (1965); for Semakhidai see Bicknell (1978).
17. A house at Bate, an *oikopedon* by the Pythion, *khōria* at Bate, by the Lan . . ., by the Pythion, and by the Herakleion, and an *orgas* half at the Pythion and half 'in Kukale'. Pythion without qualification ought to refer to that near the Ilissos, despite Milchhoeffer (1892) 35f., *AM* 18 (1893) 302 who wanted to put the whole property near Marathon.
18. Stele 7 (i³ 427) 72–7: these items of agricultural land, some arable, some vineyards, fetch very high prices.
19. Stele 7 (i³ 427) 23–6, 33f.
20. One man, the son of Diodoros of ?Eitea, appears to have had only one item, a house at Kollytos (stele 6 (i³ 426) 13–15.
21. See Arist. *Ath. Pol.* 47.2, and Harrison (1971) 178–9.
22. Walbank (1982).
23. The long fourth-century inscription ii² 1582 + *Hesperia* 5 (1936) no. 10. The cases of property confiscation are in part of the portion

published in *Hesperia* (cf. above, chapter 1). The third-century inscription was published as *Hesperia* 4 (1935) no. 41 with some rather adventurous restoration. Crosby (1950) no. 14 includes a fragmentary record of two sales of confiscated property, but no details are recoverable.

24. Some of the uncertainty in the figures arises from the possible consequences of accepting Walbank's view that the demarkhs are responsible for all the registrations of confiscated property in the 402/1 cases.

25. *Hesperia* 5 (1936) pp. 393ff., no. 10, lines 120f., 156; ii² 1579.3.

26. For Philokrates' condemnation see Hypereides 4.29; D. 19. 116ff.; Aiskhin. 2.6, 3.79–81; Dein. 1.28. For the confiscation see *Hesperia* 5 (1936) pp. 393ff., no. 10, lines 10–73. (Through the kindness of David Lewis I have been able to consult his revised reading of this text.) The list of properties opens with a [χωρίον κ]αὶ οἰκίαν at Hagnous, which like the second item, ἕτερο[ν χωρίον] has on one border a property described as ...]αττος Μυρ[. Lewis believes this to be an ... attos at Myrrhinous, but it might be the property of one ... attos of Myrrhinous. Since the first property, at least, is certainly itself in Hagnous the latter interpretation is perhaps simpler. The third item is another *khōrion,* which is next to a *temenos* and bought by a man from Kydathenaion. Item four is bounded on two sides by an Artemision, on a third by land of the Eikadeis and on a fourth by ... attos. Item five is another *khōrion,* but no details are preserved that are any help with its location — we have one owner's name (Kleon, possibly to be associated with the deme of Kydathenaion and thus perhaps with the purchaser of item three) and mention of a road and perhaps a παγος. Item six includes an *eskhatia,* an *oikia* and more besides; it is next to the land of the Eikadeis and to land owned by a man from Paiania. From the various elements that are repeated it becomes clear that Philokrates' holding was certainly fragmented but the fragments were on the whole fairly close together and they were all in the deme. Myrrhinous is now firmly placed by cemetery finds, and the settlement may lie east of the cemeteries, where the cutting of a new track has revealed a heavy scatter of classical sherds and possibly some ancient blocks, in an area some 500 m east along the track from the pumping station (autopsy, 6 May 1981). The precise location of Hagnous is less certain: the evidence for placing it at Dankla is insufficient (Milchhoeffer (1889) 10f.) and material recently found at Markopoulo may reflect the position of the settlement more accurately (*ADelt* 26B1 (1971) 38; *AAA* 4 (1971) 143–6; *BCH* 96 (1972) 611, 75 (1951) 111). For Hipponikos see Davies (1971) 269.

27. Pp. 10–15.

28. Aresaikhmos: Davies (1971) 12888A. Meletos' name is fully preserved at Walbank (1982) stele II, 17ff.; it may be restored at stele III, 3f., but see Walbank's commentary.

29. The most recent survey of the Attic leases is by Behrend (1970) who is mainly interested in the legal questions. To his collection must now be added the Eleusis quarry lease (below) and the leases of religious property to which Walbank has recently added new fragments, Walbank (1983). Local information is sparse in these new fragments, and hence although they offer scope for more or less plausible speculation they have not been considered in detail here.

30. *REG* 91 (1978) 289f.

31. Peiraieus theatre: ii^2 1176.32f.; Teithras property: *AM* 49 (1924) 4, no. 2; Rarian field: ii^2 1672.253.

32. The demesmen were pleased enough with the deal done over the theatre to honour Theaios 'who made the theatre fetch 300 dr. more' (ii^2 1176.25ff.). The *ergasterion* at Peiraieus is in ii^2 2496, a lease notable for the fact that the surety is the lessee's father.

33. Pleket (1964) 43. 11–16. Any building has to be removed at the end of the lease.

34. Dyaleis lease: ii^2 1241; Aixone lease: ii^2 2492.

35. On Moirokles see further below, chapter 4 n. 44. Diodoros of Myrrhinous might be another example, but we cannot be sure that the man in the Dyaleis lease and the man acquiring property in the *hekatostai* inscription are one and the same (ii^2 1241, 1601a).

36. See Davies (1971) 67f., 160, 517–20. The entry for Diopeithes of Sphettos misses the reference to his renting activity.

37. For claims about the traditional and patriarchal character of property leasing see Andreyev (1967).

38. The first suggestion was made by Andreyev, the second (very tentatively) by Lewis, and the third by Humphreys (1978, 289 n. 18).

39. Andok. 1.134 makes it clear that the *poletai* auctioned off taxes, and although Aristotle (*Ath. Pol.* 47) is not explicit about it it is almost certain that confiscated property was also auctioned. The demes certainly used the auction: *REG* 92 (1978) 289ff. lines 23f.; i^3 84; ii^2 334, 1241; Pleket (1964) 25.

40. ii^2 1597.15ff., and probably ii^2 1598B.17ff., 1603.27–32. See Lewis (1973) 194f.

41. For 8% (or thereabouts) see Is. 11.42 (2 cases) and ii^2 2496 (if the *eisphora* assessment is realistic). But ii^2 1241 seems to attest a rent of either 12% or 5.36% (Behrend (1970) 118f.).

42. The terminology of sales (ὠνητής, ἀποδίδεσθαι) is used, but so it is regularly in leases, see Harrison (1968) 203 n. 1, 234 n. 2.

43. Lewis has shown that the stelai all refer to one occasion, and

believes that dates under Lykourgos, Antipater, or Demetrios are equally possible. My impression is that the prosopographical data favour an earlier rather than a later date, and thus more, rather than less, normal circumstances. The inscriptions could be the result of a decision, on some religious pretext, to have demes pay one-eighth of their income from new leases for one year over to a sacred fund, a decision which might be coupled with a drive to get demes to lease out more land. The particular circumstances materially affect the question of whether the information about property acquisition given here is representative.

44. Lewis suggests 2 columns per stele and not many more than 20 entries per column (p. 191). In total 130 entries are preserved, 63 with price.

45. Lessees from the same deme acquire eighteen *khōria*, seven *eskhatiai*, two *khōria* and *oikopeda*, one *oikia* and . . . , and one *kēpos*; non-local men acquire five *khōria*, four *eskhatiai*, and one *khōrion* and *oikia*; neighbouring demesmen acquire six *khōria* and one *eskhatia*.

46. Phrynaios' son from Athmonon, Karkinos and Mantitheos of Thorikos, Philippos of Halai Aixonides, Nikias of Xypete, Kharias of Pallene, and Nikokles of Kydantidai. For all these men see further Davies (1971).

47. Phrynaios' son buys land at Prasiai, and Nikias of Xypete land in the neighbouring deme of Phaleron.

48. For Diodoros of Myrrhinous see n. 35 above; Diophantos and Thymokhares of Sphettos and Diokles of Sounion all have mining interests. Of the rest (Blepyros of Teithras, Eukles Lakleous, Polykrates, Drakontides and Molottos of Aphidna, and Mnesimakhos of Kothokidai) even the least certainly wealthy were of hoplite status (Molottos was *diaitetes*, Mnesimakhos ephebe).

49. The cases are ii^2 1594B.42, 1598A.16, 20–3, 1601.27f.

50. Auctions may not lead to the highest bidder taking the property, see Arist. *Ath. Pol.* 47.2.

51. A 50-drachma property at Aphidna goes to a son of Drakontides of Aphidna, descendant of one of the Thirty and probably to be identified with Euthykrates the *epistatēs proedriōn* in 337/6 and *epimeletēs* of the Mysteries in 329/8 (ii^2 242.5, 243.5, 1672.244); a 50-drachma *khōrion* at Pallene goes to the son of the propertied Kharias (Davies (1971) 243). That these small plots pass to men of means suggests that the plots were not the product of artificial division (contrast Lewis (1966) 197). There are certainly some very large lots: a property at Rhamnous fetches 20,000 dr.

52. Recent *horoi* are now collected and discussed in Millett (1982). For the purposes of this analysis it makes no difference whether

the property was used as collateral or substitutive security, and no distinction has been made here between *horoi* for *apotimema* transactions and those for *hypotheke* and *prasis epi lusei*.

53. Fifty-eight cases of land and house(s), fifty-three of land alone, forty-five of house alone, five of the next largest category — *ergasteria* with or without slaves.
54. For the kudos of having a house at Eleusis cf. D. 21.158.
55. Xenophon (*Poroi* 4.50) says land near the city is particularly valuable. *Khōroi* in this text surely includes agricultural land, and this would explain the contrast with *Poroi* 2.6 which worried Finley (1952, 253 n. 50). Aristotle (*Pol.* 1319a6ff.) also suggests that land prices were enhanced near the city. For a more complex case cf. D.S. 12.9.2, 12.11.1.
56. Phainippos' *eskhatia* at Kytherros had no *horoi* but was clearly a major part of his land (D. 42.5, 28, with de Sainte Croix (1966)).
57. n. 26 above. Compare the estates of Pherekles (n. 17) and the anonymous figure with Athmonon interests (n. 19).
58. A suggestion reinforced by the number of (marginal) *eskhatiai* in the *hekatostai* inscriptions, and by the possibility that those inscriptions include land leased for the first time (above n. 43).
59. Cf. intra-deme solidarity: e.g. D. 35.6,10, 43.37f., 57.10; Lys. 31.15; inter-deme prejudice: e.g. (possibly) Plut. *Thes.* 13.3; D. 43.64, 44.34—9. On all this see below, chapter 7.
60. Lys. 7 is our best evidence for the merits and demerits of leasing land, but we do not know where this land was, nor how typical there wartime events were. The land rented out in Lys. 17.5 might be in the deme of the speaker or near it. Xenophon (esp. *Oik* 20.22f.) suggests that distant lands are dealt with through *epitropoi*. The property Stratokles leases (Is. 11.42) is central to the area of his interests.
61. See Davis (1969) Fragmentation of farm land has been said to be a product of partible inheritance, but Davis (1977) has stressed that inheritance systems alone will not cause fragmentation. On the relationship between inheritance and land-holding see Goody, Thirsk and Thompson (1976).
62. Fragmentation as inefficient: Chisholm (1962), Shaw (1963); as a deliberate strategy: Davis (1977), Forbes in Dimen and Friedl (1976). On climatic variability see Gallant (1982).
63. Cf. stele 1 (i^3 421) 123ff., stele 2 (i^3 422) 83ff.
64. Fragmented land-holding and the growing of a variety of crops need not rule out commercial agriculture, but it is likely to limit its scope especially when, as in classical Athens, the number of cash crops is limited. This is far from meaning, however, that no agricultural produce would ever be exchanged.

4. Demes and democracy

1. The institutional approach to democracy as a whole is encouraged by the Aristotelian *Ath. Pol.*, and has been perpetuated at deme level by Haussoullier (1884) and Traill (1975). David Whitehead is working on a definitive account of the deme which has more respect for that of Haussoullier and more institutional bias than this study. Cf. Whitehead (1981) which I know through the kindness of the author.

2. Lloyd (1979) 242.

3. Finley (1973C) 17.

4. Laslett (1956). Compare the similar distinction made by Tönnies between natural communities (*Gemeinschaft*) and competitive societies (*Gesellschaft*), with the upper limit of population of 500 for the former.

5. Finley (1973C) 24 has a limited acknowledgement of this. For the fallacy cf. Jones (1957) ch. 5 on the working of Athenian democracy.

6. Cf. Lukes (1974).

7. Hierokleides: ii^2 206, 209 (the former a *probouleuma*, the latter not); Kallikrates: ii^2 215, 233; Brakhyllos: ii^2 223, 408; Demosthenes: ii^2 360, *IG* vii 4254.

8. Euboulides: D. 57.8; Polykrates: ii^2 207, 1745 (Polykrates' grandsons, ii^2 678); Theodoros: ii^2 330, 1750; Nothippos ii^2 349 (Tod 193); Lysias: ii^2 455, 456, 460; Phyleus: ii^2 360, 330; Phileas: ii^2 348, 410; Epiteles: ii^2 365, at Amphiaraon, *AEph* (1891) 87, at Delphi, *BCH* 24 (1900) 464 line 22, 475 line 25 with 503f., see Walbank (1981B) 173f.

9. *Exetastēs*: ii^2 1270; *probouleuma*: ii^2 360 with discussion of Rhodes (1972) 66f. For Telemakhos see chapter 1.

10. Philotades: ii^2 136; grandfather: i^3 281.4; father: Plut. *Mor.* 833e; brother: ii^2 109, 111; son: ii^2 410. Phanodemos: ii^2 223B. 1f. with Jacoby *FGH* iiib 1. 171–4. Kteson: ii^2 1928, D. 59.48; son: *SEG* 21.310; sister: Finley (1952A) 135a; see Davies (1971) 338.

11. Prokleides: ii^2 354; *diaitetes*: ii^2 2409; son: ii^2 4404; grandson: ii^2 1247. Kteson: above n. 10. Philotades: Thompson (1970C). For the status of *diaitetai* see chapter 2.

12. Kephisophon: ii^2 223, 244; military activity: ii^2 1623.35, 1628.438, 1629.484, 959, 1675.33; D. 45.19 (Davies (1971) 291–3); Philemon: ii^2 381; father: *ML* 77.21, Paus. 7.16.4, Plut. *Mor.* 844b (Plutarch gets the demotic wrong, confusing Kallistratos with the more famous figure from Aphidna); mother: ii^2 1523, 1524. The others are: Telemakhos and Demophilos of Akharnai, Aristophon of Azenia, Lykourgos of Boutadai, Stephanos of Eroiadai, Andration of Gargettos, Polyeuktos of Kydantidai, Diophantos of

Myrrhinous, Kephisophon, Demosthenes and Demades of Paiania, Epikrates of Peiraieus, Hegesippos of Sounion, Diopeithes, Euetion and Polyeuktos of Sphettos.

13. Hegesippos: ii² 125, 237; brother's decree: ii² 123; for the rest of the family see Davies (1971) 209f.

14. For Telemakhos' wealth see chapter 1; Stephanos is prominent in D. 59; Polyeuktos was active in the courts and is the object of Hypereides 3; Philemon of Oe is of a strategic family; Epikrates was prominent enough to come to a nasty end in 322 (Lucian, *Dem. Enc.* 31); Polyeuktos of Sphettos figures in mining leases (Crosby (1950) 9.16f.). Davies himself argues for a decline in the power of wealth in the fourth century (1981), but his arguments are idiosyncratic.

15. Rhodes (1972) 52—81; Hansen (1981).

16. For fifteen miles as a practical limit cf. the figure of 120 stades for how far outside Athens men have to live before they have recourse to a different refuge in the decree (perhaps not genuine) at D. 18.38.

17. See e.g. Theoph. *De Elig. Mag.* ed. Keaney and Szegedy-Maszak, *TAPA* 106 (1976) 250ff., and Davies (1981). Note that one of the proposers from outside the 15-mile circle is the general Kallistratos of Aphidna.

18. Patterson (1981). Patterson believes that citizenship was always decided by small groups and that the deme simply took over the rôle of the phratry.

19. Euboulides' father had let Halimous' copy get destroyed (D. 57.26, 60), and it was the demarch who was corrupted to enter a name illegally (D. 44.37). Pollux, *H* 104 might be interpreted as saying that the *lexiarkhoi* derived their name from the *grammateion*, rather than vice versa. Recent work: Koch (1894), Toepffer (1895), Hondius (1922), Jameson (1963) 399f., van Effenterre (1976).

20. *Genē* scattered: D. 59.61, *SEG* 21.527 (Salaminioi); uncertainty over membership: Clinton (1980) 27—9 (but note that Clinton (1974) 51 line 54 suggests that the *grammateion* of the Kerykes was hellenistic, a point that I owe to David Lewis). For recent and radical work on phratries and *genē* see Roussel (1976), Bourriot (1976).

21. *FGH* 328 F 35; ii² 1237.

22. Land: ii² 1241, 2621; *SEG* 12.100.17f. Democratic multiplication: Arist. *Pol.* 1319b20.

23. Apatouria: see chapter 7 n. 37; homicide: *ML* 86 (i³ 104) (phratry), D. 43.57f., ii² 1672.119f. (deme).

24. Theatres are known from remains at Eleusis, Rhamnous, Thorikos, Peiraieus, and Ikarion; they are epigraphically attested at Kollytos,

Aixone, Plotheia and Akbarnai. Brauron had a gymnasium and Eleusis had gymnasiarkhs. Kephisia had a palaestra and Pausanias says there was one at Eleusis; Brauron also had one. See *ADelt* 24A (1969) 6 for Kephisia; *Ergon* (1961) 25 for Brauron; Paus. 1.39.3 for Eleusis.

25. Demarch and assembly: Harpokration s.v. *demarkhos; REG* 91 (1978) 291 line 38; D. 57.8f., 13; executive: cf. e.g. ii² 1176.5, 18, 1177.22, 1187. 18ff., 1188.31, 1193.29, 1198.18ff., 1199.14f., 1202.20, 2492.21; *SEG* 2.7.21, 22.116.24; *REG* 91 (1978) 290f.; *AEph* (1925/6) 168.17.

26. *Hesperia* 8 (1939) 178.7. But see p. 77 below for Peiraieus demarch. Demarchs are also honoured in ii² 1173, 1178, 1179, *SEG* 22.117, D. 57.64. It is curious that three of these cases come from Ikarion.

27. At Peiraieus: ii² 1177 (*SEG* 21.517, 25.143); organising festivals elsewhere: ii² 1173, 1178–9, 1183.36f.; prosecuting: ii² 1177, 1362.15; special share of sacrificial meat: cf. *SEG* 21.541.558; distribution of meat: ii² 1183.34, 1187.20f., and possibly i² 188A.13 (but see Lewis ap. i³ 244), *AEph* (1925/6) 168.9f.; providing victims: *Hesperia* 8 (1939) 178. Some inscriptions talk of the demarch 'sacrificing' (ii² 1183.33, 1358.23;*SEG* 22. 117.1f.) but despite Burkert (1977) 157 priests appear indispensable for public sacrifices (cf. e.g. Ar. *Birds* 848f., 862, and Durand in Vernant and Detienne (1979) 155–6, Martha (1882) 78).

28. *ML* 73 (i³ 78); ii² 140; ii² 1672.273. The exact position of the Amphiaraon demarch is not clear: Whitehead argues that he is demarch of Sounion ((1982) 40–2), but the open significance of δῆμος might allow a δῆμος which was not a deme to have a *demarkhos*.

29. Overseeing *tamiai*: ii² 1198.15, 1202.14, 1206.4f.; cf. ii² 1174. In i³ 253–4 the demarch seems to bear the financial responsibilities alone. *Enktetikon*: ii² 1214.26, cf. D. 50.8. Absence of land register: Finley (1952A) 13f. and nn. 19, 20. Receiving rent: *REG* 91 (1978) 290f., 31f.; ii² 2493.14, cf. *SEG* 24.151.33. Aixone committee: ii² 2492.35.

30. Euxitheos: D. 57.63; chasing debts: ii² 1183.34f., Harpokration, Souda s.v. *demarkhos*, Zonaras p. 494, Bekker, *Anec. Graec.* 1.242; listing property for confiscation: i³ 425.23, 26, 30, 41, 44; Walbank (1982); Plut. *Mor.* 834.

31. Clear cases: D. 57, Is. 12.11; Arist. *Ath. Pol.* 42.1. There are two epigraphic cases of deme action in the courts but in neither case is the nature of the action clear (ii² 1177, 1205).

32. Responsibility of demesmen for election: *SEG* 2.7.6ff. (cf. D. 57.46 for priests); Peiraieus demarch: Arist. *Ath. Pol.* 54.8; Eleusis decrees: *REG* 91 (1978) 290f.; elections in Theseion: Arist. *Ath.*

Pol. 62.1 (cf. D. 44.39 where the elections are referred to as an *agora tōn arkhontōn*). The interpretation offered here is not without difficulties — it is hard to see why the allotment of the demarch should require an agora of the demesmen — and the demand that the rent be paid in the city remains odd on any view.

33. On *euthunoi* see Haussoullier (1884), 81, Hignett (1953) 204f., Piérart (1971). For *euthunoi* in demes as central officers see Dunst (1977), Kirchner ap. ii² 1183. Tetrapolis decree: ii² 1243.17f. (but Lewis has doubts about the text here); Thorikos calendar: *SEG* 26.136.12, 57. *Horkōmosion*, building: Plut. *Thes.* 27.7; sacrifice: Pl. *Criti.* 120b; dealings with *kata dēmous dikastai*: Arist. *Ath. Pol.* 48.4f.; Halai Aixonides: ii² 1174; Myrrhinous: ii² 1183.16ff., cf. also ii² 1216, 1243, i³ 244B, *REG* 91 (1978) 291.42.

34. *Tamiai*, one: Eleusis, ii² 1185.8, cf. 1220.3; Akharnai (?) ii² 1206.3, 8; Halai Aixonides, *ADelt* 11 (1927/8) par. 40; Eitea, *ADelt* 25A (1970) 206 line 16; Gargettos, *AM* 67 (1942) 7 no. 5.7; two: Plotheia, i³ 258.3; plural: ii² 1198.16, 1202.14, 2492.22, 35, 1212.12, 1175.23; *AM* 66 (1941) 218.9f. The restoration is dubious at ii² 1175.21ff. where a *tamias* helps to administer a curse. Heralds: ii² 1176.7, 1178.4, 1199.21, 1214.28; *SEG* 21.541.55; *Polemon* 1.229.14, 23; central importance of: Arist. *Pol.* 1326b6ff.; menial status of deme employees: D. 44.3. *Grammateis*: ii² 1206.13, (1195.1f.). *Antigrapheus*: ii² 1182.23 (Harpokr. s.v. knows only the central official of this name). *Logistēs*: ii² 1183 (but if the *euthunoi* are central officials the *logistēs* might be also). *Horistēs*: ii² 1177.22. Committees: ii² 2492.35; *SEG* 21.519.11, 24.151.26.

35. ii² 1202.1, cf. 2493.15.

36. Eleusis lease: ii² 2500; back-up of central authority: ii² 2492 with Lewis (1974) 82 n. 7; honouring central officials: cf. ii² 1187 with Mitchel (1964).

37. Taxes: ii² 1214.26, 1187.16, 1188.29f., 1204.12, cf. 1185.4f., 1185.25; loans: Finley (1952A) nos. 5, 67a, *Hesperia* 41 (1972) 279; by-law: ii² 1196A. The inscription i³ 2 has been claimed to show that Kleisthenes put minor judicial matters in the hands of the deme, but the stone is reused in the fifth century and its original context unclear. Neither it nor the garbled scholiast on Ar. *Clouds* 37 are sufficient to establish deme judicial authority; cf. Vanderpool (1942), Whitehead (1981).

38. Cf. Bloch (1975). One of the clearest specific examples of traditional language in (honorific) decrees is the use of the concept of *philotimia*, on which see now Whitehead, 'Competitive outlay and community profit', *Classica et Mediaevalia* 34 (1983) 55–74.

39. Prominent politicians on *boule*: Demosthenes (D. 19.154, 234, 286);

Demades (*SEG* 19.149.144); Lykourgos (ii² 1672.302). Cf. also D. 21.111, 59.3f. Social composition: Lys. 13.20; Sundwall (1906) ch. 1; Rhodes (1972) 4f.; Ruschenbusch (1979B, 1981).

40. Arist. *Ath. Pol.* 62.1, Andok. 1.84; cf. Whitehead (1981).

41. See in general Arist. *Ath. Pol.* 53. Arbitrating for tribe other than their own: D. 21.93f.

42. Arist. *Ath. Pol.* 16.5, 48.5, 53.1f.; Bekker, *Anec. Graec* 1.310.21ff. For argument over whether they dealt with their own tribe see Rhodes (1981) 590, Harrison (1971) 19.

43. Service in deme units: Is. 2.42 with Wyse (1904) 268; Polystratos: Lys. 20.23; Mantitheos: Lys. 16.14.

44. Demophanes: *ML* 53.32; ii² 1622.676; Euthydemos: priest of Asklepios: ii² 47.24; Moirokles: proposes to honour Xenokles: ii² 1191; makes dedication to Dionysus: ii² 2845. The problem is whether he is to be identified with the Moirokles active in mid-fourth-century politics: D. 19.293, 58.53,56, D. *Ep.* 3.16, Arist. *Rhet.* 1411a, Arr. 1.40.4, Plut. *Dem.* 23, Harpokr. s.v., Souda s.v. Antipatros. See Ampolo for a case (not final) for identity: Ampolo (1981).

45. Kleokhares: Pouilloux (1954) no. 6; brother Strombikhos: Pouilloux (1954) no. 15.46; Kleodorides: Meritt and Traill (1974) 72.189; Antiphilos: ibid. 62.282; Kleokhares (II): ii² 1217. Thoukydides: *SEG* 22.117.7, ii² 2409.17f.; son and nephew: Meritt and Traill (1974) 61.44,47. Arkhias: *AEph* (1925/6) 168f., Apollodoros, ii² 1749.51. Antipatros: ii² 1601.16f. with Lewis (1973) 192 n. 2; Phoxias: ii² 2411 and Meritt and Traill (1974) 72 (ii² 7504 makes a connection with the propertied family of Xenokles of Sphettos possible). Prokles: ii² 1672.273. See Whitehead (1982) 39 for rebuttal of a further claimed demarch – *bouleutes* connection.

46. Kybernis: *SEG* 2.7.20; descendant: ii² 680. Euainetos: *ML* 53.27; descendant: ii² 785.3; *Hesperia* 5 (1936) 422, 10 (1941) 276 no. 73.2; Euthydomos: ii² 2394, i³ 475.247; relative: ii² 1668.3, ii² 2825.7.

47. We know of no man who was demarch more than once, and it is likely that there was some limit on repeated holding of this office. The allotment was presumably from men who put themselves forward, rather than from all who were not disqualified. The strong disincentive to service as demarch probably helped to make so powerful an office more acceptable in the democracy.

48. Glaukides: ii² 1202.2, *AM* 66 (1941) 218; Sosippos: *AEph* (1957) 45.2; Smikythos Sosippou in ii² 1955 suggests that the family was of *hippeis* census.

49. Men with only bouleutic connections: Theophilos of Halimous, *SEG* 2.7, ii² 212; Menestratos of Ikarion: i³ 254 (descendants, Meritt and Traill (1974) 136.64); Diodoros of Peiraieus: ii² 1214

with ii² 449, Meritt and Traill (1974) 72.140; son of Philistides of Peiraieus: *Hesperia* 3 (1934) 44; father: Meritt and Traill (1974) 62.249; ancestor: i³ 102. Menyllos' lekythos, *AAA* 10 (1977) 226–41. Athmonon deme list: *ADelt* 21A (1966) 134f. Note also Hegesippos Hegesiou of Melite, proposer of *SEG* 22.116, perhaps son of the *diaitetes* of 325/4 (ii² 1926) who may feature in ii² 2383 of 360–350, and grandson of the *epimeletes neoriōn* of 366/5 (ii² 1622.506). Timokrates son of Timokles, proposer of *ADelt* 25A (1970) 204ff. seems a descendant of Timokles *tamias* of Athena in the 420s (i³ 302, 303, 369.36) and of Timokrates the hero of Phyle (*Hesperia* 10 (1941) 288.37).

50. Pheidippos: see Meritt and Traill (1974) 49.37; Neoptolemos: Conophagos (1980) 389 no. 2, Davies (1971) 399f.; Philoxenides: *AM* 66 (1941) 218.1, Finley (1952A) 87; daughter: Plut. *Mor.* 843a; Demokrates: ii² 1198; family: Davies (1971) 359f.; Kallias: ii² 1199.24, 5430; son: ii² 1197.8 (perhaps *grammateus* in 285/4, ii² 360.26). For deme pride in competition victories cf. the celebration of a torch-race victory by his tribe by the potter Nikias son of Hermokles of Anaphlystos (exceptionally recording his deme in his signature) *ARV²* 1333.1.

51. Men with bouleutic connections: Nearkhos, ii² 1199.9, father *bouleutes* ii² 2375.11; Athenokles: ii² 1212; perhaps *bouleutes*: Meritt and Traill (1974) 86.59; Polystratos, *ADelt* 11 (1927/8) 40.4; related to Polystratos, *bouleutes*: Meritt and Traill (1974) 72.95; Pantikles honoured in the same decree seems connected with Sokrates, *bouleutes*: Meritt and Traill (1974) 61.197. Cf. Leophilos Eudikou honoured in ii² 1199.8f. who appears in the puzzling list ii² 1927. Men known from other deme contexts: Antikharmos, ii² 1199.8, perhaps mentioned at 1197.7, son of Nauson, ii² 2492.47; Phalanthos, father of Smikythion of Athmonon (ii² 1203) in the catalogue of the deme, *ADelt* 21A (1966) 134f. 10; Pantikles (above) and Theodotos, honoured together, appear together in ii² 2820 among these responsible for the statue.

52. Cf. Barnes (1969), Boissevain (1974).

53. Gellner (1977), cf. Davis (1977) ch. 3.

54. *Trittys* with property: ii² 2490; cults: i³ 255, 258 (not certain); election of tribal officials: ii² 1151f. 2818 (cf. 2824 (restored)); trittyarchs: Pl. *Rep.* 475a; *trittyes*' part in naval system: D. 14.22f.; *horoi* of *trittyes* from Agora: *AJA* 60 (1956) 279–82.

55. The other five *trittyes* unrepresented are: inland and coastal of Hippothontis, coastal of Akamantis, inland of Aiantis, coastal of Antiokhis.

56. Ruschenbusch (1979B, 1981), Rhodes (1980) and chapter 2. It seems quite likely that perhaps 70% of Athenians over thirty served at least once.

5. Athenian stone resources and their exploitation

1. On ancient classification of stones see Orlandos (1968) 1ff., Wycherley (1974A). All the primary and secondary material on quarrying in Greece is reviewed by Dworakowska (1975, cf. 1968 on Attika), but without any autopsy. The best work has been done outside Attika: Adam (1966), Koenigs (1972), *Etudes Thasiennes* (1980), and now M.K. Durkin and C.J. Lister, *ABSA* 78 (1983) 69–96.

2. In antiquity the mountain was called Brilessos and the marble named Pentelic after the particular area from which it came. The mountain then came to be called Pendele and Leake was the first correctly to identify Brilessos (1841, 4ff.).

3. *Mélanges Nicole* (1905) 401–5. A second unfinished statue was found high up in the area of the classical quarries (*AJA* 72 (1968) 75).

4. Ladas (1952) has the fullest, but not entirely accurate, modern account of the Spelia quarry. See pl. 4.

5. Lepsius (1890) 20. Lepsius claims that the marble of the Erekhtheion is better quarried; Tschira (1940) claims that the marble in the later Parthenon is better than that in the earlier because the lower levels of the quarry had been reached.

6. Dworakowska (1968) lists seven locations where Hymettan marble was extracted, Petropoulakou and Pentazos (1973) eight. The shallow workings were reported by Dow (1935): they may have been abandoned because they had served their purpose.

7. The Dragon House is published by Boyd and Carpenter (1977); it is slightly misplaced on Blatt V of the *Karten von Attika*. The Cethegus graffito published by Ober (1981) indicates that there was a Roman interest in the slope, but that that particular quarry was not exploited subsequent to Cethegus' presence. The traces of the quarry road (pl. 5) are exiguous: it cannot have been more than 3.1 m wide (autopsy 10 April and 13 June 1981).

8. Lepsius (1890) 27. For the Cliff Tower quarry see Langdon and Watrous (1977) 172, Waelkens (1982).

9. Velatouri: Fiedler (1840) 42, 70; cf. Lepsius (1890) 30. Stephani: Kordellas (1870) 48 (quoted by Milchhoeffer (1889) 27). The 0.97-m diameter column reported by Kordellas is no longer there (autopsy 14 May 1981).

10. Papageorgakis (1967). For Agia Marina see Milchhoeffer (1889) 50, Tomlinson and Trevor Hodge (1969) 142, *AEph* (1979) 47, 52.

11. See Travlos in Shoe (1949) 341, and contrast Travlos (1949) 144 n. 8. The quarry north of Eleusis is reported by Gell (1819) 13, 17, but neither Edmonson nor I have been able to trace it.

12. Peiraieus quarries: Pritchett (1965) 97, 99, Lolling in Curtius

(1884) 6f.; *ADelt* 28B1 (1973) 46—8, 29B1 (1974) 99f., 102, 149.

13. Lepsius (1890) 123, Dworakowska (1968) 89 n. 9, Kourouniotes and Thompson (1932) esp. 139—43, and cf. *Hesperia* 12 (1943) 269ff.

14. Milchhoeffer (1889) 19. Searched for 30 April 1981.

15. Marked on *Karten von Attika,* Blatt XVII. For desertion cf. Pomponius Mela 2.46, Wheler (1682) 448f., Eliot (1962) 81.

16. i³ 395 (cf. i³ 386 92ff.). Vallois (*REA* 35 (1933) 199f.) argues that it is the Eleusinion in the city that is in question. For the quarry see Iakovides (1969) 5. Lewis argues that the Peisistratid road to Steiria may imply that the quarry was being exploited in the sixth century, cf. Pl. *Hipparkhos* 228b—e and *SEG* 15.53.

17. Milchhoeffer (1889) 7, *Ergon* (1960) 20, *BCH* 86 (1962) 664, 671, Kondis (1967). The quarries extend some 30 m up the slight slope and stretch *c.* 100 m along it. They are about 500 m from the sanctuary, across the Eridanos.

18. The modern debate about marble identification was begun by Pritchett and Herz (1953) and Renfrew and Peacey (1968). For two recent contributions see Coleman and Walker (1979) and Germann *et al.* (1980).

19. Wycherley (1973, 1974A) with Renfrew and Peacey (1968) on the distinctive iron oxide content of Pentelic.

20. See Orlandos (1968) 4 (speculative). Despite the obvious translation these are not 'field stones', for which see Thuc. 4.4.

21. Suggested by Holleaux (1906) and approved by Dörpfeld ad. loc., this identification is not at all certain.

22. See Wycherley (1974A).

23. (1762) vol. 1, ch. 2, p. 7, note b.

24. Fifth century: i³ 395, 386.92ff. Fourth-century *telesterion*: ii² 1670—3, 1675, 1680; *SEG* 19.148, and cf. ii² 204. Tower: *SEG* 19.146.

25. Arsenal: ii² 1668; temple of Zeus: ii² 1669.

26. For Sounion see Dinsmoor (1971) and above chapter 2, n. 1.

27. For the fort see Pouilloux (1954), who suggests (ch. 4) that differences in masonry style between Attic forts may be a product of local builders.

28. Autopsy 25 April 1981.

29. For Oinoe see Vanderpool (1978) 231f. For Mazi tower see Chandler (1926) 15, McCredie (1966) 89f., Wrede (1933) 24. Autopsy 25 April 1981.

30. Munter (1893), Milchhoeffer (1895) 6, Arvanitopoulou (1958) 27ff., (1959) 17f.

31. The dimensions of the column seen by Kordellas are suitable for any but the lowest part of the columns of the Thorikos temple.

32. In view of the variation in detail of method between quarries

and rock types, generalising about 'ancient quarrying methods' needs to be done with greater caution than has often been the case in the past. For small quarries there are very good English parallels: at Adderbury (Oxon.) stone for the church was specially dug out from the rectory garden. Much of the stone for Oxford colleges was dug at Headington, and the quarries of the Oxford Dominicans and of Merton college, at Wheatley and Headington, were both smaller than 100 yards square, and the latter was not more than eight feet deep.

33. Tomlinson and Trevor Hodge (1969). Again there are English parallels: when Cardinal Wolsey planned to build a school at Ipswich the first attempt was to quarry stone at Harwich, and only when it was found that 'it does not last' did they go so far as to procure Kentish rag. Note also the letter written to Protector Somerset in 1549 which stresses that the lower beds are better than the upper and that he should see to it that the stone be set in the same position in the building as it was in the quarry. Just as poor quarrying leads to poor weathering in the Parthenon, so there are cases of disastrous results in England after masons have set the stone the wrong way for the grain. For all this see Salzman (1952).

34. Lepsius (1890) claims work in Pentelic marble from Athens, Spata, Lamptrai, Sounion, Peiraieus, Salamis, Aigina, Eleusis, Tanagra, Oropos, Thespiai, Ptoon, Atalante, Euboia, Korinth, Aigion, Epidauros, Argos, Thyrea, Mantineia, Ithome, Olympia, Delos, Rheneia, and Kythnos. Many of these cases are of sculptural use. He finds Eleusinian stone at Khalkis and Olympia.

35. Burford (1969) 155f.

36. *Hesperia* 5 (1936) 401 no. 10, lines 138ff., ii^2 47.30, *REG* 91 (1978) 289–306. Ampolo (1982) has a full discussion of the problem.

37. The lessee fails to pay the fourth and fifth instalments of rent on the quarry, but all payments from the fourth to the tenth on these other public contracts. It seems unlikely that he resumed payment on the quarry while continuing to default on the rest.

38. For the rent compare the 152 dr. per annum of the Aixone agricultural lease (ii^2 2492).

39. Cf. Burford (1969) 171–5. No land in Attika is referred to simply as 'public land'. The case of the quarries at Carrara is an instructive parallel: here the earliest exploitation is by non-local men sent in by various towns in north Italy, and particularly Florence, to get marble. All they had to pay was an export tax, not anything for the stone itself. For all this see Klapisch-Zuber (1969).

40. *Lithotomia*: i^2 336 (i^3 395) 7, 11, ii^2 1672.17, cf. 21–2. *lithotomoi*: i^2 339.24, 347.37, 348.70, 349.20, 350.44 (i^3 436–451), i^2 364

(i^3 463) 21–3, ii^2 1680.4, cf. 1666.A8, B1,72 etc., 1669.14. *timē*: ii^2 1672.49, cf. 52, 132. Only in the case of rubble does there seem to be a price for the stone: ii^2 1672.197ff.

41. ii^2 1672.49: Demetrios, Ergasion, Kyprios, Euarkhos, and Milakos.

42. ii^2 1672.51ff.: there are five men responsible for quarrying 304 stones at 1 dr. 1 ob. each (1 dr. 3 ob. more for transport). If each earns the day rate of 1 dr 3 ob. (line 46) then each has about 47 days of work here. The other *lithoi arouraioi* required in that year are 165 @ 3 dr. 4 ob. each for quarrying and transport together. If the quarrying cost is assumed to be 1 dr. and the same five labourers are employed then each had twenty-two days of work out of this order.

43. Above n. 24 for evidence; Clinton (1971) for discussion. The calculations use Stanier's 55 dr. per ton quarrying cost and 8 tons for the weight of the drums (Glotz (1923) reckoned $5\frac{1}{2}$ tons): Stanier (1953). The 'year' here is 300 man-days.

44. The Pentelic in the ceiling coffers at Epidauros has been estimated to weigh 140 tons. On the same basis as the above calculations this is a year's work for 35 men. Pentelic was also used in the walls of the cella and in the inner colonnade, and in the absence of estimates of weight for these I have allowed a generous figure. None of these calculations is meant to be considered precise, simply somewhere in the right order. Work in the English medieval quarries was similarly sporadic.

45. This is one of the major theses of Burford (1969). Neither her claims of skilled use of materials in temples (1969, 168) nor her claims that using stone from far off is common (1965, 24), are supported by the evidence.

46. i^2 373. 3,5,6,11,16; cf. i^2 374.211, [248] (i^3 475f.).

47. ii^2 1657, ii^2 351.

48. Plut. *Per.* 12, i^2 339–53 (i^3 436–51).

49. Road repairs: ii^2 1672.28, 63. Compare refurbishing the Portland stone quarries for the building of St Paul's cathedral. 333/2 accounts: ii^2 1673. Separate payments for transport: ii^2 1672.49f.; single payment: ibid. 17f.

50. i^3 436–51.

51. Daos of Eleusis: ii^2 1672.54, 133; Neokleides of Kephisia: ibid. 51, 53f.; the Ergasion who appears in 49 and 54 may be the slave of Daos. For Ergasion as a slave name see Reilly (1978) 43 nos. 959–61.

52. In the Peiraieus generally and in Eleusis in the late 330s demand for stone can be expected to have been high. It is notable that the first private commercial quarries in England were those that supplied the Oxford colleges, and for a long time the only others were the Maidstone rag quarries supplying London.

53. Clinton (1971) argues that payment was at the rate of 4 dr. per yoke per day with a bonus of 6 dr. for arriving within three days. Cost per drum still varies between 228 and 402 dr.
54. ii² 1672. 130ff. The stone is not quite clear at this point.
55. ii² 1672. 48ff. Fourth-century records from Delphi show that it cost twice as much to transport stone from Korinth to Kirrha as to quarry it, and four times as much to transport it from Kirrha to Delphi: Fouilles de Delphes iii.5 (1932) 19. 47,54,14,87; 23.1, 39. Cf. Burford (1969) 184–91, Snodgrass (1983) 20.
56. Glotz (1923), Clinton (1971).
57. See above chapter 2, n. 79. It is not known if the Kolonai demes were Kleisthenic, but they certainly existed by the middle of the fifth century: i³ 472.
58. ii² 1673.37 with Clinton (1971) 94f.
59. Note that Phainippos, whose deme is unknown but whose mother was daughter to a man of Kolonai, has his sizeable land-holding at Kytherros, D. 42.5.
60. Cf. Abrams in Abrams and Wrigley (1978) 27. Note that one of the factors which made for the large-scale exploitation of Carrara marble was the way in which it served as a convenient return cargo on the grain ships from the Naples area, which helped to establish a regular market. See Klapisch-Zuber (1969) ch. 7.

6. Patterns of exploitation in the Athenian silver mines

1. Cf. Finley (1973B) 123–49 (the quotation is from p. 134).
2. Spartan interest: Thuc. 6.91 (cf. 2.55); deserting slaves: Thuc. 7.27; Xenophon's scheme: Poroi 4.23f.; Conophagos' calculation: (1980) 341ff. For another recent calculation see Kalcyk (1982) who suggests that 54,100 were employed per year in the fifth century, 22,100 in the fourth century (the addition in his final table is incorrect).
3. Kallias and Nikias: cf. Davies (1971) s.vv.
4. MIGRA 1 (1975) 45–54, Mussche, Thorikos III.70f., AR (1981–2) 13.
5. Washery excavations: of Conophagos: Conophagos (1980) 375ff., AAA 12 (1979) 15–23; of J.E. Jones: AC 45 (1976) 147–72; BCH 102 (1978) 651f.; AR (1979–80) 17–19, (1981–2) 12f. For excavations on the coast see AAA 9 (1976) 24–43, PAA (1959) 259–63, Ann. Géol. Pays Hell. 11 (1959) 137ff., Hesperia 10 (1941) 168, ADelt 27B1 (1972) 147.
6. Allusions in Aristophanes: Ar. Knights 362, cf. Birds 593, 1105f. and schol. on Peace 451, Frogs 1422; orators: D. 37 (with Finley (1952A) 52–5, Hopper (1953) 204ff., Harrison (1968) 274,

282, 289, Hypereides 4; *poletai* leases: Crosby (1950, 1957). Until recently the basic works have been Ardaillon (1897), Hopper (1953), Eliot (1962) (for toponymy), and Lauffer (1979). However, Conophagos (1980) and Kalcyk (1982) have reopened many areas for discussion. The latter, a somewhat raw work, became available to me too late for full reference to be included here or in chapter 2.

7. That the surviving leases are random selections depends on the rejection of Conophagos' unnatural interpretation of συγκεχωρήμενα and his forced reading of the *Ath. Pol.* There is some bias introduced by the fact that the leases are more or less arranged by locality, so that e.g. all the Anaphlystos mines known, bar two, are recorded in just 32 lines of ii² 1582.

8. The terminology of the leases seems generally informal and non-technical, reflecting the way the registrants themselves described the mines. *Edaphos*, however, seems from stele 4 on, to be used as a technical term meaning 'someone's mining land', distinct from *khōrion* and from *metallon*. The detailed survey of mining remains suggests that, if a lot of structures are not to go unmentioned in the leases, *ergasterion* probably refers to any non-domestic buildings and not simply to washeries (*contra* Hopper).

9. Meidias: ii² 1582.44, 82; Diopeithes: *SEG* 12.100.53, 78; Lysitheides: Crosby (1950) 5.55, 6.9f., 14.5f., 19.6f., 20.27; Diophanes: Crosby (1950) 1.59f., 13.68. Timarkhos: Aiskhin. 1.101.

10. Kallias of Lamptrai: Crosby (1950) 1.73f., 5.70.

11. Lysitheides' children: Crosby (1950) 29.4,7; Arkhestratos: 5.21, ii² 1585.15; Aspetos: ii² 1582.55; Crosby (1950) 15.21, (1957) S2.6; father at *SEG* 12.100.58; Diokles and Diokhares: Crosby (1950) 1.58, 14.19, 15.25f. For the location of Nape see above p. 35 n. 60 referring to *SEG* 26.266; Crosby (1950) 1.57, 14.11.

12. Thrasylokhos and Meidias: *SEG* 12.100.49; Crosby (1957) S2.12; ii² 1582.44, 82. Family of Pheidippos: Crosby (1950) 1.46f., 81, 13.103, 15.42–5, 18.70–2, 19.4–9, 20.25f., (1957) S2.29; son: ii² 1582.25f.; Crosby (1950) 13.64, 71; brother: 13.64; for the stemma see Lauffer (1957).

13. For the exceptions see Crosby (1950) 15.23, (1957) S2.21 for Apolexis of Aithalidai, whose father also both leased a mine and owned property (*SEG* 12.100.51f., 71–6), and Crosby (1950) 16.56–60, 18.65–9 for Euthykrates. Teisarkhos of Aixone (*SEG* 12.100.50) is a third exception if he is the . . . khos of Crosby (1950) 3.12. Note that in all these calculations only men with demotics preserved have been considered identifiable, and that registrants have been numbered, rightly or wrongly, among the lessees, on the grounds that in a very large number of cases the registrant is also lessee.

14. Kephisodoros and Euphemides: Crosby (1950) 9.9, ii² 1587.17–19; Isandros and Stratokles: ii² 1582.92, 98; Crosby (1950) 18.17f.; Epikles 1.71, 5.36.
15. Kallias: *SEG* 12.100.42, 48, 65; Pheidippos, above n. 12; Kephisodotos is father to Apolexis, n. 13. Cf. also Diotimos of Euonymon: Crosby (1950) 26.7f., (1957) S2.15f., 24; ii² 1582.65f., cf. 103f.; Mnesidamos of Myrrhinous: *Hesperia* 5 (1936) 393ff. no. 10, lines 3f., 7, 9; Diodoros of Themakos: Crosby (1950) 19.16; Eudraon of Thorikos: Crosby (1950) 5.52f., 20.17–19.
16. Hdt. 7.144, Arist. *Ath. Pol.* 22, Thuc. 1.14, D.S. 11.41, 43, Polyain. *Strat.* 1.30.5, Plut. *Them.* 4, Nepos, *Them.* 2.1–3. See Labarbe (1957) (tendentious).
17. Conophagos (1980) 438n. argues that only *kainotomiai* paid the $\frac{1}{24}$ tax. The amount of public income varies enormously according to whether the sums mentioned in the leases were paid once a lease (Conophagos), once a year (Crosby), or once a prytany (Hopper).
18. Gauthier (1976) 142 for the quotation. Davies (1971) 403–7 for Nikias and his descendants.
19. *SEG* 12.100.64. Davies' (1971, 260ff.) suggestion as to how Kallias Lakkoploutos acquired his wealth demands land ownership in the mining area.
20. Xen. *Poroi* 4.15, ii² 2368 with Crosby (1950) 16A and B, AII.65ff.
21. Teisiakon: ii² 1582.59; Euthykrates: n. 13 above and Hyp. 4.34; Epikrates: Crosby (1950) 1.70f., 20.5, 11.
22. E.g. Crosby (1950) 201f., Conophagos (1980) 350ff.
23. For earlier speculation on related lines see Hopper (1968) 320.
24. Previous analysis by Gomme (1933) 46 (on limited data), Crosby (1950) 205, Hopper (1953) 245. Crosby includes Kikynna, Kephale, and Potamos Deiradiotes in the mining demes, Hopper Aigilia, Hagnous, Myrrhinous, Prasiai, Prospalta, Kephale, Steiria and Thoraia! Mining demes here means demes where mines are attested in the leases. A total of 239 individuals with demotics appear in the leases.
25. Leukios owns property at Besa and leases at Thrasymos (only probably in Sounion): Crosby (1950) 1.46, 80; 5.5, 16.AII.70, 20.5f; Philinos leases at Sounion but owns at Thorikos: Crosby (1950) 1.60, 14.2, ii² 1582.47, 50.
26. Only demes from which more than one individual has been recorded in the leases are plotted. Locations generally follow Traill. Potamioi have been credited to Potamos Deiradiotes.
27. See schol. Ar. *Knights* 899 and *Hesperia* 22 (1953) 175f. (a third-century grave stele).
28. The distribution of rich demes (see above, chapter 2) will not entirely explain the distribution of those involved in the mines.

29. Gargettos decree: *AM* 67 (1942) p. 7, no. 5; Kotzias, *Polemon* 4 (1949) 4f.; Epikydes in mining lease: ii² 1588.3f.
30. Hopper (1954) 249–54; Lauffer (1957).

7. *Kinsmen and neighbours, choosing and using*

1. Previous work on kinship has tended to concentrate on quite narrow questions: cf. Bicknell (1972, 1974) on political families, Harrison (1968) for family law, Glotz (1904), Lacey (1968), Dover (1975) on family solidarity. Only recently has important work begun to be done on the basic nature of kinship (Humphreys (1978)) and some basic data collected (cf. Thompson (1967, 1972)). The work in this chapter is heavily indebted to Davies (1971), through which a vast amount of information is easily accessible.
2. Cf. Is. 2.10f. On this aspect see Raepsaet (1971) and Raepsaet and Charlier (1971).
3. Cf. D. 41.3.
4. D. 44.63 with Harrison (1968) 85–7.
5. Is. 2.20; cf. Is. 2.10–12 and the assumption at Is. 3.73 that the adopted son would come from the circle of kinsmen.
6. For a list of who is adopted see *REG* 33 (1920) 139. Daughter's son: D. 42.21, 27; D. 43.37; Plut. *Them.* 32.1; Is. 10.4f.; Plut. *Mor.* 843a; nephews: Is. 6.6, 11.41f.; D. 43.77; cousins: Is. 5.6; wife's son: Is. 8.40; half-sister: Is. 7.9.
7. Links with another deme: cf. the classic case of manoeuvres involving Eleusis and Otryne, D. 44; deme connection, kinship unclear: *Thrasy*boulos Aiskhinou of Lousia adopted by Hippolokhides of Lousia, Is. 7.23, noting that Hippolokhides is the son of *Thrasy*medes.
8. See Davis (1977) 197–222 for a discussion of such questions with reference to the modern Mediterranean.
9. E.g. at ii² 7763, 7629, *SEG* 21.855.
10. ii² 6963, if Kirchner is right in identifying the father. Euphronios is not a sufficiently rare name for this to be beyond doubt.
11. Cf. Mair (1971) 44, 81.
12. Etienne (1975); cf. Humphreys (1980) 114–5.
13. For Hybadai see *RE* suppl. 10 s.v.
14. Yet people from Oe and Hybadai do occur in this part of Attika: there is a woman from Oe among the Brauron dedicants, and two brothers from Hybadai made a dedication at a Heraklion apparently at Philaidai, see Kirchner ad ii² 3205, Davies (1971) p. 520.
15. Davies (1971) 4549.
16. Davies (1971) 3773 and Wyse (1904) 402f. (on Is. 5).

17. Davies (1971) 12267 and esp. p. 474. (Davies appears to equivocate over the exact relationship between Aristogeiton (II) and Ando-kides' children, saying one thing in the text but showing another in his stemma.) Note also the family from Anaphlystos which, from the five stelai relating to it found in the Kerameikos (ii^2 5652, 5676–8, 5685), would seem to be based on the *astu* and which forms one marriage alliance with a family from Agryle, which may have been promoted by propinquity of that deme to the *astu*, and one with a family of Akharnai, where locality is less clearly impor-tant. A further case of a family from elsewhere having a base near the city is provided by ii^2 5479 which seems to show that a family from Kothokidai, normally resident in Salamis (ii^2 6474f., 6480), had a base at Sepolia. (The presence of Demokleia's brother makes it more likely that the base was of their family than, *pace* Davies, that it was of Demokleia's husband, Exopios of Halai (Davies (1971) 4719).)

18. Humphreys (1980) 115.

19. Davies (1971) 10807.

20. Davies (1971) 9576. Although we know a lot about Antikrates' family we do not know the origins of any other spouses.

21. Davies (1971) 5791.

22. See Davis (1977) 207, 210. Prohibited marriages are so restricted under Athenian law that local exogamy cannot have been entailed by such prohibitions (cf. Mair (1971) 28).

23. Davies (1971) 5638.

24. E.g. Is. 2.3, 9; 5.5, 26; 7.18; 10.4; cf. 6.22; D. 40.6; 43.48; 39.2, 23; 40.24f.; 59.58; Lyk. *Leok.* 22–4; Plut. *Mor.* 843a.

25. See Davies (1971) table 1.

26. For a discussion of marriage strategies see Davies (1977) 216ff., and more generally Mair (1971) 74–87 and Bloch (1973). The discussion of the use of kin in section 2 of this chapter is relevant here.

27. For regulations about *epikleroi*: Plut. *Sol.* 20.2f.; D. 46.18f., 43.54. For concern to preserve the *oikos*: D. 43.75, Is. 7.30, D. 43.11, Arist. *Pol.* 1274b2ff. For children preserving the *oikos* see esp. Is. 2.36, D. 44.48.

28. Political marriages: Davies (1971) 11793 VI–VII, 8429 XII, 10808, 8157, 7737; Bicknell (1974) 157f., Vernant (1974) ch. 3. For parental decision: Xen. *Oik.* 7.10f. This is not to deny the considerable informal rôle of women, as in Arab societies today, nor the importance of the decision of the daughter. Hdt. 6.122 would be an example of daughters deciding, if it were genuine or genuinely informed.

29. Humphreys (1980) 116. It is worth noting that there is only one certain case of a marriage outside the deme of Oion in the Bouselid *oikos*: see the stemma in Davies (1971) table V.

30. Dowries: jewels/linen: Is. 8.8.; *sunoikia*: Is. 5.26; jewels and *sunoikia*: D. 45.28. Cf. D. 41.5. Mortgaging land to raise dowry: Finley (1952A).

31. Relatives present: Is. 5.26; giving away the basis: D. 44.49, 46.18.

32. Contrast Is. 8.19.

33. Harrison (1968) 1. For a rather different discussion of this problem see Vernant (1974) 44ff.

34. Compare Aristotle's discussion in *Pol.* 1.

35. Is. 2.7—9. There seems to be a fair amount of decoration of the events to give a specious appearance in the way they are presented in the speech.

36. D. 43.74 for a clear case. Cf. D. 43.48—50, 58.16; Is. 3.30, 2.36.

37. Vidal-Naquet (1968), Schmitt (1977).

38. Competition over who should bury: Is. 8.21f., 3.8f.; D. 43.65, 54.32; Lys. fr. 64. Expense: D. 45.79, 40.52, 48.12; Pl. *Ep.* 361e; cf. borrowing money for: D. 40.52; Is. 8.23, 25, 38f. *SEG* 12.100.28f. has burial expenses of 30 dr. Helping non-kin with expenses: Lys. 19.59.

39. Intra-deme marriages of men of Sounion: ii² 7412, 7425, 7442, 7448 (two cases on the last stone).

40. Humphreys (1980); Pouilloux (1954), *AEph* (1961) Chr. 9ff.; *Praktika* 1975A, 1976A, 1977A, 1978A, 1979A; *AEph* (1979).

41. Inter-deme: ii² 6006 (?), *SEG* 26.303; Phanokrates of Rhamnous and Arkhestrate daughter of Mnesarkhos of Oinoe from the peribolos of Phanokrates, *Praktika* 1978A. Inter-deme marriages of Rhamnous families are also known from outside the deme: ii² 7365, 7372, 7376.

42. Nemesis: cf. *ML* 53; garrison, Pouilloux (1954) no. 17 (third-century).

43. Note the way that members of this deme are found as creditors upon local *horoi*: in particular one Hieron, whose family has a prominent funerary enclosure, is found as joint creditor with another man of Rhamnous (name unknown) on a stele found at Marathon (*SEG* 21.656) and as creditor on another *horos* from Rhamnous itself (*AEph* (1979) 42).

44. Dionysius of Halikarnassos on Lys. 34 claims that Lysias alleged that restricting franchise to landowners would exclude 5,000 from citizenship.

45. Cf. Xen. *Oik.* 4.4, despite the light-hearted manner of presentation.

46. But the use of women and children as agricultural labour is considered a mark of poverty: Arist. *Pol.* 1252b, Pl. *Laws* 805e, Arist. *Pol.* 1323a5, cf. D. 57.45.

47. De Sainte Croix (1981) argues (208ff.) that the ancient Greek world should be considered a world of peasants, but not all of us find his superimposed classes of money-lenders and town-dwellers

in classial Attika. In fact neither of the two traditions of anthropological thought about peasants, one from Redfield stressing peasant culture, the other, from Steward, stressing exploitation, will fit the Attic data. See Silverman (1979).

48. Compare the convolutions of the argument employed in D. 42 to try to show from his holding that Phainippos was an exceptionally wealthy man.

49. Hired labour: D. 53.20 (where it is *not* certain that it is slaves that are hired); of low status: Solon 1.47f. (individual specialist), Theoph. *Char.* 4.3, Ar. *Wasps* 711f.; hired gangs (low status): D. 57.45, 18.51; Xen. *Oik.* 18.2, 5; cf. Xen. *Oik.* 20.16. *Misthōtai* slavish: Is. 5.39; cf. Isok. 14.48, 18.48; Xen. *Mem.* 2.8; Pl. *Pol.* 290a.

50. Ndendeuli: Gulliver (1971); Panama: Gudeman (1976).

51. As de Sainte Croix assumes: (1981) 576 n. 16.

52. There is another strong case if the *sungeorgountes* of Is. 9.18 are 'men helping with the farm-work', and not just 'men who were also busy in the fields'.

53. Bloch (1973). Compare Is. 1.6, 5.24f. Men of Rhamnous are not the only ones to provide loans for other local men, to judge from the find-spots of a number of *horoi*: see above, chapter 3.

54. This is the case regardless of the motivation behind Kleisthenes' reforms.

55. The inspiration for this discussion came from a paper by Sally Humphreys on the use of kin as witnesses, now in *History and Anthropology* (1983).

56. For the scrutiny: Aiskhin. 1.77 and schol., 86, 114 and schol., 2.182; Harp. and Soud. s.v. *diapsephismos*; D.H. *De Din.* 11, *De Is.* 16f.; Bekker, *Anec. Graec.* 1.236; D. 18.132 and schol.; Soud. s.v. *apepsephisato*.

57. Cf. Lacey (1980).

8. The religious factor: confirmation or alternative?

1. Paus. 1.23.7. Archaeology and literary sources agree that Brauron was deserted in Pausanias' time (Plin. *NH* 4.24, Pomponius Mela 2.46), so that his information about Brauron itself must be second-hand.

2. Rhodes and Dobbins (1979), cf. Stevens (1936), Dinsmoor (1947) with Edmonson (1968).

3. Akropolis dedications: Raubitschek (1949), Langlotz and Graef (1925). *Krateriskoi* in general: Travlos (1960) 55 n. 20, Threpsiades and Vanderpool (1964) 33–5, Kahil (1965, 1977). From Akropolis: Kahil (1981).

4. Earliest Brauron records from Akropolis: i³ 403. 416/15 inscription

from Brauron: *Ergon* (1958) 37, *AJA* 63 (1959) 280.

5. Early occupation: *Praktika* (1949) 79, (1955) 168; *Ergon* (1961) 128. Temple: *Praktika* (1945–8) 86, Kondis (1967) 168, Travlos (1976). Pottery: Kahil (1963).

6. Temple of Iphigeneia: *Ergon* (1957) 20, Euripides, *IT* 1465. Stoa: *Ergon* (1958) 37, (1962) 28f.; *Praktika* (1959) 18; Bouras (1967) 149ff.; Kondis (1967) 171; Coulton (1976) 226f. Edmonson would argue for a fourth-century date. Activity elsewhere in Attika: Boersma (1970). 'Periklean' building outside Athens is known at Eleusis (Telesterion), Akharnai (Ares), Rhamnous (Nemesis), Thorikos (?Eleusinion), Sounion (Poseidon). With the possible exception of Cape Zoster no Attic sanctuary investigated archaeologically has failed to reveal building activity at this date. Stoa rooms: Linders (1972) 72.

7. *Ergon* (1961) 24, *REG* 75 (1963) for the third-century inscription; later there is the Polydeukion stele (*Ergon* (1961) 35), which does not imply use as a sanctuary.

8. The Brauron site had to be drained before excavation, and inundation may have caused the abandonment of the sanctuary. Associations of Artemis: Nilsson (1941) 463f., Farnell (1896) 2. 558f., Calame (1977) 174–90. Euripides, *Hippolytus* 73ff., 148ff.; with Barrett (1964) ad locc.; and cf. Eur. *IT* 1103f., 1234ff. Oinoe: ii^2 5116 (cf. i^2 845.5).

9. For the dedications see Linders (1972); ibid p. 13 for the new coverlet, and 58f. for refutation of the not unattractive view of A. Mommsen that *rakos* in the inscriptions is to be associated with menstruation. The garbled statement of the scholiast on Kallim. *Hymn* 1.77 seems to indicate that Brauron recieved dedications of clothes on parturition, and the inscriptions would support this.

10. The other demes involved are: Eroiadai, Phaleron, Melite, Kydathenaion, Perithoidai, Aphidna, Lamptrai, Oe, Teithras, Paiania, and Halai.

11. Grave stele only: ii^2 7129; Hieronymos: Davies (1971) 243f.; Kallistratos of Aphidna: Davies (1971) 280ff., Lysikrates' wife: ii^2 1524. If Davies (1971) 421 is right, then the first known dedicant at Brauron also comes from a wealthy family from far away (Melite).

12. 401/0 inventory: ii^2 1381 and 1386; silver *hydriai*: ii^2 1424a, 1425, 1429, 1437, 1444; box from Brauron: ii^2 1388.73. Examination of priests etc. Aiskhin. 3.18, ii^2 410.22, 354.21.

13. Hierokles' case is also mentioned at Dein 2.12. For another case of *hierosulia* involving another with a priestly name, Theosebes, see above p. 5 and n. 25.

14. D. 54.25, Hypereides fr. 199 Jensen (201 Blass). Cf. Schaps (1977) for the non-naming of respectable women.

15. Ar. *Peace* 874. For *double entendre* cf. schol. ad loc. and the variant textual tradition. Rhapsodes: Hesykhios s.v. *Brauroniois*. *Kanephoroi*: Philokhoros, *FGH* 328 F 101 (but F 100 has *arkteuomenai*). Note that schol. Theokr. 2.66 has it required that one be a *kanephoros* for Artemis before marriage. Cf. Walbank (1981A).
16. Hdt. 4.145, 6.137–40. Jacoby, *FGH* 3b suppl., commentary, vol. 1, 409, notes 24ff. Philokhoros' embroidered version: *FGH* 328 F 99ff. Plutarch's independent version: *Mor.* 247b, 296b.
17. All the relevant texts are set out by Brelich (1969) 240ff.
18. Cf. Montepaone (1979A).
19. Euripides, *IT* 1462f. The text of the *Lysistrata* passage and the link with Iphigeneia have been established by Sourvinou-Inwood (1971) and Stinton (1976). Walbank (1981A) does not convince. On Artemis and Iphigeneia see now P.H.J. Lloyd-Jones, *JHS* 103 (1983) 87–102.
20. Kahil (1965, 1977).
21. Necessary for marriage: schol. Ar. *Lys.* 645, Bekker, *Anec. Graec.* 1.444, Harpokr. s.v. *arkteusai*, Souda s.v. *arktos*. Age of menarche: Amundsen and Diers (1969). Age of *arktoi*: schol. Ar. *Lys.* 645, Souda s.v. *arktos. Arrephoroi*: Burkert (1966) with further parallels. Link with periodicity of Brauronia: Sourvinou-Inwood (1971). Pre-menarche pubescence: Tanner (1978) 60ff., 197ff., esp. 62 fig. 22, 200 fig. 77. Aristotle: *HA* 7.1 (581a). First menstruation during illness: Hippokrates, *Epidemics* 1, Littré 2. 646–8, *Epidemics* 3, cases 7 and 12, Littré 3. 122, 136. On menstruation and its overtones in myth and ritual see now Helen King, 'Bound to bleed' in A. Cameron and A. Kuhrt, eds., *Images of women in antiquity* (London, 1983). Statues of boys found at Brauron have been claimed as 'bears', but although puberty rites that are to some degree mixed are known elsewhere (G. Lewis (1980)) boys have no part in the *arkteia* mythology and its whole structure is geared to the female nature. The boy statues may be a product of Artemis' more general concern for birth and growth. For the statues in general see *Praktika* (1949) 90 pl. 19, (1950) 173 pl. 5, (1959) pl. 12; *Ergon* (1958) 36 pls. 38f., (1959) 16f., (1960) 23f.; *AEph* (1961) 68–83.
22. See Gould (1980) 53.
23. *Katakontizein*: Hdt. 9.17, Thuc. 8.108, D. 18.151.
24. Aristotle on bears: *HA* 2.17, *HA* 6.18, 30, *HA* 8.5, 8, 30. Untameable: Ael. *NH* 4.45, Galen 5.40.
25. Souda s.v. says that *arktoi* act ἀπομειλισσόμεναι τὴν θεόν. For Kallisto see Apollodoros.
26. Amphidromia: Hesykhios s.v. *dromiamphion hēmar.* Cf. Nilsson (1941) 104f.

27. For Artemis and the dance see Calame (1977). The quotation is from D'Aquili and Laughlin (1979) 159.
28. For the Thesmophoria at Halimous see Plut. *Solon* 10.3, Clement, *Protr.* 2.34.2, and schol. on Ar. *Thesm.* 80. For the demes and the Thesmophoria see Is. 3.80, 8.18f. For symbolic antistructure see Turner (1974) ch. 5, cf. Turner (1969) and Sallnow (1981). On the Thesmophoria in general see Detienne in Vernant and Detienne (1979), Zeitlin (1982).
29. Abuse: Hesykhios s.vv. *gephuris, gephuristai.*
30. The finest analysis of the Brauronia to date is Vidal-Naquet (1974), who perhaps puts too heavy a stress on the 'wildness'.
31. Cf. Ar. *Lys.* 645ff., Harpokr. s.v. *dekateuein,* Vidal-Naquet (1974) 155, Walbank (1981A).
32. Thus the Artemis sanctuary can be seen to contribute to the discourse over the rôle of women in the polis which Loraux has shown to be taking place in the other cults on the Akropolis (Loraux 1981B).
33. For the position of Philaidai see appendix B. The sanctuary is about a kilometre from the settlement. A similar separation of sanctuary and settlement occurs at Rhamnous, Sounion and Marathon (Herakleion). Sounion and Marathon both had major festivals.
34. For claims about the political 'take-over' of the Eleusis cult see Solders (1931), Bonner (1933) 132f., Nilsson (1951A) 38 and Boardman (1975). The supposed evidence for Eleusinian independence in the archaic period is non-existent: *sunoikismos* stories are firmly tied in with the distant past, and Herodotos 1.30 does not indicate a seventh-century war between Athens and Eleusis (see How and Wells (1912) ad loc.).
35. For the Eumolpos myth see Lyk. *Leok.* 98f., and schol. Eur. *Phoin.* 854. For a different view (not argued for) see Boardman (1975).
36. For the Lesser Mysteries and problems with the tradition about them see Dowden (1979). For a political interpretation see Boardman (1975).
37. For the members of the families see Clinton (1974).
38. Herakles in Akris: *REG* 91 (1978) 289ff. lines 36–9; i^3 5: see Healey (1962), Simms (1975), Clinton (1979); i^3 391: Ἐλευσῖνι may go closely with the verb rather than with the *hieropoioi,* and mean that the *epistatai* were to receive the money 'at Eleusis'. Fourth-century law on *aparkhe*: ii^2 140, which may also have set up the '*hieropoioi* from the *boule*', see ii^2 140 add.
39. Phrearrhioi: Vanderpool's comment (1970, 50) that 'The mention of the Phrearrhians in line 12 shows that we have to do with the cult regulations of that deme' is a *non sequitur.* Thorikos building:

Boersma (1970) 78f., dedication: i^2 869/ii^2 2600 with *MIGRA* 1 (1975) 17. Thorikos is the landing place for Demeter in the *Homeric Hymn* (line 126). A remarkable number of vessels particularly associated with Eleusinian rites have been found in the Laurion area, Jones (1982B).

40. *SEG* 21.541.101ff., 201ff., 313ff., 413ff. Ἐλευσι. ἐν ἄστει must mean 'at the city Eleusinion' (*contra* Mikalson (1972) 39).

41. It is thus vital that the *Homeric Humn* make no mention of Athens, and the absence of any mention cannot be treated to a political interpretation (*contra* Walton (1952), cf. Richardson (1974)).

42. For demes at the Panathenaia cf. ii^2 334.24, D. 44.37, Souda s.v. *demarkhos*, schol. Ar. *Clouds* 37. For the Panathenaia and empire see *ML* 46.

43. Tauropolis: Menander, *Epitrep.* 451ff., 471, 476. Decrees: *AEph* (1925–6) 168ff., (1932) 30–2.

44. Thorikos: Kephalos, *SEG* 26.136.15ff., Thorikos, ibid. 18, 28ff., 54. Erkhia: Zeus Epakrios, *SEG* 21.541.560, Nymphai, ibid. 114, 544, Leukaspis, ibid. 350 and Dunst (1964). Tetrapolis: ii^2 1358.15, 24 with Peek, *AM* 67 (1942) 12f.)

45. See Jameson (1965), Salviat (1964), Mikalson (1972) 49f., Dunst (1977).

46. Cf. Snodgrass (1977) 16, 30.

9. The replacement of Athens

1. Cf. Gernet (1968) 371ff.
2. Cf. Loraux (1981A) 124ff.
3. Ar. *Clouds* 138f. and Dover (1975) 113.
4. E.g. (although no great confidence should be put in some of this information) Aigilia for figs: Theokritos 1.147f. and schol. 75 (ed. Wendel), Athen. 652e; Akharnai for charcoal: Ar. *Akh passim*, and for ivy: *Anth. Pal.* 6.279, 7.21, 9.286; Statius, *Theb.* 12.623; Soud. s.v. *Akharneitēs*, cf. Paus. 1.31.6; Athmonon for vines: Ar. *Peace* 190; Kephisia for turnips: Athen. 369c; Lakiadai for radishes: Hesykh., Soud., s.v. ō *Lakiadai*. Cf. Aixone for red mullet: Athen. 325d–f; Hesykh. s.v. *Aixōnida triglēn*.
5. For the links between productive system and social organisation cf. Goody (1976) *passim*.
6. This is true whether or not the figure in Thucydides is sound. For an argument that it is, see Thompson (1964) on Thucydides 2.20f.
7. A recent study of a French village has shown a complete contrast in social organisation between *gens du finage* and *gens du bois*: Jolas and Zonabend (1973). The dichotomy is not likely to have been so marked in Attika.

BIBLIOGRAPHY OF WORKS CITED IN
ABBREVIATED FORM

Abrams, P. and Wrigley, E. A. (1978) ed. *Towns in societies*. Cambridge.

Abramson, H. (1980) 'A hero shrine for Phrontis at Sounion', *Cal. Stud. Class. Ant.* 12.1–20.

Adam, S. (1966) 'The technique of Greek sculpture in the Archaic and Classical periods', *BSA* suppl. vol. 3. London.

Ampolo, C. (1981) 'Tra finanza e politica: carriera e affari del Signor Moirokles', *Riv. Fil.* 109.187–204.

(1982) 'Le cave di pietra dell' Attici: problemi giuridici ed economici', *OPUS* 1.251–60.

Amundsen, D. W. and Diers, C. J. (1969) 'The age of menarche in classical Greece', *Human Biology* 41.125–32.

Amyx, D. A. (1958) 'The Attic Stelai Part III. Vases and other containers', *Hesperia* 27.163–310.

Andreyev, V. N. (1960) 'The price of land in Attika in the C4th B.C.', *VDI* 2.47–57.

(1967) 'Public land in Attika in the 5th to 3rd centuries B.C.', *VDI* 2.48–76.

(1974) 'Some aspects of agrarian conditions in Attica in the fifth to third centuries B.C.', *Eirene* 12.5–46.

Ardaillon, E. (1897) *Les Mines du Laurium dans l'antiquité*. Paris.

Arvanitopoulou, T. A. (1958) Δεκέλεια. Athens.

(1959) Ὄστρακα ἐκ Δεκελείας. Athens.

Barnes, J. A. (1969) 'Networks and political process', in J. Clyde Mitchell, ed., *Networks in urban situations*, 51–76. Manchester.

Barrett, W. (1964) *Euripides' Hippolytus*, ed. with an introduction and commentary. Oxford.

Behrend, D. (1970) *Attische Pachturkunde: ein Beitrag zur Beschreibung der μίσθωσις nach den griechischen Inschriften*. Vestigia 12. Munich.

Bicknell, P. (1972) *Studies in Athenian politics and genealogy*. Historia Einzelschrift 19.

(1974) 'Athenian politics and genealogy: some pendants', *Historia* 23.146–63.

(1975) 'Kleisthenes and Kytherros', *Mnemosyne* 4th series 28.57–62 = following entry.

(1976) 'Clisthène et Kytherros', *REG* 89.599–603.

(1978) 'Akamantid Eitea', *Historia* 27.369–74.

Bloch, M. (1973) 'The long term and the short term: the economic and political significance of the morality of kinship', in J. Goody, ed., *The character of kinship*, 75—87. Cambridge.

(1974) 'Symbols, song, dance and features of articulation', *Archiv. Europ. de Sociol.* 15.55—81.

(1975) ed. *Political language and oratory in traditional society.* London.

Boardman, J. (1975) 'Herakles, Peisistratos, and Eleusis', *JHS* 95.1—12.

Boersma, J. S. (1970) *Athenian building policy from 561/0 to 405/4 B.C.* Groningen.

Boissevain, J. (1974) *Friends of Friends: networks, manipulation, and coalitions.* Oxford.

Bonner, R. J. (1933) *Aspects of Athenian democracy.* New York.

Borgeaud, Ph. (1979) *Recherches sur le dieu Pan.* Paris.

Bouras, M. (1967) Ἡ ἀναστηλώσις τῆς στόας τῆς Βραυρῶνος. *ADelt* suppl. 11. Athens.

Bourriot, F. (1976) *Recherches sur le nature du genos.* Lille.

Boyd, T. and Carpenter, J. (1977) 'Dragon houses: Euboia, Attika, Karia', *AJA* 81.189—215.

Bradford, J. (1956) 'Fieldwork on aerial discoveries in Attica and Rhodes', *Antiquity* 36.172—80.

(1957) *Ancient landscapes.* London.

Brelich, A. (1958) *Gli eroi greci: un problema storico-religiose*, Roma.

(1969) *Paides e Parthenoi*, vol. 1. Roma.

Burford, A. (1965) 'The economics of Greek temple building', *PCPS* n.s.2. 21—34.

(1969) *The Greek temple builders of Epidaurus.* Liverpool.

Burkert, W. (1966) 'Kekropidensage und Arrephoria', *Hermes* 94.1—25.

(1977) *Griechische Religion der archaischen und klassischen Epoche.* Stuttgart.

(1979) *Structure and history in Greek mythology and ritual.* Berkeley.

Calame, C. (1977) *Les Choeurs de jeunes filles en Grèce archaique*, vol. 1 *Morphologie, fonction religieuse et sociale;* vol. 2 *Alcman.* Rome.

Carter, J. (1981) 'Rural settlement in Metaponto', in G. Barker and R. Hodges, eds., *Archaeology and Italian society. BAR* 102, 167—77. Oxford.

Chandler, L. (1926) 'The North-West frontier of Attica', *JHS* 46 (1926) 1—21.

Cherry, J. F. (1978) 'Generalisation and the archaeology of the state', in D. Green, C. Haselgrove and M. Spriggs, eds., *Social organisation and settlement. BAR* S47 411—37. Oxford.

Chisholm, M. (1962) *Rural settlement and land use.* London.

Chorley, R. and Haggett, P. (1967) *Models in geography.* London.

Clastres, P. (1974, translated 1977) *Society against the state.* Oxford.

Clinton, K. (1971) 'Inscriptions from Eleusis', *AEph* (1971) 83—113.
(1974) *The sacred officials of the Eleusinian Mysteries. TAP Soc.*
64, part 3. Philadelphia.
(1979) 'IG i^2 5, the Eleusinia and the Eleusinians', *AJPh* 100.1—12.
(1980) 'A law in the city Eleusinion concerning the Mysteries',
Hesperia 46.258—88.
Coleman, M. and Walker, S. (1979) 'Stable isotope identification of
Greek and Turkish marbles', *Archaeometry* 21.107—12.
Conophagos, C. (1980) *Le Laurium antique.* Athens.
Coulton, J. J. (1976) *The architectural development of the Greek
stoa.* Oxford.
Crosby, M. (1941) 'Greek inscriptions: a poletai record of the year
367/6', *Hesperia* 10.14—30.
(1950) 'The leases of the Laurion mines', *Hesperia* 19.189—312.
(1957) 'More fragments of mining leases from the Athenian agora',
Hesperia 19.189—312.
Curtius, E. (1884) *Historische und philologische Aufsätze Ernst Curtius
zu seinem siebenzigsten Geburtstage gewidmet.* Berlin.
D'Aquili, E. G. and Laughlin, C. D. (1979) 'The neurobiology of myth
and ritual', in E. G. D'Aquili, C. D. Laughlin and J. McManus,
eds., *The spectrum of ritual: a biogenetic structural analysis.*
Columbia.
Daux, G. (1963) 'La grande démarchie: un nouveau calendrier sacrificial
d'Attique (Erchia)', *BCH* 87.603—34.
Davies, J. K. (1971) *Athenian propertied families 600—300 B.C.*
Oxford.
(1978) *Democracy and classical Greece.* London.
(1979) 'A reconsideration of i^2 847', *LCM* 4.151—6.
(1981) *Wealth and the power of wealth in classical Athens.* New
York.
Davis, J. (1969) 'Town and country', *Anthropological Quarterly*
42.171—85.
(1977) *People of the Mediterranean.* London.
Day, J. (1942) *An economic history of Athens under Roman
domination.* New York.
Detienne, M. (1963) *Crise agraire et attitude religieuse chez Hésiode.*
Bruxelles—Berchem.
(1972, translated 1977) *Les Jardins d'Adonis.* Paris.
(1977, translated 1979) *Dionysos mis à mort.* Paris.
Deubner, L. (1932) *Attische Feste.* Berlin.
Dilettanti, Society of (1817) *The unedited antiquities of Attica.*
London.
Dimen, M. and Friedl, E. (1976) eds. 'Regional variation in modern
Greece and Cyprus: towards a perspective on the ethnography
of Greece', *Annals of the New York Academy of Sciences,* 268.

Dinsmoor, W. B. (1947) 'The Hekatompedon on the Athenian
    Acropolis', *AJA* 51.109–51.

Dinsmoor, W., Jnr (1971) *Sounion*. Athens.

Dover, K. J. (1975) *Greek popular morality in the time of Plato and
    Aristotle*. Oxford.

Dow, S. (1935) Report in Blegen, 'News items from Athens', *AJA*
    39.267–70.

    (1942) 'The Aigaleos–Parnes wall', *Hesperia* 11.193–211.

    (1965) 'The greater demarchy of Erchia', *BCH* 89 180–213.

Dowden, K. (1979) 'Grades in the Eleusinian Mysteries', *RHR*
    197.409–31.

Dunst, G. (1964) 'Leukaspis', *BCH* 88.482–5.

    (1977) 'Der Opferkalender des attischen Demos Thorikos', *ZPE*
    25.243–64.

Dworakowska, A. (1968) 'Starozytne Kamieniolomy Attyki. Materialy
    do inwentaryzacji', *Archaeologia* (Warsaw) 19.85ff.

    (1975) *Quarries in ancient Greece*. Warsaw.

Edmonson, C. (1966) 'The topography of North West Attika' (Ph.D
    thesis, unpublished).

    (1968) 'Brauronian Artemis in Athens', *AJA* 72.164f.

Effenterre, H. van (1976) 'Clisthène et les mesures de mobilisation',
    REG 89.1–17.

Ehrenberg, V. (1969) *The Greek State* (ed. 2). London.

    (1973) *From Solon to Sokrates* (ed. 2). London.

Eliot, C. W. J. (1962) *Coastal demes of Attica: a study of the policy of
    Cleisthenes*. Toronto.

    (1967) 'Aristotle *Ath. Pol.* 44.1 and the meaning of trittys', *Phoinix*
    21.79–84.

    (1968) 'Cleisthenes and the creation of the 10 phylai', *Phoinix*
    22.3–17.

Etienne, R. (1975) 'Collection Dolly Goulandris II. Stèle funéraire
    attique', *BCH* 99.379–88.

Farnell, L. R. (1896, 1907, 1909) *Cults of the Greek states* (5 vols.).
    Oxford.

Feaver, D. (1957) 'Historical development in the priesthood of Athens',
    YCS 15 123–58.

Fiedler, K. G. (1840) *Reise durch alle Theile des königreiches
    Griechenland in Auftrag der königl. Regierung in den Jahren
    1834 bis 1837*, vol. 1. Leipzig.

Fine, J. (1951) *Horoi. Studies in mortgage, real security, and land
    tenure in ancient Athens. Hesperia* suppl. 9.

Finley, M. I. (1952A) *Studies in land and credit in ancient Athens*.
    New Brunswick.

    (1952B) 'Multiple charges on real property in Athenian law. New
    evidence from an Agora inscription', in *Studi in honore de
    Vincenzo Arangio Ruiz*, vol. 3, 474–91.

(1963) *The ancient Greeks*. New York.

(1973A) ed. *Problèmes de la terre en Grèce ancienne*. Paris.

(1973B) *The ancient economy*. London.

(1973C) *Democracy ancient and modern*. London.

Forbes, H. and Foxhall, E. (1982) 'Σιτομετρεία: the rôle of grain as a staple food in classical antiquity', *Chiron* 12.41–90.

Friis Johansen, H. and Whittle, E. (1980) *Aeschylus, The Suppliants* (3 vols.). Gyldendalske Boghandel.

Gallant, T. W. (1981) 'A fisherman's tale: an analysis of the potential productivity of fishing in the ancient world'. (Unpublished manuscript.)

(1982) *The Lefkas–Pronnoi survey* (Ph.D. thesis, Univ. of Cambridge.)

Gauthier, Ph. (1976) *Un Commentaire historique des Poroi de Xénophon*. Genève–Paris.

Geertz, C. (1966) 'Religion as a cultural system', in M. Banton, ed., *Anthropological approaches to the study of religion*. ASA monographs 3, pp. 1–46, London, reprinted in G. Geertz (1975), *The interpretation of cultures*, 87–125. New York.

(1980) *Negara. The theatre state in nineteenth-century Bali*. Princeton.

Gell, W. (1819) *The itinerary of Greece, containing one hundred routes*. London.

Gellner, E. (1977) 'Patrons and clients', in E. Gellner and J. Waterbury, eds., *Patron and client in Mediterranean societies*. London.

Germann, K., Holzmann, G. and Winkler, F. (1980) 'Determination of marble provenance: limits of isotopic analysis', *Archaeometry* 22.99–105.

Gernet, L. (1968) *Anthropologie de la Grèce antique*. Paris.

Glotz, G. (1904) *La Solidarité de la famille dans le droit criminel en Grèce*. Paris.

(1918) 'Le date des comptes relatifs au portique d'Eleusis', *REG* 31 207–20.

(1923) 'Un transport de marbre pour le portique d'Eleusis', *REG* 36.26–45.

Gomme, A. W. (1933) *The population of Athens in the fifth and fourth centuries BC*. Oxford.

(1956) *A historical commentary on Thucydides Books II–III*. Oxford.

Gomme, A. W. and Sandbach, F. (1973) *Menander, a commentary*. Oxford.

Goody, J. (1976) *Production and reproduction*. Cambridge.

Goody, J., Thirsk, J. and Thompson, E. (1976) *Family and inheritance: rural society in Western Europe 1200–1800*. Cambridge.

Gould, J. (1980) 'Law, custom and myth: aspects of the social position of women in classical Athens', *JHS* 100.38–59.

Grote, G. (1851) *History of Greece* (11 vols., ed. 3). London.

Gudeman, S. (1976) *Relationships, residence and the individual: a rural Panamanian community*. London.

Guiraud, P. (1893) *La Propriété foncière en Grèce jusqu'à la conquête romaine*. Paris.

Gulliver, P. (1971) *Neighbours and networks: the idiom of kinship in social action among the Ndendeuli of Tanzania*. Berkeley.

Hansen, M. (1976) 'How many Athenians attended the ecclesia?', *GRBS* 17.115–34.

(1981) 'Initiative and decision: the separation of powers in C4th Athens', *GRBS* 22.345–70.

Harrison, A. W. (1968) *The law of Athens*, vol. 1 *The family and property*. Oxford.

(1971) *The law of Athens*, vol. 2 *Procedure*. Oxford.

Haussoullier, B. (1884) *La Vie municipale en Attique*. Paris.

Healey, R. (1962) Summary of dissertation, 'Eleusinian sacrifices in the Athenian Law code', *HSCP* 66.256–9.

Higgins, W. (1977) *Xenophon the Athenian*. New York.

Hignett, C. (1953) *A history of the Athenian constitution*. Oxford.

Holleaux, M. (1906) 'Inscriptions d'Athènes', *AM* 31.134–44.

Hondius, J. J. E. (1922) 'Quod sit τὸ κοινὸν γραμματεῖον?', *Mnemosyne* 50.87–90.

Hopkins, M. K. (1966) 'The probable age structure of the Roman population', *Population Studies* 20.245–64.

Hopper, R. J. (1953) 'The Attic silver mines in the fourth century B.C.', *ABSA* 48.200–54.

(1961) '"Plain", "Shore" and "Hill" in early Athens', *ABSA* 56.189–219.

(1968) 'The Laurion mines: a reconsideration', *ABSA* 63.293–326.

How, W. and Wells, J. (1912) *A commentary on Herodotus*. Oxford.

Humphreys, S. C. (1977) 'Public and private interests in classical Athens', *CJ* 73.97–104, reprinted in Humphreys (1983) 22–32.

(1978) *Anthropology and the Greeks*. London.

(1980) 'Family tombs and tomb cult in ancient Athens: tradition or traditionalism?', *JHS* 100.96–126, reprinted in Humphreys (1983) 79–130.

(1983) *The family, women and death: comparative studies*. London.

Iakovides, S. E. (1969) Περατί: τὸ νεκροταφεῖον. Athens.

Jameson, M. H. (1963) 'The provisions for mobilisation in the decree of Themistocles', *Historia* 12.385–404.

(1965) 'Notes on the sacrificial calendar from Erkhia', *BCH* 89.154–72.

(1977) 'Agricultural slavery in classical Athens', *CJ* 73.122–45.

(1982) 'The leasing of land at Rhamnous', *Hesperia* suppl. 19.60–74.

Johnson, G. (1977) 'Regional analysis in archaeology', *Annual Review of Anthropology* 6.479–508.

Jolas, T. and Zonabend, F. (1973) 'Gens du finage: gens du bois', *Annales ESC* 28.285–305, reprinted and translated in R. Forster and O. Ranum, eds. (1977), *Rural society in France*, 126–51. Baltimore and London.

Jones, A. H. M. (1957) *Athenian democracy*. Oxford.

Jones, J. E. (1975) 'Town and country houses of Attica in classical times', *MIGRA* 1 'Thorikos and the Laurion in archaic and classical times', 63–136.

(1982A) 'The Laurium silver mines: a review', *Greece and Rome* 29.169–84.

(1982B) 'Another Eleusinian kernos from Laureion', *ABSA* 77.191–9.

Judeich, W. (1931) *Topographie von Athen* (ed. 2). Munich.

Kahil, L. Ghali (1963) 'Quelques vases du sanctuaire d'Artémis à Brauron', *Antike Kunst Beiheft* 1.1ff.

(1965) 'Autour de l'Artémis attique', *Antike Kunst* 8. 20–32.

(1977) 'L'Artémis de Brauron. Rites et mystères', *Antike Kunst* 20.86–99.

(1981) 'Le "cratérisque" d'Artémis et le Brauronion de l'Acropole', *Hesperia* 50. 253–63.

Kahrstedt, U. (1932) 'Die Landgrenzen Athens', *AM* 57.8–28.

Kakovogiannis, E. (1982) Σουνιακά-Λαυρεωτικά, *ADelt* 32A.182–217.

Kalcyk, H. (1982) *Untersuchungen zum attischen Silberbergbau. Gebietstruktur, Geschichte und Technik*. Frankfurt.

Karouzou, S. (1963) Ἀγγεῖα τοῦ Ἀναγυροῦντος. Athens.

Kent, J. H. (1948) 'The temple estates of Delos, Rheneia and Mykonos', *Hesperia* 17.243–338.

Kirsten, E. (1952) Contributions to A. Philippson, *Die griechischen Landschaften*, vol. 1. *Der Nordosten der griechischen Halbinsel*. Frankfurt am Main.

Klapisch-Zuber, C. (1969) *Les maîtres de marbres: Carrare 1300–1600*. Paris.

Knell, H. (1983) 'Der Tempel der Artemis Tauropolos in Lutsa', *AA* (1983) 39–43.

Koch, E. (1894) Ληξιαρχικὸν γραμματεῖον, in *Griechische Studien H. Lipsius zum sechzigsten Geburtstag dargebracht*, 11–17. Leipzig.

Koenigs, W. (1972) 'Beobachtungen zur Steintechnik aus Apollon-Tempel von Naxos', *AA* (1972) 380–5.

Kondis, I. D. (1967) 'Artemis Brauronia', *ADelt* 22A.156–206.

Kordellas, A. (1870) *Le Laurium*. Athens.

Kotzias, N. (1925) Δημοτικὸν ψήφισμα Ἁλῶν τῶν Ἀραφενίδων, *AEph* (1925–6) 168–77.

Kourouniotes, K. and Thompson, H. (1932) 'The Pnyx in Athens', *Hesperia* 1.90—217.

Kuenen-Janssens, L. J. (1941) 'Some notes on the competence of the Athenian woman to conduct a transaction', *Mnemosyne,* 3rd ser. 9.199—214.

Labarbe, J. (1957) *La Loi navale de Themistoclé.* Paris.

Lacey, W. C. (1968) *The family in classical Greece.* London.

(1980) 'The family of Euxitheos', *CQ* 30.57—61.

Ladas, G. (1952) 'Ἡ σπηλιὰ τῆς Πεντέλης', *Συλλέκτης* 1.137—68.

Langdon, M. (1976) 'A sanctuary of Zeus on Mount Hymettos', *Hesperia* suppl. 16.

(1982) 'Some Attic walls', *Hesperia* suppl. 19.88—98.

Langdon, M. and Watrous, L. V. (1977) 'The farm of Timesios: rock-cut inscriptions in South Attika', *Hesperia* 46.162—77.

Langlotz, E. and Graef, B. (1925) *Die antiken Vasen von der Acropolis zu Athen.* Berlin.

Laslett, P. (1956) 'The face to face society', in P. Laslett, ed., *Philosophy, politics and society: first series,* 157—84. Oxford.

Lauffer, S. (1957) 'Prosopographische Bemerkungen zu den attischen Grubenpachtlisten', *Historia* 6.287—305.

(1979) *Die Bergwerksklaven von Laureion* (ed. 2). Wiesbaden.

Lauter, H. (1980A) 'Zu Heimstätten und Gutshaüsern im klassischen Attika', in *Forschungen und Funde: Festschrift Bernhard Neutsch,* 279—86. Innsbruck.

(1980B) 'Ein ländliches Heiligtum hellenistischer Zeit in Trapuria (Attika)', *AA* (1980) 242—55.

(1981) 'Klassisches Landleben in Attika', *RUB-Aktuel* 76 for 19 October 1981.

(1982) 'Zwei Horos-inschriften bei Vari. Zu Grenzziehung und Demenlokalisierung in südost-Attika', *AA* (1982) 299—315.

Lauter-Bufé, H. (1979) 'Das "Wehrdorf" Lathouresa bei Vari. Ein Beitrag zum Dekeleischen Krieg', *AM* 94.161—92.

Leake, W. M. (1841) *The Demi of Athens.* London.

Lechtman, H. and Merrill, R. S. (1977) eds. *Material culture, styles, organisation and dynamics of technology.* Proc. of American Ethnological Society. St Paul, Minnesota.

Lepsius, G. R. (1890) *Griechische Marmorstudien.* Berlin.

Lewis, D. M. (1955) 'Notes on Attic inscriptions II', *ABSA* 50.1—36.

(1963A) 'Cleisthenes and Attica', *Historia* 12.22—40.

(1963B) Review of Eliot (1962) in *Gnomon* 35.723—5.

(1966) 'After the profanation of the Mysteries', in E. Badian, ed., *Ancient society and institutions: studies presented to Victor Ehrenberg,* 177—91. Oxford.

(1973) 'The Athenian Rationes Centesimarum', in Finley (1973A) 181—212.

(1974) 'Entrenchment clauses in Attic decrees', in D. W. Bradeen and M. F. McGregor, eds., *Phoros: tribute to B. D. Meritt*, 82—9. New York.

Lewis, G. (1980) *Day of shining red. An essay on understanding ritual.* Cambridge.

Linders, T. (1972) *Studies in the treasure records of Artemis Brauronia found at Athens.* Acta Instituti Atheniensi Regni Sueciae 4.19.

(1975) *The treasurers of the other gods.* Beiträge zur klassischen Philologie 62.

Lloyd, G. E. R. (1979) *Magic, reason and experience. Studies in the origin and development of Greek science.* Cambridge.

Loraux, N. (1973) 'Marathon ou l'histoire idéologique', *REA* 75.13—42.

(1979) 'L'autochthonie: une topique athénienne', *Annales ESC* 34.3—26. reprinted with revisions in Loraux (1981B) 35—73.

(1981) *L'Invention d'Athènes. Histoire de l'oraison funèbre dans la 'cité classique'.* Paris.

(1981B) *Les Enfants d'Athéna. Idées athéniennes sur la citoyenneté et la division des sexes.* Paris.

Lukes, S. (1969) 'Alienation and anomie', in P. Laslett and W. Runciman, eds., *Philosophy, politics and society: third series.* Oxford.

(1974) *Power: a radical view.* London.

McCredie, J. (1966) *Fortified military camps in Attica.* Hesperia suppl. 11.

MacDowell, D. (1978) *The law in classical Athens.* London.

Maier, F. G. (1959) *Griechische Mauerbauinschriften,* teil 1. Vestigia 1. Heidelberg.

Mair, L. (1971) *Marriage.* Harmondsworth.

Manville, B. (1980) 'Solon's law of stasis and ἀτιμία in classical Athens', *TAPA* 110.213—21.

Marinos, G. and Petrascheck, W. (1956) *Laurium.* Athens.

Martha, J. (1882) *Les Sacerdoces athéniens.* Paris.

Meritt, B. D. and Traill, J. S. (1974) *The Athenian Agora, vol. 15 Inscriptions: the Athenian councillors.* Princeton.

Mikalson, J. D. (1972) *The sacred and civil calendar of the Athenian year.* Princeton.

Milchhoeffer, A. (1883) *Karten von Attika* (Curtius and Kaupert) *Erläuternder Text,* heft II. Berlin.

(1889) *Karten von Attika,* heft III—VI. Berlin.

(1892) *Untersuchungen über die Demenordnung des Kleisthenes.* Berlin

(1895) *Karten von Attika,* heft VII—VIII. Berlin.

(1900) *Karten von Attika,* heft IX. Berlin.

Millett, P. (1982) 'The Attic Horoi reconsidered in the light of recent discoveries', *OPUS* 1.2 219—40.

Mitchel, F. (1964) 'Derkylos of Hagnous and the date of ii^2 1187', *Hesperia* 33.337—51.

Montepaone, U. (1979A) 'Il mito di fondazione del rituale Mounychio in honore di Artemis', in *Recherches sur les cultes grecs et l'occident 1*. Cahiers Centre Jean Bérand 5.65—76.

(1979B) 'L'ἀρκτεία à Brauron'. *Stud. Stor. Rel*. 3.2.

Münter, L. (1893) *Das Grab des Sophokles*. Athens.

Murray, O. (1980) *Early Greece*. London.

(1981) 'The Greek symposion in history', *TLS* 4,101, 6 November 1981, 1307—8.

Mylonas, G. (1961) *Eleusis and the Eleusinian Mysteries*. Princeton.

Nemes, Z. (1980) 'The public property of demes in Attica', *Acta Classica Univ. Sci. Debrecen* 16.3—8.

Nilsson, M. (1941) *Geschichte der griechische Religion*. Munich.

(1951A) *Cults, myths, oracles and politics in ancient Greece*. Lund.

(1951B) 'Die Prozessiontypen in griechischen Kult', in *Opuscula Selecta* 1.166—214. Lund.

Ober, J. (1981) 'Rock-cut inscriptions from Mount Hymettos', *Hesperia* 50.68—77.

Oikonomides, A. N. (1957) Σούνιον. Athens.

Orlandos, A. (1968) *Les Materiaux de construction et la technique architecturale des anciens Grecs,* part 2. Paris.

Osborne, R. G. (1983) 'Beans mean . . . ', *LCM* 8.111.

(forthcoming) 'The nature of Athenian legal actions', *JHS* 105.

Papageorgakis, J. (1967) 'Τὰ εἰς τὴν μαρμαρικὴν τέχνην χρήσιμα πετρώματα τῆς Ἑλλάδος', *Ann. Géol. Pays Hell.* 18.193—268.

Parke, H. W. (1976) *Festivals of the Athenians*. London.

Patterson, C. (1981) *Perikles' citizenship law of 451—50 B.C.* New York.

Pečirka, J. (1970) 'Country estates in the polis of Chersonesos in the Crimea', in L. de Rosa, ed., *Ricerche storiche ed economiche in memoria de Corrado Barbagello* 1.457—77. Naples.

(1973) 'Homestead farms in classical and hellenistic Hellas', in Finley (1973A) 113—47.

Pečirka, J. and Dufkova, M. (1970) 'Excavation of farms and farmhouses in the chora of Chersonesos in the Crimea', *Eirene* 8.123—74.

PECS (1975) *Princeton Encyclopedia of Classical Sites,* ed. R. Stillwell. Princeton.

Petrakos, B. (1967) 'Νέαι πηγαὶ περὶ τοῦ Χρεμωνιδείου πολέμου', *ADelt* 22A.38—52.

(1979) 'Νεές ἔρευνες στὸν Ῥαμνούντα', *AEph* (1979) 1—81.

Petropoulakou, M. and Pentazos, E. (1973) Ἄττικα. Οἰκιστικά στοιχεῖα — πρώτη ἔκθεσῆ. Athens.

Philippson, A. (1952) *Die griechischen Landschaften*, vol. 1 *Der Nordosten der griechischen Halbinsel*. Frankfurt am Main.

Phythian-Adams, C. (1976) 'Ceremony and the citizen: the communal year at Coventry 1450–1550', in P. Clark, ed., *The early modern town*, 106–28. London.

(1979) *Coventry: desolation of a city.* Cambridge.

Picard, C. (1940) 'L'héroon de Phrontis au Sounion', *Rev. Archéol.* 16.5–28.

Piérart, M. (1971) 'Les euthynoi athéniens', *Ant. Class.* 40.526–75.

Pleket, H. (1964) *Epigraphica 1. Texts on the economic history of the Greek world.* Leiden.

Pouilloux, J. (1954) *Le Forteresse de Rhamnonte.* Paris.

Pritchett, W. (1953) 'The Attic stelai. Part 1', *Hesperia* 22.225–99.

(1956) 'The Attic stelai. Part 2, *Hesperia* 25.178–317.

(1965) *Studies in ancient Greek topography,* vol. 1. Berkeley and Los Angeles.

Pritchett, W. and Herz, N. (1953) 'Marbles in Attic epigraphy', *AJA* 57.71–81.

Radcliffe-Brown, A. (1940) Preface to E. Evans-Pritchard and M. Fortes, eds., *African political systems.* Oxford.

Raepsaet, G. (1971) 'Les motivations de la natalité à Athènes', *Ant. Class.* 40.80–110.

Raepsaet, G. and Charlier, M.-T. (1971) 'Etudes du comportement social: les relations entre parents et enfants dans la société athénienne à l'époque classique', *Ant. Class.* 40.589–606.

Raubitschek, A. (1949) *Dedications from the Athenian acropolis.* Cambridge, Mass.

Reilly, L. C. (1978) *Slaves in ancient Greece. Slaves from Greek manumission inscriptions.* Chicago.

Reinmuth, O. (1971) *The ephebic inscriptions of the fourth century B.C.* Leiden.

Renfrew, A. C. and Peacey, J. S. (1968) 'Aegean marble. A petrological study', *ABSA* 63.45–66.

Renfrew, A. C. and Wagstaff, J. M. (1982) eds. *An island polity.* Cambridge.

Rhodes, P. J. (1972) *The Athenian boule.* Oxford.

(1979) 'Athenian democracy after 403 BC', *CJ* 75.305–23.

(1980) 'Ephebes, bouleutai and the population of Athens', *ZPE* 38.191–200.

(1981A) *A commentary on the Aristotelian Athenaion Politeia.* Oxford.

(1981B) 'Members serving twice in the Athenian boule', *ZPE* 41.101–2.

Rhodes, R. F. and Dobbins, J. J. (1979) 'The sanctuary of Artemis Brauronia on the Athenian acropolis', *Hesperia* 48.325–41.

Richardson, N. J. (1974) *The Homeric hymn to Demeter.* Oxford.

Robinson, R. (1962) *Aristotle Politics Books III and IV. Translated with introduction and comments.* Oxford.

Roussel, D. (1976) *Tribu et cité*. Paris.

Ruschenbusch, E. (1979A) 'Die soziale Herkunft der Epheben um 338', *ZPE* 35.173—6.

(1979B) 'Die soziale Zusammensetzung des Rates der 500 in Athen im 4 Jh.', *ZPE* 35.177—80.

(1981) 'Epheben, bouleuten und die Bürgerzahl von Athen um 330 v. Chr.', *ZPE* 41.103—5.

Sainte Croix, G. E. M. de (1966) 'The estate of Phainippus (Ps. Dem. xlii)', in E. Badian, ed., *Ancient society and institutions: studies presented to Victor Ehrenberg*, 109—14. Oxford.

(1981) *The class struggle in the ancient Greek world*. London.

Sakellariou, M. and Pharaklas, N. (1972) Μέγαρις, 'Αιγόσθενα, 'Ερένεια: Athens.

Sale, W. (1975) 'The temple legends of the arkteia', *Rh. Mus.* 18.265—84.

Sallnow, M. (1981) 'Communitas reconsidered: the sociology of Andean pilgrimage', *Man* 16.2.163—82.

Salviat, F. (1964) 'Les théogamies attiques, Zeus Teleios et l'Agamemnon d'Eschyle', *BCH* 88.647—54.

Salviat, F. and Vatin, C. (1974) 'Le cadastre de Larissa', *BCH* 98.247—62.

Salzman, L. (1952) *Building in England down to 1540*. Oxford.

Schaps, D. (1977) 'The woman least mentioned: etiquette and women's names', *CQ* 27.323—30.

Schmitt, P. (1977) 'Athéna Apatouria et la ceinture. Les aspects feminins des Apatouries à Athènes', *Annales ESC* (1977) 1059—73.

Shaw, D. (1963) 'The problem of land fragmentation in the Mediterranean', *Geog. Journ.* 53.40—51.

Shoe, L. (1949) 'Dark stone in Greek architecture', *Hesperia* suppl. 8.341—52.

Siewert, P. (1982) *Die Trittyen Attikas und die Heeresreform des Kleisthenes*. Vestigia 23. Munich.

Silverman, S. (1968) 'Agricultural organisation, social structure, and values reconsidered', *Amer. Anthrop.* 20.1—20.

(1979) 'The peasant concept in anthropology'. *Journ. Peas. Stud.* 7.49—69.

Simms, R. (1975) 'The Eleusinia in the C6th to C4th', *GRBS* 18.269—79.

Skinner, Q. (1978) *The foundation of modern political thought*, vol. 1. Cambridge.

Smith, E. and Lowry, H. (1954) 'A survey of mountain-top sanctuaries in Attica, with an appendix on the fortifications of Attica'. ASCS Papers (unpublished).

Snodgrass, A. M. (1977) *Archaeology and the rise of the Greek State*. Cambridge.

(1980) *Archaic Greece: the age of experiment*. London.

(1983) 'Heavy freight in Archaic Greece', in P. Garnsey, M. K. Hopkins and C. R. Whittaker, eds., *Trade in the ancient economy*. London.

(forthcoming) 'The site of Askra', in *Proceedings of the 4th International Conference on ancient Boiotia*, Lyon, May 1983.

Solders, S. (1931) *Die ausserstädtische Kulte und die einigung Attikas*. Lund.

Sourvinou-Inwood, C. (1971) 'Aristophanes, *Lysistrata* 641–647', *CQ* 21.339–42.

Sparkes, B. and Talcott, L. (1970) *The Athenian Agora* vol. 12 *Black and plain pottery of the 6th, 5th, and 4th centuries*. Princeton.

Stanier, R. S. (1953) 'The cost of the Parthenon', *JHS* 73.68–76.

Starr, C. (1965) *A history of the ancient world*. Oxford.

Stevens, G. P. (1936) 'The Periklean entrance court of the Acropolis', *Hesperia* 5.459ff.

Stinton, T. C. W. (1976) 'Iphigeneia and the bears of Brauron', *CQ* 26.11–13.

Stuart, J. and Revett, N. (1762) *The antiquities of Athens*. London.

Sundwall, J. (1906) *Epigraphische Beiträge zur sozial-politischen Geschichte Athens im Zeitalter des Demosthenes*. Leipzig.

Tanner, J. M. (1978) *Foetus into man: physical growth from conception to maturity*. London.

Thompson, H. A. (1938) 'Note on the identification of the property at Sounion', *Hesperia* 7.75–6.

Thompson, W. (1964) 'Three thousand Akharnian hoplites', *Historia* 13.406–13.

(1966) 'Τριττὺς τῶν πρυτάνεων', *Historia* 15.1–10.

(1967) 'Marriage of first cousins in Athenian society', *Phoenix* 21.273–82.

(1969) 'Kleisthenes and Aigeis', *Mnemosyne* 4th series 22.137–52.

(1970A) 'Notes on Attic demes', *Hesperia* 39.64–7.

(1970B) 'The kinship of Perikles and Alkibiades', *GRBS* 11.27–9.

(1970C) 'Regional distribution of Athenian Pentakosiomedimnoi', *Klio* 52.137–51.

(1971) 'The deme in Kleisthenes' reforms', *Symbolae Osloenses* 46.72–9.

(1972) 'Athenian marriage patterns: remarriage', *Cal. Stud. Class. Ant.* 5.211–25.

(1976) *De Hagniae Hereditate. An Athenian inheritance case*. Leiden.

Threpsiades, J. and Vanderpool, E. (1964) 'Themistocles' sanctuary of Artemis Aristoboule', *ADelt* 19A.23–36.

Toepffer, J. (1895) 'Das attische Gemeindebuch', *Hermes* 30.391–400.

Tomlinson, R. A. and Trevor Hodge, A. (1969) 'The temple of Nemesis at Rhamnous', *AJA* 73.185–92.

Traill, J. S. (1975) *The political organisation of Attica. Hesperia* suppl. 14.

(1981) 'Athenian bouleutic alternates', in G. Shrimpton and D. McCargar, eds., *Classical contributions: studies in honour of M. F. McGregor.* New York.

Travlos, J. (1949) 'The topography of Eleusis', *Hesperia* 18.138—47.

(1960) 'Eleusis (1950—1960)', *ADelt* 16B.43—60.

(1976) 'Τρεῖς ναοὶ τῆς Ἀρτέμιδος: Αὐλιδίας, Ταυροπόλου καὶ Βραυρωνίας', in U. Jantzen, ed., *Neue Forschungen in griechischen Heiligtümern,* 197—205. Tübingen.

Tschira, A. (1940) 'Die unfertigen Saülentrommeln auf der Akropolis von Athen', *JdAI* 55.242—61.

Turner, V. (1969) *The ritual process.* London.

(1974) *Dramas, fields and metaphors: symbolic action in human society.* New York.

Ucko, P., Tringham, R. and Dimbleby, G. W. (1972) eds., *Man, settlement and urbanism.* London.

Ussher, R. G. (1960) *The characters of Theophrastus.* London.

Vanderpool, E. (1942) 'An archaic inscribed stele from Marathon', *Hesperia* 11.329—37.

(1965) 'The location of the Attic deme Erchia', *BCH* 89.21—6.

(1966) 'The deme of Marathon and the Herakleion', *AJA* 70.319—23.

(1970) 'A lex sacra of the Attic deme Phrearrhioi', *Hesperia* 39.47—53.

(1974) 'The Attic deme Phegaia', in *Mélanges Helléniques offerts à Georges Daux,* 339—44. Paris.

(1978) 'Roads and forts in Northwestern Attica', *Cal. Stud. Class. Ant.* 11.227—45.

(1982) *Studies in Attic topography and history presented to Eugene Vanderpool. Hesperia* suppl. 19.

Vernant, J.-P (1974) *Mythe et société en Grèce ancienne.* Paris.

Vernant, J.-P. and Detienne, M. (1974) *Les Ruses de l'intelligence: le mètis des Grecs.* Paris.

(1979) (eds.) *La Cuisine du sacrifice en pays grec.* Paris.

Vernant, J.-P and Vidal-Naquet, P. (1973) *Mythe et tragédie en Grèce ancienne.* Paris.

Vidal-Naquet, P. (1968) 'The Black hunter and the origin of the Athenian Ephebeia', *PCPS* n.s. 14.49—64. Revised version printed in Vidal-Naquet (1981) and in R. Gordon, ed. (1981), *Myth, religion and society,* 147—62. Cambridge.

(1974) 'Les jeunes: le cru, l'enfant grec, et le cuit', in J. Le Goff and P. Nora, eds. *Faire de l'histoire* 3.137—68. Revised reprint in Vidal-Naquet (1981) and in R. Gordon, ed. (1981), *Myth, religion and society,* 163—85. Cambridge.

(1981) *Le Chasseur noir*. Paris.

Waelkens, M. (1982) 'A new rock-cut inscription from the "Cliff Tower" in S. Attica', *MIGRA* 5.149—62.

Wagstaff, J. M. (1965) 'Greek rural settlements: a review of the literature', *Erdkunde* 23.306—17.

Walbank, F. (1957) *A historical commentary on Polybius,* vol. 1. Oxford.

Walbank, M. (1981A) 'Artemis bear-leader', *CQ* 31.276—81.

(1981B) 'The decree for Lapyris of Kleonai (*IG* 2^2 365)', in G. Shrimpton and D. McCargar, eds., *Classical contributions: studies in honour of M. F. McGregor,* 171—5. New York.

(1982) 'The confiscation and sale by the Poletai in 402/1 B.C. of the property of the Thirty Tyrants', *Hesperia* 51.74—98.

(1983) 'Leases of sacred properties in Attica', *Hesperia* 52.100—35, 177—231.

Wallace, W. (1947) 'The demes of Eretria', *Hesperia* 16.115—46.

Walton, F. R. (1952) 'Athens, Eleusis, and the Homeric Hymn to Demeter', *HThR* 45.105—14.

Wheler, G. (1682) *A journey into Greece by Geo. Wheler Esq., in the company of Dr Spon of Lyons.* London.

Whitehead, D. (1977) *The ideology of the Athenian metic. PCPS* suppl. 4.

(1981) 'Deme and polis: local government and central government in classical Athens.' (MS dated 27 December 1981.)

(1982) 'Notes on Athenian demarchs', *ZPE* 47.37—42.

Wickens, J. (1983) 'Deinias' grave at Timesios' farm', *Hesperia* 52.96—9.

Wrede, W. (1933) *Attische Mauern.* Athens.

Wycherley, R. E. (1957) *The Athenian Agora,* vol. 3 *The testimonia.* Princeton.

(1973) 'Pentelethen', *ABSA* 68.349—53.

(1974A) 'Poros: notes on Greek building stones', in D. W. Bradeen and M. F. McGregor, eds., *Phoros: tribute to B. D. Meritt,* 179—87. New York.

(1974B) 'The stones of Athens', *Greece and Rome* 21.54—67.

Wyse, W. (1904) *Isaeus, the speeches with critical and explanatory notes.* Cambridge.

Young, J. (1941) 'Studies in South Attica. The Salaminioi at Porthmos', *Hesperia* 10.163—91.

(1956) 'Studies in South Attica. Country estates at Sounion', *Hesperia* 25.122—46.

Zeitlin, F. (1982) 'Cultic models of the female: rites of Dionysos and Demeter', *Arethusa* 15.129—57.

Zvorykin, I. and Saul, P. (1948) *Soil map of Attica.* Drapetsona, Peiraieus.

INDEX OF PASSAGES CITED

43.65	139 n. 38	57.23f.	148
43.74	139 m. 36	57.26	72, 148
43.75	136 n. 27	57.28	148
43.77	128 n. 6	57.29	148
44	135	57.31f.	147
44.3	79 n. 34	57.33	150
44.10	136	57.38	149
44.34ff.	61 n. 59	57.40	149
44.37	72, 75, 179 n. 42	57.43	149
		57.44	149
44.39	77 n. 32	57.49	142 n. 46, 144 n. 49
44.48	136 n. 27		
44.49	138 n. 31	57.46	77 n. 32
44.63	127 n. 4	57.47f.	150
45.19	68 n. 12	57.52	149
45.28	4 n. 18	57.58	148
45.79	139 n. 38	57.60	73 n. 19
46.18f.	136 n. 27, 138 n. 31	57.63	54, 76 n. 30, 150
		57.67	149
47.52f.	41 n. 82	58.16	139 n. 36
47.53	18	58, 53, 58	84 n. 44
48.12	49, 139 n. 38	59	68 n. 14
48.27	49	59.3f.	81 n. 39
49.6, 11, 26	48 n. 7	59.39	48 n. 6
50.6f.	82	59.48	67 n. 10
50.8	48, 76 n. 29, 82	59.58	135 n. 24
52.28	42 n. 88	59.61	73 n. 20
53	6, 17	Ep. 3.16	84 n. 44
53.1	6	DIODOROS SIKELOS	
53.2	4 nn. 16, 17	11.41, 43	116 n. 16
53.4	17 n. 9, 146	12.9.2	60 n. 55
53.5	146	12.11.1	60 n. 55
53.13	4 n. 18	DIONYSIUS HALIKARNASSIOS	
53.15f.	17 n. 9	De Dinarch 11	147 n. 56
53.15	48 n. 6	De Isaeo 16f.	147 n. 56
53.20	144 n. 49	DIPHILOS	
54.25	161 n. 14	2.549 (Kock)	165
54.32	139 n. 38		
55	17, 34 n. 58		
55.11	18 n. 10	EURIPIDES	
55.13	17	Hippolytos 73ff., 148ff.	157 n. 8
55.23f.	18 n. 10	Iphigeneia in Tauris	
55.26	18	1103f.	157 n. 8
57	76 n. 31, 88, 146–151, 184	1234ff.	157 n. 8
		1462	164 n. 19
57.3	147	1465	156f.
57.6	147	Phoinissai 854 schol.	174 n. 35
57.8	67 n. 8, 75 n. 25, 148		
57.9	148	FINLEY	
57.10	61 n. 59	Studies in Land and Credit	
57.12	148	no. 5	80 n. 37
57.13	75 n. 25	no. 67A	80 n. 37
57.15	148	no. 87	87 n. 50
57.20f.	148		

GENERAL INDEX

adoption, 62, 127f., 135
Agia Marina, quarry, 95, 100, 101
agora: of Athens, 99, 147f.; of
  Sounion, 31, 35
agriculture: factors affecting, 16, 47,
  62f., 152; carried out from
  nucleated centre, 17, 62f., 142;
  variety of agricultural land, 19−21;
  exploiting marginal land, 20f., 41
  with n. 82, 142; for subsistence, 63;
  labour for, 142−6
Agrileza valley, 31−5; quarries in, 31f.,
  95, 100ff.
agroikos, 185
agronomoi, 18
agros, 18, 19f., 49
Aiantis, 5 n. 24, 57
Aigilia, 186 n. 4, 192
Aigina, stone from, 98f., 103, 106
Aixone, 2, 25, 55, 74 n. 24, 76, 79,
  84, 85, 104 n. 38, 120, 186 n. 4,
  192
Akharnai, 44, 48, 67, 74 n. 24, 122,
  123, 133 n. 17, 157 n. 6, 158,
  186 n. 4, 188f.
Akropolis: quarried, 96; stone in
  buildings on, 98f., 106, 107;
  sanctuary of Artemis Brauronia,
  154−7, 158, 172ff., 176; *hekatostai*
  inscriptions set up on, 56
Alkibiades, 47 n. 5, 50 n. 12
Amphiaraon, 67, 75 with n. 28, 86, 100
Amphidromia, 169
Amphitrope, 113
Anagyrous, 25−9, 35, 39, 120, 192
Anaphlystos, 87 n. 50, 113 with n. 7,
  114, 119, 133 n. 17, 192
Andokides, family of, 135f.
Angele, 131f., 158, 192
Apatouria, 74, 139
Aphidna, 5 with n. 24, 37 with n. 68,
  51 n. 16, 53, 59 n. 51, 132f., 158
  n. 10, 192
apographē, 1 n. 1, 2 n. 5, 4−6, 10
Apollo Zoster, 23f., 25, 35
Apollodoros, 6, 17, 48, 67, 82, 146
Araphen, 39 n. 75, 194
Aristotle: on nature of polis, 9; on
  demes as *koinoniai*, 42; on

democracy, 65, 71; on agricultural
  labour, 143; on menarche, 165; on
  bears, 167
arkteia, 162−73
army, rôle of deme in recruitment, 42
  n. 88, 82
Artemis: Attic shrines of, 157; Aristoboule, 86, 88, 155; Brauronia, 154−
  72, 176, on Akropolis, 154−6,
  dedications to, 158−61, 170, 172,
  treasure records of, 155f., priestess
  of, 160f., relations with Artemis
  Mounykhia, 162f.; Mounykhia,
  155, 162f., 180; connection with
  Iphigeneia, 164, 169
Asklepios: tax for, 1, 3; dedications to,
  67, 159; priest of, 55, 67, 84 n. 44;
  altar of, 4f.; sanctuary of, in
  Peiraieus, 3, 5; mines named after,
  3 with n. 11
assembly, 6f., 65, 69, 79, 91; of deme,
  79f.
asteios, 185
astu, 8 n. 32, 13, 16, 19, 49 n. 9, 50,
  51, 53, 56, 59, 60, 61, 69, 70, 78,
  81, 87, 91, 144, 176f., 184, 185,
  186−9
astynomoi, 18
Athena, 31, 55, 56, 68, 86 n. 49, 132,
  155
Attic Stelai, 47 n. 3, 50f., 63
auction, 57 with n. 39

bears, 162−6, *and see arkteia*
beekeeping, 27 with n. 43, 32, 193
Besa, 1, 3, 114, 115, 117, 119, 192
boule, 42, 67f., 77, 80f., 84, 86, 91, 173
bouleutai, 83, 84, 85, 86, 91, 184;
  quotas of, 42f., 46, 80f.; as indication of population, 43−5, 69;
  proposing decrees, 66−9; organising
  deme *proeisphora*, 82; raising
  troops, 82
Brauron, 154−174, 187; natural environment, 157; quarries for, 97,
  100, 102; temple, 156; stoa, 156;
  gymnasium and palaestra, 74 n. 24;
  stables, 160; hunt at, 160f., 167;
  ritual at, 157−72, 177; dedications